JOHN DAVISON

JOHN DAVISON

LITTLE MAN, BIG HEART

JOHN BLAKE

Published by Metro Publishing, an imprint of John Blake Publishing Ltd,
3 Bramber Court, 2 Bramber Road,
London W14 9PB, England

www.blake.co.uk

First published in hardback in 2007

ISBN: 978-1-84454-442-4

British Library Cataloguing-in-Publication Data:

A catalogue record for this book is available from the British Library.

Design by www.envydesign.co.uk

Printed in Great Britain by William Clowes Ltd, Beccles, Suffolk

1 3 5 7 9 10 8 6 4 2

Papers used by John Blake Publishing are natural, recyclable products made from wood grown in sustainable forests. The manufacturing processes conform to the environmental regulations of the country of origin.

Every attempt has been made to contact the relevant copyright-holders, but some were unobtainable. We would be grateful if the appropriate people could contact us.

This book is dedicated to the memory of my mother and father who taught me the virtue of courage. Also to Dave, my brother, R.I.P, and to Ruben, a true champion.

CONTENTS

THANKS

It would take another book to thank and mention all the people and fans who I met along the way. You know who you are. Big thanks for all the support. A special word of thanks has to go to Martin Rankin and Chris Cartwright for helping the memories flow. Without them this book could not have happened. Thanks also to Tommy Conroy and John Gibson for your time and advice, and to Stephen Richards for all you did to help. And finally to Jimmy Wilde, a great boxing fan and a great friend who I hope is resting in peace.

JD
Newcastle upon Tyne 2007

1

MY TIME

'I felt as if I were walking with destiny, and that all my past life
had been but a preparation for this hour and for this trial.'
WINSTON CHURCHILL, *DIARIES*, 1940

*Standing in a boxing ring, battered and bruised, awaiting
the decision of the biggest fight of his life, John Davison
surveys the scenes of mayhem around him. It's 17 April 1993
and he has just fought for the WBO World Featherweight
Title. Detached and dejected, the world is a painful haze of
colour and sound. As he glances at the referee and judges, the
people already clambering into the ring, his heart is pounding
in his chest, his breathing short and laboured. Through dulled
senses somewhere, a million miles away, he can just make out
the primeval chant of thousands.*

'Dava! Dava! Dava!'

*He's heard it from the second he entered the ring. It has
rolled around the hall all night, reaching a crescendo in the
final round.*

'Dava! Dava! Dava!'

His fans, the supporters he has cherished since the day he

1

began his remarkable and completely unexpected journey.

'Dava! Dava! Dava!'

It's a chant he's heard many times before in the last five years. But tonight it has a special significance. His vociferous supporters know the agonies he has endured in the last two days. They have seen the newspaper reports and watched the television coverage with the same feeling of disbelief. They can understand his mental torture.

But he has locked the pain and anguish inside, as he has done on every other occasion he has ever stepped inside a boxing ring. John Davison has always come out to entertain, to give his last ounce of strength, his last breath, to repay his fans' loyalty and deliver to them the victory they have craved almost as much as he desired it for himself. And his supporters know it and have responded as only they can, with an electric atmosphere completely befitting the coronation of a new king. But tonight their support has been more poignant, more meaningful. Tonight, on John Davison's biggest of trials, they have tried to carry him.

'Dava! Dava! Dava!'

His people are willing him home. And he's almost there, almost achieved the casual immortality that comes from sporting genius. To be known and remembered as the best there is in a world of billions like him. But something is wrong. Something is very, very wrong.

Even through blurred vision, John Davison knows this is not the picture he'd imagined he'd see if he made it to this point. The man in the corner to his right, his opponent through 12 rounds of torture, is not the man it should have been. It's not the man who has invaded his dreams for the last six months, the opponent that he had lived and breathed and fought over and over again in his mind.

MY TIME

As John Davison surveyed the scene before him, he was certain of only one thing. That it was never meant to be like this. This was not the way it was supposed to happen. How had it all come to this...?

John Davison exploded into boxing in the most violent of ways. Aged 25, he was unemployed and going nowhere. He'd never been in a boxing ring in his life until the fateful day his mates had dragged him to a local gym 'to mess around'. He had nothing better to do at the time, stuck in his flat in the suburbs of Newcastle, with no money and no plan.

That single event had changed his life beyond all comprehension. Within 12 months, he was in the final of the ABAs, the most prestigious amateur boxing competition in the world. On the way, he'd destroyed two England Internationals with first-round KOs. One of his victims, Birmingham's Colin Lynch, was highly experienced, having fought with distinction for England 18 times. The other, Paul Hodkinson, was England Boxing Team Captain and one of the finest amateurs in Europe. He would go on to lift the British, European and WBC World Featherweight Titles as a professional. Neither opponent would ever forget what John Davison had done to them.

The England selectors immediately snapped up this raw, new talent. Davison would go on to represent his country all over the world over the next three years, captaining the National Team eight times. He was a firm favourite to be selected for the 1988 British Olympic Team. But, when a man he had beaten twice was selected in his place, and thinking he would be too old for the next games in four years' time, he decided to hang up his gloves. Boxing was for young men, he told himself, and he was just weeks from his 30th birthday.

But he was addicted. There was something about boxing

3

that filled a void he hadn't known existed before he'd walked into that gym. Boxing pushed him to fanatical training, mental preparation, the fusion of body and spirit for an ultimate test where he alone was responsible for his destiny. He loved his new and unexpected life. Not the travel, the trophies or the minor adulation he received. He loved it for the challenges it gave him, the trials he had to endure and overcome. He loved it for what it had taught him about himself, things he would never otherwise have known. Life on the dole in the North-East of England was grim and he wasn't quite ready to give up the roller-coaster ride.

A local boxing manager convinced him to turn professional. It was not a decision taken lightly. Barry McGuigan, the most successful British featherweight in the last decade, had retired, burned out at 28, and most boxers are finished long before their 30th birthdays. The difference between brilliant amateur and decent professional was huge. Surely he would be too old to bridge so wide a gap? But he had a young family to support and the dole queues were long. There wasn't really any choice.

What he achieved in the next five years had been beyond his wildest dreams. A Davison fight night became a special occasion, a unique experience of raw power and aggression as he attacked his opponents from the very first bell. It was a white-knuckle ride, which left fans feeling that they, too, had been in the ring, taking and giving punches in an all-out war. Davison gained a reputation as one of the best-value British boxers around, packing out venues every time he fought. He defined all that was simple and brutal about the noble art. Seek and destroy as quickly as possible, not one step backwards. His army of fans loved him because he was one of them – a happy-go-lucky Geordie, a smile on his face, the life and soul of the party. He was the man on the street, albeit with a unique and completely natural talent. Drop this prince of jokers into a boxing ring and he became a fearless hunter, a no-holds-barred action man who destroyed reputations. It was Roy of the Rovers with boxing gloves.

Now, at the age of 35 and in complete defiance of the laws of boxing, he'd almost reached the pinnacle of sporting brilliance. He was just one more fight from the ultimate accolade. To sit with the immortals of boxing, to be one of the few to be called Champion of the World. To live the dream.

Then, in the last 48 hours, the dream had turned into a nightmare. The world had continued to spin upon its axis but Davison's had fallen apart at the seams. Twice before, the fight had been cancelled and rescheduled, throwing meticulous preparations into disarray. He'd ended up training for six long months but, eventually, the Champion had flown to Britain and Davison had been sure that, at long last, he would face his moment of destiny.

Then it had all gone spectacularly wrong. The Champion, the man whose face he saw every time he closed his eyes, had been stripped of his title in a scandal that was the first of its kind and that had rocked the sporting world. The news had been transmitted around the globe within hours. In the meantime, in his little corner of planet earth, his fight was cancelled. His chance was over. His dreams were shattered.

No one can comprehend the mental preparation a professional boxer makes before so huge a fight, unless you are one of only a select band of mortals to have undertaken such a test. Every second of every day, every piece of food, every ounce of liquid, every breath, every fibre of your being is channelled into that single moment when the bell rings and you step out alone to face your destiny. He had lived the fight every single day for six months. And now it was over he had broken down and cried.

And then, unbelievably, he'd been told to pick himself up again. He was to fight someone else. A man he'd never heard of, a style he didn't know. Same time. Same place. Tickets had been sold. TV schedules had been booked. Cameras were ready to flash. Get out there, boy! Go do your stuff! He was expected to put the pieces back together and to go out in front of the whole world, yet again risking his life in pursuit of his dream.

John Davison did what he always did, what his unique character allowed him to do. He bowed his head in determination. He had 24 hours to prepare for a World Title fight.

Now, standing in the ring, surrounded by his family and supporters, the disorganised mayhem at the end of a World Title fight, he felt numb. Like the whole world, he was still stunned at the events of the last few days and what fate had conspired to throw at him.

The referee came over to him and nodded once. He knew it was time. Led into the middle of the ring, he stood waiting on the biggest decision in his life. He had come further than anyone could ever have imagined, a comet, literally exploding from nowhere and dazzling all who saw him. And this was it. This was his moment. He'd given more than anyone would ever know to stand in this place, at this time, and face his day of judgement. He saw nothing and he heard nothing but his own voice, repeating over and over again the mantra that he carried in his head – 'This is my time... this is my time... this is my time... this is my fucking time...'

②

BASIC INSTINCT

'Champions are not made in the gyms. Champions
are made from something they have deep inside them –
a desire, a dream, a vision.'

MUHAMMAD ALI

I suppose that life is all about choices. When you're thrown
into this world, kicking and screaming, everyone gets the
same basic equipment – a body with two arms, two legs, a
head; two eyes to see with; a matching pair of hands and feet.
It's all pretty standard stuff. Added to that, you might get a
natural gift thrown into the overall package, an 'optional
extra' so to speak. Something you can do simply because you
can. Not everyone gets one but, if you do, it's all about
recognising it, harnessing your natural talent early.

What you choose to do with your gift can make you special.
When I was young, everyone wanted to be the next Bobby
Charlton or George Best, the next Muhammad Ali. But you
need a natural gift to accompany the dream. And, even then,
you have to be dedicated from an early age, to take your gift
and polish it up so it shines brightly. For a chosen few, those
years of self-sacrifice will pay off. They'll score the winning
goal, they'll conquer the world... they'll live the dream.

JOHN DAVISON: LITTLE MAN, BIG HEART

I never had any dreams when I was young. And, as I got older, all I ever wanted was to have a laugh, get pissed, protect my family and survive. It took a long time for fate to knock on my door, for me to realise that I had a gift. Once it had, all I remember was boxing. Before, all I remember was fighting. In one way or another, I've been fighting since I was five years old.

I originally wanted to call this book *Size Doesn't Matter*. Carry on reading and you'll see why. Growing up on the mean streets of Newcastle, I had to be able to look after myself or I'd have been chewed up and spat out. It was survival of the fittest, or maybe the hardest. But if my natural weight was only 9 stone when I was 25, can you imagine what I was like when I was a teenager? I could hide behind lamp-posts and, on windy days, I had to put lead in my shoes to stop myself being blown away. But, in spite of that supposed 'handicap', I gained a reputation. I never started fights but I always finished them. People weren't usually stupid enough to fuck with John Davison.

Fighting, be it in the street or in the ring, is all about bottle. I can honestly say I've never been scared of anything or anyone in my life. I've always thought that worrying wastes energy and gets in the way of action. If I've got something to do, I do it. If there's a problem, I sort it. You could call it being strong willed, supremely focused. Maybe. Whatever it is, I've always looked on it as being a gift. It's the only gift I was given to complement my standard equipment. That and the ability to punch people so they'd fall over.

I was born on 30 September 1958 in Newcastle upon Tyne. My parents passed on to me that brand of determination and humour so particular to Tyneside. My mother, Margaret, worked as a cleaner and usherette in the local cinema. My dad,

John – known to one and all as 'Jake the Rake' – worked on the roads laying tarmac, hence his nickname. I was their fourth child, coming after my brother Davie, who was head of the brood, and my sisters Sheila and Margie. I was soon to be followed by my younger sister Alison and my baby brother Tom, making six in all. Tragically, my mother would lose another six children to miscarriages.

We were a big family but that wasn't unusual in those days. There was a family down the street that had 11. God knows how they squeezed them all in the house! Most of my friends seemed to have loads of brothers and sisters. Big families were commonplace; it was par for the course. We lived in the West End of Newcastle and the people there were so poor they couldn't afford to go out to cinemas or pubs at night and they certainly couldn't afford televisions. So there wasn't much else to do when the lights went off! Even now, I still think the best things in life are free.

Home for the Davison clan was a rotting Victorian terraced house in Lancaster Street in Elswick, which was an old working-class suburb that overlooked the city. Looking down to the river, you could see the huge Armstrong Vickers factory, which snaked along the banks of the Tyne on the Scotswood Road. The factory, and the shipyards further downstream, had supported the area for generations and the people of Elswick were as tough as the steel they shaped into tanks, guns and ships. The ships built in the yards had confronted the Kaiser's navies – and later Adolf Hitler's – when they threatened these shores. The assembly lines had been manned around the clock throughout both World Wars, the blood, sweat and tears of the locals producing thousands of tanks and guns that rolled out the factory gates and straight into battle. The people of Elswick were skilled in producing war machines.

JOHN DAVISON: LITTLE MAN, BIG HEART

It was a hard place, where men were men and the women were grateful. Looking at the area from the opposite side of the river was like looking at a patchwork quilt; blocks of old Victorian terraced housing criss-crossing the landscape into what seemed like infinity. Parts of it were later used for the backdrop to the cult film *Get Carter!*. The scenes of decaying houses, washing lines and outside toilets were not the creation of some London film-set designer. They were people's homes.

The locals were proud of their heritage. As a boy, I loved to hear my mother tell me stories of watching dogfights over the Tyne when the Germans tried to bomb the munitions factories during the Second World War. Spitfires would be spinning majestically in the sky, while, below, the locals stayed determinedly at their posts. She would also tell me of the night the Luftwaffe had destroyed the massive goods station at Manors, on the other side of the city. It had been full of sugar and butter and had burned for days. The locals, barely surviving on war rations, had been tortured by the smell of toffee wafting over the city. I would fall asleep at night dreaming of a world made of thick, rich, creamy toffee.

By the early 1960s, the heavy industry along the banks of the Tyne was rapidly declining and so was Elswick. Whole swathes were being demolished to make way for a brave new world of high-rise flats. When Prime Minister Harold McMillan had famously proclaimed, 'You've never had it so good!' he hadn't been picturing Elswick. The cobbled streets were straight out of a Catherine Cookson novel, but without any chance of a happy ending. My parents worked hard to make ends meet but, with six hungry mouths to feed, it was never going to be enough. We were evicted for non-payment of rent in the early 1960s and moved to Shieldfield, on the other side of the city. To compound my parents' shame, the story appeared in the local paper with their photograph.

Our new house in Rosedale Terrace was even worse than the one we'd vacated. Eight people were crammed into a mouldy old house with just one fire in the kitchen, no bathroom and an outside toilet. It was long before the days of double glazing and central heating and my abiding memory of childhood is the cold we had to endure each winter. It was literally freezing in the house, with ice on the inside of the windows each morning. You'd wake up and the first thing you would see was your own breath. It was probably warmer in the street outside! We were sleeping three to a bed and, at night, Davie, Tom and I would fill old pop bottles with hot water from the kettle in a desperate attempt to stay warm. This could have catastrophic consequences though. If a bottle leaked, the bed would be soaked and we'd have to lie there, shivering uncontrollably, until morning. Sometimes, I'd sneak downstairs and get my mother's coat from the chair in the kitchen and wrap myself in it, with my legs down inside the arms for added warmth. She would always be wondering how her coat was so creased. It used to end up looking like it had been dragged through a hedge by Steptoe's horse.

For my parents, life was a constant struggle and a balancing act between the grocery store and the pawnshop. There were times when we had nothing, not even enough money for coal for the fire. We'd burn pieces of furniture, old rags, anything to keep those precious flickering flames alive. I remember once having a piano; fuck knows where we got it. It was in a shit state and hadn't been tuned for years, not that anyone was taking piano lessons! One morning, with a foot of snow outside, Dad simply chopped it up with an axe and started feeding it on to the fire. A potential career as a concert pianist literally went up in smoke! Another time, we ripped up the lino from the kitchen floor and that, too, went on the fire, sending thick, black, oily smoke curling up the chimney and poisoning pigeons for miles around. I'm sure to this day there'll be a hole in the ozone layer right above where that house used to be.

Clothes were bought from one of the many second-hand shops that lined Shields Road. In many ways, I was lucky. I didn't need a fashion designer or personal shopper to tell me what I'd be wearing the following year. I already knew as my brother Davie would be wearing it at the time. I'd hear my mother tell him, 'Careful with that, Davie, you'll be giving it to John soon.' I'd look at the fucking horrible jumper he'd be wearing and pray it would fall apart before it got to me. It was the same with haircuts. My mother would put a bowl over my head and cut round it. Everyone's mother did the same thing.

My dad loved his beer. Even years later when he was getting on, he had the ability to sit up drinking rum until the early hours, then be out to work at six the following morning. He never missed a day's work in his life. When I was little, he'd send me down the pawnbroker's with some of his 'bits and bobs', old jewellery, tools, anything to get a little money for some bottles of brown ale. He'd send us all out around the doors doing 'penny for the guy' for bonfire night, which we usually started doing in July. He'd have us carol singing from October! We were practically the Geordie Osmonds. But money was always tight. We used the previous day's newspaper for toilet paper. Most Sundays, I could stick my head between my legs and read the sports results!

One Christmas Eve, when I was about five, I'd seen the bike that my parents had got me, even though they'd gone to great pains to hide my surprise in the toilet at the bottom of the yard. They had no idea I'd seen it but, as I burst through the sitting-room door, I instantly gave the game away.

'Where's me bike, Ma?' I said, eyes wide with excitement.

'What bike, John?' my mother joked, trying to keep the surprise going just a little bit longer.

'Me bike. I saw it last night. Where's me bike?'

'What bike?' she said again.

'Me bike! It was hidden in the toilet. Me bike! Where is it?'

'You haven't got a bike,' said my dad, as he gave me my present.

If I did have a bike, it was fucking small. A midget bike, in fact. I pulled off the wrapping paper. It was a Tonka toy, a truck with animals in the back. It was all they could afford.

'But… me bike…' I said, confused.

'You've been dreaming,' said my dad.

It was true. There was no bike. I was gutted and they could both see the disappointment on my face.

The following day, my dad made me a bogey out of pram wheels and planks of wood. It wasn't a bike but it was as good as and I loved it. It was the fastest one in Shieldfield and I raced it round the streets for years.

My parents were both very strict. One of my earliest memories is of being smacked by my dad. It was summertime and I was playing in the street when I was stung by a bee. I know that things always look bigger to you when you're a kid, but this was the biggest bee in world history. It was the size of a fucking helicopter and it jabbed a sting into my arm as big as a spear. I ran home in tears, looking like an extra from *Zulu*. I flew through the front door bawling out my story, expecting some parental sympathy. I didn't get it. My dad gave me a backhander for being so soft and I was unceremoniously despatched to bed without any tea.

Another time, when I was eight, I had a job in the summer holidays, running errands for the local garage for an old penny a day. I'd done a full week, been paid and was looking forward to a weekend of stuffing my face with sweets. Gloria, the gorgeous girl who worked behind the counter, had asked me to go and fetch her lunch. Even then I was a bit of a ladies man, so I was only too happy to oblige.

In the middle of the street a stranger stopped me. 'Excuse me, son, do you know where Saddler Street is?'

'Never heard of it, mister,' I replied, urchin-like.

As I turned to go, he grabbed hold of me, put his hand across my mouth and started fumbling through my pockets. The bastard nicked my hard-earned wages!

Again, I ran home crying. Again, I got a smack, this time for talking to strangers. Again, I was dumped in bed. I was lying there a little while later, wondering why it was that all adults were completely mad, when Dad burst in. He'd been sitting downstairs, brooding about what had happened and the penny had just dropped, so to speak. Now he was angry. Very fucking angry.

'Get your clothes on, John, we're going out.'

'Where we going, Da?' I asked, pulling my jumper over my head.

'Get your clothes on,' he repeated as he threw me my shoes. 'Come on, son, hurry up.'

'Where we going?' I asked again, excited.

'We're going looking for the bastard who robbed you. No fucker turns over a Davison!'

To me, it was obvious that he'd be long gone but I didn't say a word. Dad and I ran the streets of Shieldfield for the next couple of hours, him pointing at every bloke he saw and asking, 'Is that the bastard, John?' with murderous intent.

BASIC INSTINCT

Dad was a hard bloke, a real disciplinarian. He had a reputation as someone you didn't mess with. Not so much because he was a fighter, but because of the knife he always carried in his boot. He never looked for trouble but people knew he wouldn't be afraid to use his weapon of choice, so they left him well alone.

My mother, however, was a proper battler. She was hard as nails, and could use her fists to devastating effect. She was so strong she could still do 100 press-ups when she was 60! I've always said that I inherited my natural strength and knock-out punch from her.

A neighbour down the street asked to borrow a cup of sugar one day. We didn't have any to give her, but she was now bad-mouthing our family to the whole street, saying that we were tramps who couldn't afford to buy food. My mother bided her time, keeping a dignified silence. We were walking down the street a few days later when my mother spotted her on the other side of the road. We crossed over and my mother walked calmly up and truly lamped her! One lethal right hook put the neighbour straight on her arse. My mother never said a word to her. She just took me by the hand, saying, 'Come on, John, we'll be late for your tea.' We left her sitting in the middle of the street, seeing stars.

I suppose it was a tough brand of love my parents gave us, as we always got a smack if we misbehaved. There we were, six kids in a small house, fighting like cat and dog all the time. Dad's word was law, however, and the threat of his belt was enough to stop even the biggest of rows. It does sound hard today but it's the way people were brought up in those days. It was long before the days of the anti-smack brigade and it taught you respect and discipline, as well as instilling in you a sense of right and wrong that is definitely lacking in today's kids.

JOHN DAVISON: LITTLE MAN, BIG HEART

I started school at Sandyford Primary when I was about four. I had no interest in classwork whatsoever, only in messing around and having a laugh. I was good at sport and drawing and also had an active imagination. I was great at making up stories, especially ghost stories. I used to sit under the blankets at night scaring Tom and Alison senseless with my tales. As I couldn't write, they are now lost to the literary world, but they would have made Stephen King shit a brick. No one in the class was interested in lessons and the teachers didn't really bother trying to teach anyone. They were just concerned that you didn't kill either yourself or someone else on school premises.

I can vividly remember my first ever fight. I can't remember my opponent's name, but he was a bully of the worst kind, the type I fucking hate. He'd pick on all the smaller kids, using his size to intimidate and get his own way. He was two years above me and one day he decided that I was going to be his victim for the day, probably because I was the smallest in the class. We were in the yard when he grabbed me by the throat and tried to nick my dinner money. There was no fucking way I was going to hand it over, even though he was from the 'big class' and was twice my size. He punched me in the face, bursting my nose, and then pulled my duffel coat over my head. I was completely defenceless as he started using me as a punch bag. I was crying my eyes out. But I wasn't crying because I was hurt or scared. It was sheer frustration. Even though he was giving me a hiding, I managed to unravel the coat from around me and free my arms. And that was it! I was off, swinging wildly, blood and snot flying everywhere. Although I'd later refine my technique, it worked a treat at the time. In an example of what could later be termed 'powerful counter-punching', I well and truly nailed the fucker. But I didn't stop once he was down. I'd lost it completely and had to be pulled off by a teacher as I was mashing the poor kid's face into the schoolyard. The fight was probably not down to my being brave as such, more the fact that I was fucking starving. It's fair to say that it's a brave man that comes between me and my food! However, it was an indicator that, although I was only small, I was strong and I had a big temper. The result was that I suddenly had a little bit of credibility by primary-school standards! The other kids in my class were already starting to treat me differently. I was just five years old.

By the time I hit Manor Park aged 11, any chance of being a brain surgeon was already written off. I was in the bottom class for everything. All I was bothered about was having a laugh and playing sports. Like my brother Davie, I was a great footballer, even though I was tiny for my age. I was like a whippet and people struggled to shake me off the ball because I was so strong. I played left wing, drifting inside and smashing shots into the roof of the net. I think Thierry Henry might have copied my style, although there's no way he's as fast as I was in those days! These exploits earned me the nickname 'Sporty', which my brother Davie had also been called. We couldn't afford many nicknames in Shieldfield.

I'd developed a bit of a reputation as I was always fighting. As with all schools, you have competition to see who is the hardest in each year and my name was always up there in lights. I never looked to start fights but I loved the buzz I got from scrapping, so I never backed down if someone challenged me. I had no fear and would regularly be beating up lads two or three years older than me. I'd also look after mates and stop them being bullied. I'd fight anyone who challenged me. I didn't really give a fuck. Fighting came naturally to me and there always seemed to be someone else who fancied his chances. I suppose I started to play up to it, because I knew what I could do.

I could sometimes be a little bastard. I can remember hiding behind a wall and watching some lads in the year above playing pitch and toss. A line would be marked out and they would all toss their ten-pence piece, the winner of the money being the person who got his coin closest to the wall. I'd wait for all the money to be on the ground then dive out, pick it up and run off. You weren't allowed to gamble so it wasn't like they could go and tell a teacher. If any of them fancied it, I'd happily scrap for the winnings.

It was also at Manor Park that I launched a unique money-making scheme. I'd let someone punch me in the face for 50 pence. If I could take the punch without going down, I kept the cash. I used to make an absolute fortune and, again, my reputation was enhanced.

Although as a family we were close, we also kicked the living shit out of each other if we could get away with it. I can remember sitting in the tin bath one bath night, with Margie boiling water in the ancient iron kettle to pour in to keep it hot. I was ripping the piss, telling her to hurry up or I'd beat her up. It was a risky strategy because Margie was hard. She used to play football with me and my mates, and had won many a fight against them. To sort me out, she deliberately poured the boiling water all over my legs. I was screaming, my legs scalded. She just stood, laughing, triumphant.

The following night, I used a bit of cunning to get my revenge when she came back from her boyfriend's.

'Dad's left some beer in the kitchen,' I said, not looking up from the comic I was reading. 'I dare you to drink it.'

Margie could never resist a direct challenge but she looked at me suspiciously.

'I've already had some,' I lied. 'Go on, I dare you to.'

She went into the kitchen and took a massive gulp while I stayed well out of range. From the kitchen I heard her gasp. Then I heard her retching. Then I heard her finally puking her guts up into the sink. I'd half-filled an empty beer bottle with vinegar and left it on the kitchen bench. Revenge was indeed sweet!

'You little bastard!' she screamed as she chased me through the house.

I shot off up the stairs and barricaded myself in my bedroom. A few days later, she got her own back when she hit me across the head with the poker from the fire.

Manor Park provided me with some lifelong friends, in the form of Matty Wiper and Graham Morren, also known as 'Ham'. I first met Matty when he was moved to my class and was sat in front of me. As soon as the lesson started, I started cracking him round the head with my ruler. Every time he turned around, I'd be sitting there, the picture of innocence, and he would get bollocked off the teacher for not paying attention. Ham was one of Matty's mates and was in the year below. The three of us became inseparable as we tried to avoid school as much as possible.

We had two main interests, girls and money. By the time we were 13, we were randy little bastards, catchy kissy having long since been replaced by something more advanced. We fought over girls constantly and, even now, Matty claims that he always got them first. He's never been in a boxing ring in his life yet his memory is more fucked up than mine!

A load of us had started going to a weekly disco at a boys' club in the West End. There'd be me, Matty, Ham and a lad called Ernie Swinhoe who was the best dancer I'd ever seen. All the girls would be sitting on chairs, with the lads walking around them in a big circle. When you saw a girl you fancied, you'd go and ask her to dance. It was all very grown up, all very sophisticated. The club had a big screen with a light behind it and Ernie would go behind it and shadow dance. It was hilarious.

I was gorgeous, with a big blond quiff. I spent hours practising my dance moves in the house until I could really move. Dancing equalled girls and girls equalled fun. One of the gang who shall remain nameless caught crabs – pubic lice – off one girl who he'd pulled at the disco. The rest of us had already been there, so it was a lucky escape for everyone else!

One week, Matty fell in love for the first time. This gorgeous little blonde suddenly started coming to the disco. She'd just appeared from nowhere one night, as gorgeous girls do, but no one could ever get her to dance. She was the ice maiden. Matty, though, was in hot pursuit and he wasn't used to girls saying 'no' to him, but even he would crash and burn every time he tried with this particular young lady. He tried every trick in the book and spent months trying to convince her that he was a gentleman, an all-round regular good guy. He was like a lovesick puppy but eventually she put him out of his misery and said 'yes' to a dance. At the end of the night, he gave her a peck on the cheek and started counting down the hours until he would see her again.

The next week, he was expecting to move closer to his ultimate goal. He was dressed to impress and smelling of his dad's Old Spice aftershave. He was ready for action and he was not going to be denied. But, a few weeks earlier, he'd nicked one of my girlfriends, so I was ready to put a spanner in the works.

We first walked into the disco and he had a spring in his step. 'There she is,' he said looking over. I swear I saw hearts appear in his eyes. 'I'm off to check my hair,' he said suddenly and off he went to the toilets, no doubt to rehearse his chat-up lines in the mirror.

I casually wandered over to her. 'See that lad over there…' I said, pointing at Matty as he left the hall.

'Yes,' she said, smiling.

'Keep away from him. He's got so many crabs he should be walking sideways!'

She never looked at him again.

It was around this time that I became self-sufficient financially. I became a businessman, driving forward the national economy and educating myself in the school of life. Manor Park just couldn't compete with the outside world. Spending all day in the bookies working out your bets was a maths class. Buying and selling – 'dealing', as I called it – was business studies. Dealing would become a way of life with me, still is. It was soon pretty clear that I would sell my own granny. I suppose it started when I first used to sell my dad's bits and pieces for his beer money. I was haggling when I was only knee high and, by the time I was 12, I was a hard-nosed negotiator. We used to play in an old tip next to my house, where we'd build camps and lookout points and then go and set fire to the camps and lookout points of other gangs. But, while rooting around, you would find bits and pieces of scrap metal. We'd take it and sell it at the scrap yards down by the River Tyne, 'weighing it in' as it was called. Sometimes, we found old Victorian bottles or bits of china. We'd take them to the second-hand shop in Portland Road, which was owned by a gipsy family, and sell them for pennies, insisting, 'Honest, mister, it's not nicked!' The money would be blown on fish and chips, sweets and cans of pop. Living the high life indeed!

We graduated quickly. Vast areas of Old Byker and

Shieldfield were being demolished, very much like Scotswood and Elswick before. You would have whole streets of decaying old terraces, all boarded up, waiting for the wrecker's ball. But in those houses lay untold riches for nimble minds and even nimbler hands.

By the time we were 14, we were stripping the houses of anything we could sell. It wasn't exactly theft, as it would all end up in the heaps of rubble anyway. First to go was the copper wire from the ancient electrics. We'd take it and wrap it into big balls, then throw it on the fire. The flames would burn away the rubber casing, leaving a nice lump to be weighed in. Next would be the slates from the roofs. Then it was the floorboards, piping, anything that we could detach and carry. It was all sold to the various scrap men in the area and, suddenly, I had more sweets than I could eat.

I started getting flash, saying that I was going to buy and cook my own tea one night. I chose the recipe myself – Heinz beans on plain crisps. I thought I was at the Ritz! Mind, even that wasn't as strange as some of the stuff my dad used to eat. I can vividly remember him tucking into things such as tripe and cow's heel with white pepper. His favourite was pig's trotters but I can also remember him taking jelly and custard sandwiches to work for his bait.

Our little business enterprise was not without its dangers. Although the houses were getting demolished, the police still patrolled, looking for people breaking and entering. One particular night, we were stripping copper wire when the police knocked at the door. Everyone else bolted out the back door as the Old Bill came in the front. A quick check of the troops noted that I was missing in action. Missing, presumed nicked.

Only I wasn't. I'd gone 'undercover'. I'd slid under a

floorboard and was now lying silently under the floor, listening to the two coppers debating the latest football scores. Once they'd left, I re-emerged from my little hidey-hole, as black as the ace of spades, and yet another story was added to the Davison reputation.

I started trawling the second-hand shops looking for things I could buy and then sell. My auntie Nora had been a wheeler-dealer, especially buying and selling antiques. Now I found myself following in her footsteps, a vase here and a watch there. Old things fascinated me, anything from jewellery to pictures and ornaments. I'd buy them and sell them on at a profit. It was all money at the time but antiques would develop into a passion of mine, as well as a profitable sideline.

My knowledge of just how valuable old things could be came just too late for what may still be the most expensive mistake I ever made. One night, we broke into a big old derelict house on the outskirts of the city in Heaton. It was set in its own grounds and had been empty for years. We forced a door leading to a long, cavernous cellar that went right underneath the house. At the very back, covered in old heavy blankets which stank of moss, we discovered loads of old paintings, mostly with the proper gilt-edged frames. They'd been forgotten when the owners left the house to go to ruin. Well, boys will be boys! We carried them up into the garden and had competitions to see who could punch through the canvases and make the biggest hole. Then we had a bonfire. I still have nightmares now about the amount of cash that may have gone up in smoke that night.

In those days, everyone was in a gang. You had the Heaton Aggro, the Sandyford Boot Boys, the Elswick Mafia and the West Denton Wild Bunch. It wasn't like the gangs you get today, it was just kids wanting to belong, to identify with their local area. But you always had fights if two gangs were in the same place. Once, at the West End disco, I was coming out of the toilets as another lad was coming in. I'd never spoken to him before but I knew he was from a rival gang and that everyone called him 'Snake'. He was supposed to be a right hard fucker and to look at him was to invite a smack. As we passed each other at the door, he put the nut straight on me, right out the blue. It smashed my nose, and I had blood cascading down my face. I instantly went into attack mode, smacking him full on before getting him in a headlock and trying to ram his head into the wall. We were rolling around on the floor when the staff came in and dragged us apart, before throwing us out into the street.

I was ready now. It was now going to be an even fight and he no longer had the element of surprise. But he suddenly didn't fancy it any more. I'd already caught him with a couple of beauties during our scuffle in the toilet and one of his eyes was black and swollen. As I walked towards him, two of his pals came running out. Surprise, surprise! Suddenly, he was brave again.

'Come on then, you little bastard,' he jeered. 'I'm going to teach you a fucking lesson now.'

The lesson didn't last long. As Matty and Ham appeared at the door, I was just finishing him off. His two mates had only needed a couple of punches each to take them out. They didn't seem too keen on getting involved any more as I gave their mate a kicking. A police car came screaming round the corner and Snake and I broke apart. I didn't want to get nicked so I turned and started to slowly walk away. The police, seeing that the fight had broken up, drove off. In that sort of situation, three on one, you'd maybe expect them at least to have another go, even just for the sake of pride. Not a chance! The three musketeers were heading off in the other direction, nursing their various injuries. Soft bastards.

I suppose trouble seemed to follow me around. Another time, I was at Gosforth swimming baths during the school holidays, just minding my own business, when someone came off the big diving board straight on top of me. He was a big fat bastard and he nearly drowned me. We ended up scuffling in the water until the lifeguards dragged us out. Round two kicked off in the changing rooms and, again, the lifeguards pulled us apart. I got dried and dressed, feeling pissed off that my swim had been ruined by Fatman. When I walked outside, he was waiting for me. He came swinging wildly, so I ducked and rammed a jab into his face, splitting his lips. He grabbed hold of me, trying to use his weight to push me to the floor. As we struggled and our faces came close, I stuck the nut on him. He didn't want to fight after that.

Towards the end of my supposed 'education', the money I was making from dealing and copper meant I could 'speculate to accumulate'. The big fashion at the time was 'nesting', collecting birds' eggs. It was a national craze and every self-respecting lad had to have his own collection. I didn't care about collecting, but I did want to make money from them. Most collections had the standard eggs – blackbirds, starlings and wood pigeons. But the prized ones – kestrels, sparrowhawks and lynotts – were worth a fortune if you could 'acquire' them. These were the birds that built their nests high up or camouflaged them. I started dealing eggs, buying and selling them for a small profit. But, ask any businessman, there's nothing better than getting your stock for free!

So we'd go nesting in the parks around the city – Heaton, Jesmond Dene, Gosforth, Blaydon swamps. I started organising days away in the countryside where we'd leave

Newcastle at 6.00am and not get back 'til dark. They were long, lazy days spent under blue skies in the idyllic Northumberland countryside, far away from the poverty that blighted our lives. Because I was small and light, no tree was too high and no nest was ever out of reach. I found I could take risks that others wouldn't dare.

Once, 60ft up a tree and nearing my target, I slipped and fell, somehow managing to grasp a branch before I hit the ground, saving myself from almost certain death. On another occasion, I was shinning up a drainpipe on an old school building when it snapped from the wall. I fell backwards, plunging straight into the arms of an irate caretaker. I'd developed a fearless streak in the hunt for money, and I think I might be the only person to have scaled the old bridge at Byker since the men who first built it. Looking back, the risks I took were pretty stupid. I should have died a thousand times.

By this point, any interest I had in school had faded all together. No one even pretended to learn anything at school. It was a waste of time but it did have its lighter moments. One day, we were in class when the teacher, a woman in her mid-twenties, bent over the desk in front of Matty and me to help someone with their work. For a split second, her skirt rode up too high and we suddenly realised that she wasn't wearing any knickers. It was every schoolboy's fantasy. As she did it again, Matty lifted her skirt up and spanked her bare arse! She spun round, absolutely furious and slapped *my* face!

Another time, we'd bunked off in the morning, but decided to go in for the afternoon because I had some eggs I wanted to sell. When we got there, the place was like the *Mary Celeste* – the classrooms completely deserted. Apparently, everyone had been sent home after one of the girls had taken on all-comers in the girls' toilets. She'd had sex with half the school allegedly and the teachers had found out and called the police. I don't think such a thing could ever happen now.

So my school days came to an end, with me having been in the second-hand shops or the scrap yards more than the classroom. People say that your school days are the best time of your life, but I wouldn't really know. To me, the outside world was far more interesting and I couldn't wait to get out into it for real. My only interest was in making money and, this time next year, I was going to be a millionaire!

WARNINGS FROM THE MASKED MAN

'Everybody's got plans... until they get hit.'

MIKE TYSON

My first job was working in a hotel in Jesmond, a suburb on the edge of Newcastle City Centre. These days, it's all trendy bars and rich students vomiting in back alleys, but in those days it was the main hotel zone for Newcastle. The whole of Osborne Road was lined with small hotels and guesthouses and there was a running trade of businessmen who stayed there through the week if they were in the North-East.

I was taken on as a cellar-man, my main duties being to keep the beer in good condition and the bar well stocked. I was only 16, with big blond hair and an even bigger personality. I'd be strutting round the place like I owned it, balancing crates of beer on my head, laughing and joking with the guests. Although I was still tiny for my age, looks were deceiving. I was as strong as an ox, my usual party piece being to carry a barrel of beer up to the bar on my shoulder.

It was long before the days of money being paid directly into a bank account. Each week, we queued to receive a little envelope with our week's wages in cash. Most of the waiters and barman were just turned 18, with me being the baby of the gang. But, soon enough, a routine was established. Every Friday night, as soon as we'd been paid, we'd head into Newcastle for a night out. There was always a smoky pub that would happily turn a blind eye to underage drinking, as long as you were spending money and didn't puke on the jukebox. I'd already discovered the delights of the fairer sex and now booze became my next love in life. It was my first steps into a grown-up world and I couldn't get enough of it.

But working around alcohol at such a young age can lead a person to all manner of temptations and, soon, it became a regular thing for a bottle of whisky to be 'borrowed' from the hotel to kick-start our night out in style.

One afternoon, I finished early and was given a bottle of Johnny Walker's to look after for the others. I'd never tried spirits before and was usually steaming on a few bottles of brown ale. I had a few swigs, just to see what it was like. In the cowboy films, they necked it without a thought but it stripped the inside off my throat on the way down, bringing tears to my eyes. This is what being a man's about, I thought, as I forced another gulp down. By the time the others finished, I'd drunk about a quarter of the bottle and was already regretting it.

The others finished it in record time and we headed off to the city centre, with the evidence concealed in someone's jacket. I was starting to feel worse and worse as Scotland's finest started to course through my veins. Soon my legs weren't working properly. I was well and truly off my tits and the others were carrying me along.

Suddenly, there was the sound of screeching car tyres and a

car engine in reverse. A police car engine to be precise. We were in the shit.

'Stop there, all of you,' the first copper barked.

Everyone did as they were told, suddenly fine, upstanding pillars of the community.

'Look at the state of that!' the other cop said, looking pointedly at me. 'Has he been drinking?'

Everyone shrugged their shoulders, as if to say, 'Drinking, sir? Don't know what you're talking about, sir!'

The first copper looked me straight in the eye. 'How old are you?'

Fuck! I was thinking. How old am I? Who am I? Where am I? My brain was scrambled as the whisky started to take its full effect. I swayed gently in the breeze. A gust of wind could have blown me over. He noticed the bottle-shaped bulge under the jacket, walked over and lifted the empty bottle out. Exhibit A!

'Where did the whisky come from?' copper number two asked. Everyone looked at me. I was starting to fall asleep standing up.

Someone suddenly piped up: 'He nicked it.'

There was a murmur of agreement from the group as they stitched up the one person who could not speak out to defend himself. Literally.

'Is this true, son?' he asked me.

I knew I should say something, but my lips had gone numb and my eyesight was starting to fade. Instead, I replied by belching loudly as the whisky almost made a second appearance.

'Get him in the car,' said copper number two.

By the time they'd read me my rights, I'd passed out.

I was lucky. It was obvious that I hadn't been the main culprit. The hotel owners asked me who had nicked the whisky but I didn't want to drop anyone else in it, even though they'd done exactly that to me. The owners refused to press charges but they had no choice but to sack me.

Coming out of the office having just lost my job, the rest of the gang were huddled down the corridor, obviously worried that I might have spilled the beans and cost them all their jobs.

'What happened?'

An idea dawned. 'They're pressing charges' I told them. 'I'm in court next Friday morning.' I stared at the group, now white with fright. 'You'd better all be there,' I said, as I pushed my way through them. I already had a plan.

That Friday, my co-conspirators were waiting when I arrived at the Magistrates' Court in Market Street. I'd waited for Dad to go to work then nicked his only suit, the one he wore for weddings and funerals. It wasn't the best of fits. In fact, I looked like someone who'd nicked his dad's suit for a court appearance.

I looked each one of them in the eye. All were chastened, fully aware of how they'd let me down. The police walking in and out of the court entrance only served as a reminder of what would happen to them if I decided to drop them all in it.

'What are you going to say?' one asked.

'I don't know,' I said, pretending to be shitting myself. 'They might try to force me to say what really happened.'

Several of them gulped. They'd lied to the police. This was serious. Lost jobs... court appearances... prisons...

'Wait outside,' I told them. 'I don't want you to see me in the dock.'

Knowing that they were all guilty, they were more than happy to agree.

I took a deep breath, bravely stuck my chest out and mounted the steps into the Magistrates' Court to face Her Majesty's justice system. I checked I hadn't been followed and

WARNINGS FROM THE MASKED MAN

I slipped out the back entrance. I sprinted across the road and into the pub opposite without being spotted. There, I enjoyed a leisurely pint and a pork pie while I read my newspaper. I then made the return trip, again without being seen.

I walked back through the main entrance where my former colleagues waited in terror, afraid that I'd told the truth and they were all about to be nicked.

'What happened?' asked one breathlessly.

'They said I was lucky they didn't send me to prison,' I said. 'They've fined me.'

'How much?' said another, reaching for his wallet.

There were one, two, three... ten people there. 'Fifty quid,' I said, trying my luck.

Ten £5 notes were instantly handed over by the grateful group, showing that sometimes crime *does* pay.

At this time, I was playing football regularly and had started to turn out for Shieldfield Social Club on a Sunday morning. Davie played up front for them. He was a traditional centre-forward with an eye for goal. Although I was young, I soon joined him in the team, getting a regular game out on the left. Sunday-league football can be brutal at the best of times and games would regularly involve a punch-up, which only added to the buzz for me. Football was my sport and I hadn't even thought of boxing as something I could do. I don't even remember going out of my way to watch the big fights of the time. I can remember watching Ali fight on television but I was no different to anyone else in that respect. The whole world stopped when he climbed in the ring.

We'd sometimes go to St James' Park to see Newcastle play. I don't ever remember paying to get in. We always jumped over the wall at the back of the Leazes End. It was easy. Climb over the wall, on to the roof of the toilets and then into a big space that ran underneath the stand. It was nicknamed 'The Leazes Tunnel' and there'd be up to 30 people hiding in there with torches and candles before every game. Once it kicked off, everyone slipped out and dropped into the terrace below without being spotted by the stewards. At the time, Newcastle had Malcolm Macdonald – 'Supermac' – one of the finest centre-forwards in the club's history. The man was a goal machine and the crowd loved him. He was well worth the entrance 'fee' in my eyes.

One Saturday afternoon, we did our usual thing. We slipped into the tunnel with our torches and candles. It was crowded and it was clear that we were unwelcome visitors. There was a gang already inside and they obviously felt that possession was nine-tenths of the law.

'Fuck off out of our tunnel,' one of them said.

'We're not going anywhere,' Matty replied. 'The game kicks off in a couple of minutes.'

'I've told you. Fuck off out of our tunnel!' said another lad, stepping forward. He was clearly the Top Boy. I recognised him. He was massive and supposedly one of the hardest in the Leazes End. He checked us all out and decided he'd pick on the softest. So he spat on me.

I spat back, straight into his face. He went fucking mental and his mates dived between us.

'You'd better go now,' one of them said to me. 'He'll fucking kill you!'

I looked over at him. He didn't scare me. 'I'm not going anywhere until the game kicks off,' I shrugged.

Top Boy broke free of his shackles. 'You want your go, you little bastard? Come on, you and me now! In the toilets!'

I shrugged my shoulders and followed him out of the tunnel. We dropped down into the empty toilets just as the crowd's roar signalled that the game had started.

Top Boy shouted, 'Come on then!' and grabbed me in a headlock. He started punching me in the face over and over again. I managed to break free and catch him with an uppercut but it didn't stop his advance. He was punching me around the toilets and I was bouncing off the walls as I tried to defend myself. Again, I caught him with an uppercut. It burst his nose, which seemed to upset him. Now he was really fucking angry!

He picked me up and started to smash my head against the wall. He was literally using me as a battering ram! Once, twice, three times, my head was rammed off the cold concrete. Over and over again. I had to do something or he was going to cause me some serious damage. I managed to kick him in the face and he dropped me. I rolled over and was up, quick as a flash, jumping up and grabbing him. I nutted him. He didn't seem to like that! I nutted him again. And again! And again! And again! He went limp in my arms and sank to his knees. I started smashing punches into his face just as some of his mates dropped into the toilet along with Matty and Ham. Top Boy started shouting, 'I've had enough! I've had enough!'

I could have kept on going, really pasted him. But what was the point? I stood there, swaying, covered in blood, trying to get my breath back. I heard one of his mates say, 'Fuck me, he's chinned him,' and then Matty and Ham were all over me, checking I was OK.

My eyes were already swollen but he was in a shit state. His mates helped him to his feet and he walked unsteadily over to me and held out his hand. 'Fair fight, mate,' he said and we shook hands.

We walked outside to the little shop and he bought me a bottle of pop and a bag of crisps. We respected each other now. It was just the way it was and now I was Top Boy.

It was as I hit 17, though, that the party really began. The main draw was the city centre, with its numerous bars, pubs, clubs and girls. We started hitting the town on a Friday and Saturday night but it soon progressed to pretty much every night of the week. There were the favourite haunts, of course, the ones where, even as underage drinkers, we'd be able to get in with no real problem.

We'd go to the Mayfair nightclub or the Dolce Vita and get hammered as we jumped around to disco music or northern soul. The Mayfair was more of an old-fashioned ballroom, with a massive dance floor that was surrounded by tables. There was a balcony where you could go and stand and watch all the girls on the dance floor below. I'd spot a honey and then hit the floor, gliding on over to her to impress her with my silky moves and some Davison loving. The place would be full of people swaying to the Rubettes' 'Sugar Baby Love' or the Bee Gees' 'Jive Talking' or jumping to The Blue Notes' 'Don't Leave Me This Way'. I can also remember seeing Tom Jones live at the Dolce Vita, as well as The Supremes and even Black Lace.

We all looked smart when we went out, even though most of our clothes came from second-hand shops. It was the days of flares and big checked shirts. I looked deadly in my two-tone flared trousers and shirt covered in stars. I looked like one of the Bay City Rollers! I even had a pair of moon boots. They had a million laces and it used to take me an hour to get them on. I bought a pair of Sasha shoes with high heels in an attempt to make me look taller. The collars of my shirt were bigger than the wingspan of a jumbo jet. They were 'pioneering' days for fashion. Thank God, I don't have any photographs to scare the kids with.

Being so small, it was hard getting into most of the bars. Matty and me would get Margie's eyeliner and put it on the bum fluff above our top lip to make it look like we had a moustache. We'd go out looking like Errol Flynn but, later on in the night, we'd have what looked like an oil slick in our pints. The Sasha shoes, the moustache, they were all vain attempts to make us look older. But I looked like what I was: a tiny 17-year-old in high heels with his big sister's eyeliner on my lip. It got me into the bars though!

Of course, you have to finance such a lifestyle and, again, we had graduated in that respect. Copper could still provide an income of sorts but the real earner at the time was lead. We could strip a roof as fast as look at one, with the standing joke of the time being that you had to go to 'work' to pay for your new trousers for the weekend. I could make a tenner a week from lead and copper, which was good money. It kept me in the necessities that were clothes and booze. On one occasion, we broke into a derelict church with the specific intention of nicking the bells. We managed to get them out of the belfry and somehow manhandle them down the stairs. When we got to the bottom, they wouldn't fit through the door! Fuck knows how they got them in there in the first place. Instead of a nice thick wad of pound notes, all we had to show for our labours was broken fingers and strained backs! This is when I started seriously to swot up on antiques. I'd go to the library in the city centre and nick books on Doulton, Crown Derby and Wedgwood. I'd read them from cover to cover and then sneak them back in again. It never crossed my mind actually to join the library.

Newcastle City Centre was a rough place. There was always – and I mean *always* – someone looking for trouble. And they always seemed to find me. We were milling around the chip shop after closing time, when I saw some lad giving his girlfriend some stick. He was shouting and swearing at her, calling her a bitch and a whore, starting to push her around. Then he grabbed her by the hair and I heard her shriek with pain. He was just about to give her a smack when I rudely interrupted.

'Touch her and I'll fucking kill you, pal!' I said as I walked up and stood in front of him.

He turned round, looked me up and down and started to laugh. 'What the fuck do you think you're going to do, short arse?' He relaxed his grip from round her throat and she broke free and came and stood behind me. She was shitting herself and I was now cast in the role of Knight in Shining Armour.

'Why don't you pick on someone who'll hit you back, soft shite?' I said to goad him. 'Or are you really a woman yourself?' I already knew what I was going to do when he came at me.

He lunged at me but, as he did, I jumped up, grabbing him by the collars and smashing a nut straight into his face. He tried to push me off so he could start swinging but I was far too strong. I nutted him again, feeling his nose break like matchsticks. One more and his face had literally disintegrated. He started to go down. As he did, I smashed a right hook into his head, just to help him on his way. He went down on all fours, perfectly placed to get a kicking on the floor. But why would I do that? I'd already done him, it wasn't my style, even though he had been slapping a girl around. I turned to the young maiden. 'You all right?'

She was shaking, crying. 'Yes.'

'Come on, I'll make sure you get home all right.'

We left her arsehole boyfriend on all fours, vomiting on the pavement, and headed off into the night. It was cold, so, being a gentleman, I slipped my arm around her. She didn't mind. As we walked, every now and then, my hand would accidentally brush across her backside. It didn't seem to offend her. We got to her house and stood at the door.

'You going to invite me in for a coffee?'

'You'll have to be quick,' she said. 'My dad's due back in 20 minutes.'

'I'll be quick,' I reassured her as the front door closed behind me. 'I always am...'

One Bank Holiday weekend, the Dolce Vita was having a soul night but it didn't start until midnight. The pubs kicked out at 11.00pm in those days and we had time to kill. So we staggered to Bower's Café, another location used in *Get Carter!*. It was a Mecca for piss-heads all over the city at that time of night as it did the best burgers in town. Perfect for soaking up the beer! Me and a few of the lads were standing in the queue, hard as nails and pissed out of our faces, when we noticed a group of girls in front of us. We were turning the air blue with our conversation, when one girl turned round and said, 'Do you have to?'

'Have to what?' Billy asked.

'Swear like that.'

The girl was dressed in a white shirt, black skirt and a black tie. She looked like a copper and we nearly shit ourselves.

'Sorry, pet,' I slurred, trying to appear sober and reasonable. I didn't know at the time but I was speaking to my future wife.

We got talking and it turned out that she wasn't a copper after all, which was a good thing, given the number of scams I was pulling. She was a few months younger than me, just turned 17, and her name was Carol. We hit it off straight away. Well, that's my story! She thought I was a pain in the arse to be truthful, but I told her that I usually went to the Dolce Vita on a Sunday night and there she was the following week. Game on!

I was all grown up now so I took her for a meal for our first date. We went to the Wimpy for hamburger and chips. As a believer in equality, I let her pay for her own. Who said romance is dead? But it was the start of something special.

Jobs were harder and harder to come by and, a few months later, I was offered a job as a labourer on the roads, following in the footsteps of my dad and brother Davie. But there was a complication. It was an Irish company and their next big contract was going to be in Jersey. Things were going well with Carol, but it was a struggle to get any decent work. Things in the North-East were going from bad to worse and there's a limit to how much lead you can nick. Moving so far away from home didn't faze me. I suppose I had a streak of independence running through me that had developed ever since I'd started earning for myself at the age of eight. It was a big cruel bastard of a world out there and I knew that the only things I would get would be those things that I worked for, be it wheeling and dealing, lead or digging roads.

So off I went to Jersey with another mate called John Scott. I had to leave Carol in Newcastle, but I was desperate to work. We got a flat in St Helier and instantly settled into our new life. We were taken under the wing of some Irish navvies and the way they worked was a real eye-opener. We'd start work at 8.00am, me digging the trenches for the drainage that would run alongside the road. At half-eleven we'd knock off and go straight to the pub, where the Irish lads would drink four or five pints of Guinness 'to line their stomachs for an afternoon of hard graft'. And then it was full steam ahead, an absolutely punishing pace until half-five when they all went back to the pub.

At first, I was fucked. Most days, my arms and shoulders were burning by mid-morning and I was seriously flagging by the end of the day. But, as the weeks passed by, I noticed I was getting fitter and even stronger. Without even knowing it, I was building huge reserves of stamina to complement my unique upper-body strength. And it was all done on the tools, in the grime and the dirt of laying roads, as opposed to a beautiful gym with shiny machines.

In one of the *Rocky* films, Sylvester Stallone went back to basics, lifting logs, chopping wood, before his fight with the huge Russian. He should have got himself a job with tarmac instead.

St Helier was jumping most nights of the week and I was out every single night. It had a nightclub with an aeroplane in the car park and a load of bars. We'd go out straight after work and just drink until closing time. There were plenty of holidaymakers to crack on to but there was sometimes trouble with the locals.

I was standing at the bar one night talking to a couple of mates when two girls squeezed in behind me to get served. I did what comes naturally, turning round and firing off a few one-liners. I was talking to them for a good ten minutes when a lad walked up to me.

'You! Outside! I'm going to rip your fucking head off.'

'Why?' I said surprised.

'You're trying to pull my girlfriend.'

'I'm not, mate,' I said, trying to defuse the situation. 'We're just having a bit of friendly banter. I haven't even asked her name, so how am I trying to pull her?'

Even though the girl was backing me up, her boyfriend was having none of it. Honour demanded that he kick my head in.

'Outside, you little bastard!'

'You don't want to do that...'

'Get outside!' he persisted.

'Fair enough,' I replied, 'but don't say I didn't warn you.'

We walked out into the car park and he turned and swung at me. I was expecting it, ducked it easily and smashed a right hook straight into the side of his head. It took him clean out and he hit the floor unconscious. I walked back in to finish my drink.

A few minutes later, I was back at the bar when I felt someone grab me from behind. He obviously hadn't got the message in the car park. Instinctively, I slammed my head backwards, feeling it connect with his face, then I spun round to finish him off. But it wasn't lover-boy. It was a copper and I'd just done him big style.

Three more came racing into the bar when they saw what had happened and there was a bit of a scuffle, resulting in my being dragged outside. Lover-boy had obviously come round and, not being as hard as he thought he was, had run crying to the police. I was handcuffed and thrown in the back of a van. But I noticed that they hadn't closed the doors properly.

All I'd been doing was having a quiet drink. None of this was my fault! I took my chance and kicked the back doors of the van. They burst open and I was off up the street as fast as my little legs could carry me, which wasn't that fast bearing in mind I was handcuffed and had a bellyful of ale. The holidaymakers of St Helier watched my attempted escape, pursued by three very pissed-off coppers. I could hear people starting to shout, 'Go on, son! Faster! Faster!' and I didn't look back. 'They're catching you!' someone else shouted. I was getting a running commentary! The police caught me 200 yards down the road and dragged me back to the van. This time they locked the doors properly.

I was placed on remand pending a court appearance. I spent a week at Her Majesty's pleasure in La Moye Prison, which is not the most pleasant of places. I was in a cell by myself, with fuck all to do. It was just like the Oscar-winning film *Papillon*, where an incarcerated Steve McQueen starts doing sit-ups and press-ups in his cell. The only thing I had in the cell with me was a Bible. I didn't see much point in reading it when I already knew what happened at the end.

This time, there was a real appearance in the Magistrates' Court but, unknown to me, I'd had a stroke of good fortune. The copper I'd nutted had seen my details. He, too, was from Newcastle and he knew my older brother Davie. Small world! I could have been charged with resisting arrest but they only charged me with assaulting a police officer. When it came to him giving his evidence, he told the magistrate that I hadn't known what was happening and I hadn't meant to stick one on him. Nothing was mentioned of my escape attempt. I was lucky, I could have been given up to six months in La Moye but all I got was a hundred-quid fine.

In all, I was in Jersey for two years. Carol moved down to be with me and we got engaged but she missed her family so she went back to Newcastle. There seemed little point staying together when we were so young and so far apart so we broke up. But, a little while later, I was paid off and, with nothing else on the horizon, I headed back to Newcastle, to pick up the threads of my old life.

Nothing had changed. The same faces were still pulling the same scams and drinking in the same bars. It was like I'd never been away. I went straight back into the 'lead trade' and straight back on the piss with my old mates. We were stripping the roof on an old house one day when Ham dropped a big roll of lead from the roof. It landed in the next-door garden and, the next second, some old bloke, obviously a next-door neighbour, was going ballistic! He'd obviously had a fright.

'You stupid little bastards!' he was shouting. 'You could've fucking killed me!'

'Quick!' Ham shouted. 'Scarper!'

We were off across the roofs like rats as it seemed pretty obvious the neighbour would call the police.

The following day, we went back to see if we could salvage anything.

'It can't have been a neighbour,' Matty said, looking at the house. 'That one's derelict as well.'

We sneaked into the back garden where he'd been to see if the lead was still there. It was just where it had fallen. What a result! We rolled it up and were carrying it through the front gate when a police car pulled up. I think the phrase is 'caught red-handed'.

'Where you taking that, boys?' he said, laughing at how easy a collar it was.

'We were going to weigh it in,' I said innocently. 'We've just found it lying in that garden over there. Doesn't look like it belongs to anyone so we thought we'd take it.'

'Fair enough,' said the copper, obviously thinking that the brownie points he'd get for nicking us would not be worth the time filling in the charge sheets. 'It's not your lucky day, though,' he continued. 'Some old bloke found a big bag of gold sovereigns in that garden yesterday.'

There were about 20 of us from Shieldfield who would usually go out together at weekends. There were so many of us that we just walked straight into bars; we didn't bother to queue. It wasn't like three or four bouncers were going to stop such a big group doing what it wanted. We had a laugh, had a proper drink and looked after each other. By this point, most of the other gangs knew who I was as I'd normally chinned a few of them in bars or in the street if they'd started on anyone I was out with. I was always straight there and people didn't really tend to kick off with me because there would only be one winner.

WARNINGS FROM THE MASKED MAN

The others were out mob-handed as usual one Saturday night. I was out with a girl but had arranged to meet them for last orders. Matty had left the group at about 9.00pm to go and meet his girlfriend, but he'd been followed by three lads who'd jumped him and given him a proper hiding. It was obvious who had done it. A gang from the West End had been drinking in the same bars as us for months now and there'd been real needle between us. But this night it had spilled over into open war.

The Shieldfield Squad went looking for them and it all exploded in Pumphries Bar in the Bigg Market. Chairs and tables were sent flying as 40 kids steamed into each other, using anything that they could get their hands on. It was like a scene from the Wild West! Pint glasses were being used as missiles and innocent punters sent sprawling like skittles. People were diving for cover under tables to escape the mayhem. The fighting spilled out on to the street outside, the bouncers powerless to stop it. The police turned up but there was no way they were getting out of their cars! It would have needed a squad of riot police to break it up.

It soon started to die off as more left the scene to avoid being arrested when the police reinforcements arrived. The Shieldfield lads made for the Canny Lad for last orders. They knew the West End gang drank up by the civic centre so it looked like that was it for the night. It was time to compare war stories over a pint.

But, when they got to the Canny Lad, they found the West End mob waiting. It looked like it was all going to kick off again. And then I rocked up.

'What's going on here?' I asked, noticing a variety of black eyes and split lips.

Ham told me the score and I flipped my lid. I walked up to

them. 'It's not kicking off in here again,' I said menacingly. 'I'll tell you how we'll settle it, nice and fair. You all form a queue and I'll take you two at a time outside. Hardest first!'

They knew what I was capable of and didn't want to accept my kind offer, but the Shieldfield mob saw them again a few weeks later when it all kicked off for a second time in another bar. Again, it all spilled out on to the street. One of the quietest and youngest in the group, a lad called Tony, did Shieldfield proud. He was normally quiet but, when he lost it, he *really* lost it. As people were rolling round in the road, he finally flipped completely. He smashed a chair against a wall and ripped off one of the legs. Then he piled in, cracking heads and scattering his enemies for fun. He was like Genghis Khan! He chased them down the street, totally out of control, swinging wildly. I was just gutted to miss the fun.

It wasn't just other gangs you had to watch out for. Some of the bouncers were total bastards as well. We were standing in Dobson's one night when one of the bouncers spat on a lad called Billy's back. He'd had trouble with him before but the bloke was fucking huge.

'Are you going to let him do that?' I said.

'Just leave it, John.'

'Leave it? No fucking chance! If you don't do something, I will, then I'll give you a clip for being a soft shite.'

About ten minutes later, the bouncer walked over and did it again.

'Are you going to let him do that?' I repeated.

'Just leave it, John.'

'Go and knock him out!'

The bouncer overheard what I was saying to him. 'Why don't *you* do something about it then?' he said staring at me. I think he thought he might scare me.

'OK,' I said calmly.

'Outside then!' he said, laughing.

'I've paid £1.20 for this pint and I'm not going to waste it on you. As soon as I'm finished, I'll come and see you.'

I took my time in finishing my drink and, to be honest, forgot all about it. Challenges were like water off a duck's back to me by that stage and it didn't exactly put my pulse through the roof. As I was walking past Ape Man at the door, he said, 'Haven't you forgotten something, shorty?'

'Shit, yeah!' I said turning around and slamming the nut on him. It instantly broke his nose and blinded him. I dragged him out into the street, punching him repeatedly, and we ended up in the road. His nose had disintegrated into a bloody pulp. He was flailing around, trying to connect with me as a taxi screeched to a halt, only just missing the two of us. I threw him on the bonnet of the car, jumped up to stand on it and then smashed my forehead into his face again and again. He was in bits within two minutes. None of his back-up even tried to help him.

The following week, he was back on the door but in a total mess. He was telling people that six kids had jumped him and turned him over. People believed him as well.

One day, I was walking down the street when I saw two girls coming towards me. They had horrible punk hairstyles, orange and green and purple and looked fucking dreadful. I was smirking as I walked past when I suddenly recognised one of them.

'Carol?' I said as my jaw hit the floor. 'What the fuck have you done to your hair?' It probably wasn't the best one-liner I'd ever delivered.

We started seeing each other again and, a little while later, we got engaged. It was time for me to give up the follies of youth and settle down. I still had no interests other than trying to make a living in any way I could. But the industries of the North-East were terminally ill and more and more people were hitting the dole queue every day.

By the age of 21, I'd settled into a routine. I would work when the jobs were there and deal when the dole queue beckoned. By now, I had a love, a passion for antiques and I could spot little gems that kept the wolf from the door. I picked up a Royal Doulton figurine at a car boot sale for 50p and sold it the following day for 60 quid. Another time, I got some Victorian picture frames for a fiver and sold them for a ton. It doesn't sound like a lot now, but that was a fortnight's dole money and it kept me in beer.

One night, we were in the Canny Lad having a few pints when someone had an idea. The annual fair was on the town moor. It might be a laugh to head up there and go on the rides. As with all ideas, it seemed like a good one given the beer we'd already drunk.

We staggered up to the fairground where the folly of our ways soon became apparent. Beer and spinning rides don't mix and so we ended up in a tent, watching boxing and wrestling bouts. The tent was packed with a few hundred people, all hoping to see some blood.

The Fairground Champion, an ex-heavyweight pro, was challenging all-comers.

'Who will fight this man?' shouted the announcer from the middle of the boxing ring. 'Who will fight this man?'

There weren't any takers.

'Who will fight his man? Come on! Who is brave enough to take on the Fairground Champion?'

'He will,' shouted a voice. I felt a shove on my back as my supposed mates pushed me forwards.

'Aha!' shouted the announcer. 'Ladies and gentlemen, we have a challenger!'

The crowd started cheering and I suddenly realised that they were all looking at me. I looked at the size of the Fairground Champion and was suddenly sober.

'This man is too small to fight the Champion!' shouted the announcer. The crowd roared its disapproval.

'No, I'm not!' I heard myself saying indignantly.

'This man is too small to fight the Champion,' the announcer bellowed again, whipping the crowd into frenzy.

'No, I'm fucking not!' I shouted and the crowd roared.

Before I had time to think about what was happening, I'd been stripped to the waist and some old leather gloves fastened crudely on to my fists. I climbed into the ring, much to the merriment of my mates. The crowd were placing bets with some gypsy runners. Not many were backing me.

The bell rang and I walked forward, unsure what exactly I was supposed to do. If I start dancing round, I thought, I'm going to look like a right tit.

The Fairground Champion came at me, connecting with an uppercut that threw me across the ring and into the ropes. I started dancing for all I was worth.

The big man found it hard to track me as I moved around the ring, keeping out of his range. He was strong but his punches were slow and I was fast and light on my feet. Each time he swung, I ducked underneath it and punched him in the ribs. I felt him wince with pain.

The heavyweight tried to close me down, cutting down my space. It made sense for me to stay as far away as possible from him so that's what I did. As he got close, I'd smack him once then get out the way. He was getting pissed off, the crowd urging him forward to squash the little man. Suddenly, he lunged at me, swinging wildly. I hit him with lefts and rights straight into his body, and then slammed a right hook into his head. The big man was out before he hit the floor.

The crowd were stunned as they watched me jumping up and down inside the ring. I was presented with my prize money, the princely sum of £2.

As I climbed out of the ring, the owner of the boxing stall put his arm around me. 'Well done!' he said. 'Come on, I'm taking you for a drink.'

I was led to the owner's caravan. Inside, he poured me a large whisky. 'I'd like to offer you a job,' he said suddenly, pouring yet another huge measure of scotch into my glass.

'A job?'

He nodded, easing back into his chair and smiling.

'Doing what?' I asked. 'Feeding the elephants?'

'In the boxing tent,' he said, laughing. 'You'll get to travel all over Europe with the fair. You'll earn good money.'

I was tempted. The caravan was warm and, what with the adrenalin, the cheering of the crowd still echoing in my ears and the scotch, I felt almost euphoric.

'Can I have some time to think about it?' I asked.

'Of course, come back later and see me.'

I stepped into the cool night air to clear my head. I'd always wanted to see the world and the furthest I'd been so far was digging roads in Jersey. Every day would be exciting and completely different to the last. The bright lights of the huge fair seemed to hypnotise me and draw me in.

I was suddenly aware of someone emerging from the shadows behind me. A huge figure walked up to me. It was the fairground wrestler, still dressed head to toe in black.

'You did well in there,' he said as he came up close, thrusting a huge shovel of a hand forward for me to shake.

'Yeah, thanks,' I said.

'Has he offered you a job then?'

'Yeah.'

'Don't do it,' said the wrestler, shaking his head.

'Why not? There's not much else going on round here at the minute,' I said truthfully.

'Why would you want to get punched in the face a thousand times a day for a few quid?'

'You do it.'

'I don't have a choice.'

'Maybe I don't either,' I said, shrugging.

'Look, son, I live in a 12ft caravan every day of my life. Every nutter who comes to the fair wants to rip my head off. I get spat at, sworn at, bitten and even burned with cigarettes. And that's just the women! Behind the flashing lights the punters see, this is a fucking horrible way to put food on the table.'

We stood in silence, the faint screams and laughter of the latest victims to brave the fairground rides cutting through the cool night air.

'Do yourself a favour, son,' the wrestler said quietly, almost paternally. 'Go home.'

I nodded, turned away and headed back to my friends.

4

MUG'S GAME

'A champion shows who he is by what he does
when he's tested. When a person gets up and says,
"I can still do this," he's a champion.'
EVANDER HOLYFIELD

B y the age of 25, the wheels had come off my life as the
North-East underwent massive changes. By 1983, the
traditional sources of employment – the shipyards and heavy
industries of the Tyne – had been decimated. The region,
once the engineering powerhouse of the world, was now a
desolate wasteland and a whole generation of men were on
the scrapheap as unemployment figures rocketed to a record
four million.

Carol and I were married now and things were tough. We
were living in a flat in Throckley, about eight miles upstream
from Newcastle. It was on the edge of rolling countryside,
which ran all the way to Carlisle, Hadrian's Wall country. It
would have been beautiful if it weren't for the fucking horrible
estate the council had built. We lived in a third-floor flat and,
at the time, the place was a ghetto. We'd got married the
previous year at a register office, with me wearing a pale-blue

suit that I swear was the height of fashion at the time! Our daughter, Kelly, had been born in the March, which, although a joyous occasion, had put an even bigger financial strain on us. When Carol had gone into labour, I'd done the right thing, been the modern man and had been there for Kelly's birth, instead of pacing in the corridor outside with a cigarette in my hand, which was the traditional practice for blokes at the time. All I can say is that I could understand from witnessing the pain of childbirth why many women don't really fancy going through it for a second time. Neither did I. My hand was killing me for weeks after.

For most of the time we'd been married, I'd been signing on the dole. Sure, I'd get the odd bit of work here and there, mainly labouring on building sites or in factories. But the old industries were dying and in the North-East there were simply no jobs available. I worked for a little while at the Delta Steel Works as a 'slinger'. The steel works made the rails for the railways and my job was to 'sling' the red-hot rails down the rollers where they would be cooled. There was this arsehole who used to go round the factory and his favourite pastime was to come up to people from behind and slap them on the top of the head as hard as he could. He was obviously a frustrated comedian because, in my eyes, his little gag was just *so funny*. He should have been on the stage. He was a big lad and he used his size to intimidate people, a typical bully.

One day, I was standing talking with another lad when he walked past and slapped the top of my head.

'Do that again and I'll fucking kill you,' I said through gritted teeth but he'd already walked off laughing to himself.

There's only one way to handle a bully. You front up to them and watch them crumble. They're so stupid that they don't actually expect someone to challenge them. I bided my time because I knew I'd have my moment. It came a few days later.

Dickhead was walking past me, oblivious to anyone or anything. He was the big man, people showed him respect, people moved out of the way in his presence. It was just like being back in the schoolyard again. I walked up to him. 'I want a word with you.'

Before he had time to react, I slammed my forehead straight into his face. He went down like a sack of shit. I could have really put the boot in if I'd wanted to. But why stoop to his level? He knew the score now. I walked off, leaving him in a pool of blood. I bet he stopped his little game after that.

While I was at Delta, we took another hit financially when I ended up on the sick for three months. I was grafting away one day, firing the hot rails up the rollers when I slipped and fell. Instinctively, I put my arms out to break my fall. But I'd forgotten to put my safety gloves on. The palms of my hands made contact with the red-hot metal. I don't even know how loud I screamed as I watched the skin melt from the palms of my hands.

But no job lasted long and I looked on it as being up to me to try to supplement the meagre allowance of 60 quid a week that the Government said that a family of three could live on.

The flat was a shit-hole. We couldn't even afford second-hand furniture for it. We'd had to borrow stuff from family and friends and most of the toys that Kelly had were presents. Carol and I were sleeping on a mattress because we couldn't even afford a bed. But we weren't alone. There were tens of thousands of couples just like us, on the scrapheap before their lives had even begun.

My only real interests were antiques and football. I was still playing for Shieldfield Social on a Sunday. I was now the team enforcer and would be there if there was any trouble, protecting some of the younger lads. We'd just played a cup match where there had been absolute mayhem. Davie, who was still the star centre-forward, had been knocked out early in the game by the opposition centre-back. The bastard had deliberately taken Davie out with his elbow and it had all gone from there. In the ensuing brawl, which had involved all 22 players, 10 substitutes and both managers, I'd nutted three of them. The lad who had done our Davie didn't even get a yellow card and, although the game continued, it erupted at various intervals as the referee struggled to maintain any sort of control. At the end, I went looking for the centre-back. He ended up barricaded inside his changing room, petrified, with me kicking at the door.

I suppose I had a natural confidence from knowing what I could do if I did get in trouble. I'd been in town a couple of weeks earlier and a lad I barely knew from Byker had been going to get jumped by some big bodybuilder. He was literally shitting himself. I made him point the arsehole out and then said loud enough for him to hear, 'Give me two quid and I'll knock him out for you.' Mr Muscle was out the door within seconds. Did I psyche him out? Maybe. But fighting is all about bottle and confidence. I had the bottle to take him on and the confidence that I would win. I didn't even have to swing a punch.

One day, Ham and I were in town crossing the roundabout at the top of the Tyne Bridge when a car came flying round it at 50mph. It nearly hit the two of us and we both let the driver know our displeasure by giving him V-signs, and not the sort that Winston Churchill used.

He came back round and stopped the car, obviously the big man. He jumped out ready for action, clearly not coming to apologise. 'Two fucking smart-arses, eh?' he shouted as he came towards us.

I looked straight at him and said calmly and quietly, 'Get back in your car or I'll rip your fucking head off!'

He slowed down, unsettled by how sure of myself I was.

Ham laughed. 'I'd do as he says if I was you, mate. You really don't want a piece of him. He's your worst nightmare.'

It stopped him dead. Now he was really unsure. My temper, admirably held in check, was close to breaking though. I took a step towards him, slipping into Terminator mode. He backed off a little.

'Come on, then,' I said, lunging at him, 'I'll fucking kill you!'

But he was already off. He ran back to his car and burned rubber up the street.

I was still wheeling and dealing to try to make enough to get by. But it's hard when you've got nothing to work with. There was an antiques shop in Vine Lane owned by a lovely bloke called Geordie Punting and his wife Betty and they were really good to me. They'd let me buy stuff on tick and pay for it weekly, whenever I had the money. I'd drop off a quid here, a fiver there, for some piece that I thought I could sell on for more. It was a slow way of earning a crust but I had to do something to preserve both my sanity and my dignity. I would trawl the second-hand shops, trying to find things I could sell at a profit, even just a quid or two. A vase, a picture, anything really. It was pretty low-grade stuff but it kept my pride intact. I refused to give up. I wouldn't just wait for the Giro to land on the doormat.

I always saw the same faces at the antique fairs; the auction houses and the car boot sales. You would hear the rags-to-riches stories that kept your own dream alive. I heard one story about one bloke on the scene who bought a vase from an auction house for £500 and later sold it at Sotheby's in London for over 100 grand. I heard stories like that all the time. The lucky punter would always be a friend of a friend of a friend of the person telling you the story. Details were always sketchy and the exact amount was never known. But the story was true as sure as apples were apples. The optimist in me always thought it could one day be me, that I might strike it lucky rummaging through some box at a car boot sale.

Of course, you could always make the odd decent score. Most people in the antiques trade were knowledgeable, they knew what they were buying and what the going rate would be, but there were always people out to take advantage of you if you looked like an amateur. Of course, a piece didn't have to be an original to be worth something. The term 'copy' was never used; such pieces were usually called a 'replica' or a 'reproduction'. To me, they were 'snides' and they could sometimes offer a lucrative return.

I used to go to a flea market which was held at the train station at Tynemouth every week. Dealers came from miles around to buy and sell and the place was always packed. Usually, I'd be there, browsing the stalls, looking for something I could turn into a profit. But, this time, I was selling and the piece I was selling was a fucking gem.

I'd bought it about four months earlier. It was a life-size brass cast of a pit-bull terrier in a fighting stance by a French sculptor. I'd paid 80 quid for it from Vine Lane, but had paid in instalments so it had taken me a couple of months before I could put this little doggy in the window. It was beautiful and, to be honest, I'd bought it because I liked the look of it more than because I thought I could make a profit on it. It was a snide, but it was a good snide. When you turned it upside down, the finishing underneath was smooth, almost as good quality as the original would have been, rather than jagged like some mass-produced copy. But now I needed some cash and so it was up for sale.

I had a few other bits and pieces and I slung them all in the back of a car and headed down to the coast. The place was busier than usual and you always had dealers who would pounce you as soon as you opened your car boot. They'd start rummaging through your wares before you'd even got to your stall, in the hope of negotiating a quick bargain. As I opened up the boot of the car, one guy was straight over and he made a beeline for the dog.

It was a big bastard and he lifted it out with difficulty, trying to turn it over to see the signature below. I could see he was excited, while I remained poker-faced.

'How much do you want for the dog?' he asked.

I knew that if it were original it would have been worth about 800 quid. 'Er... I don't know,' I said, giving him a look that suggested that I was new to the game and didn't have a clue what I was doing. 'Give me 400 quid and it's yours.'

He almost had a hard-on when I said the price, but he was still going to be a cunt to me. 'I don't think it's really worth that much,' he said in a friendly way, patting me on the shoulder like a close mate, showing me that he had my best interests at heart.

'How much do you think it's worth then?' I said.

'Maybe 300. I'd take it off your hands for that, but I'm maybe robbing myself.'

'OK,' I said unsurely. '350.'

He pulled out a massive wad of notes and counted £350 into my hand.

'Is there anything else you'd like to look at?' I said innocently.

'No, that's fine,' he said as he struggled to get the dog into his arms. He couldn't get away fast enough. I dropped the boot, got back in the car and headed for home, having made a fortune in the space of just a few minutes.

I went back a few weeks later and saw the guy on his stall. The dog stood pride of place in the centre of the stall. It had obviously been spotted for the snide that it was. When he saw me, his face turned to thunder.

'Still got the dog I see,' I smirked.

'You bastard!' he said. 'You knew it wasn't an original.'

'Yeah, but you didn't,' I said, laughing. 'It's still a nice piece, though. I never actually wanted to sell it but I was skint at the time.'

'Do you want to buy it back?' he asked hopefully.

'Yeah. I'll give you 40 quid.'

'Fuck off!'

I was always on the lookout to make money and I had no shame. If I saw an interesting ornament in someone's window, I'd go and knock at the door and ask if I could buy it. I came out with ingenious little scams to make things look older than they were. You could take a figurine and rub mud on it from the garden, or ashes from a fire. Suddenly, it was worth an extra 20 quid if I got the right punter at my stall. But I didn't buy everything just to sell on. Yes, I could spot a bargain and, no doubt, it would be sold by the following day and the money would be spent. But I also kept quite a bit of stuff. I'd have Carol begging, 'No, John! You can't put that there. It's bloody horrible...' as I installed my latest art-deco ornament or picture in the flat. As soon as things got tight, I'd go back to selling again to keep the wolves from the door.

As with most people on our estate, our whole life was dominated by the lack of work and the lack of money. Despite the little victories, the lack of money affected almost everything. Take away a man's means of supporting his family and you take away his pride, his reason for living. Crime was on the up and, for the first time, drugs had started to become prevalent in the new working-class ghettos. It wasn't safe to walk the streets at night and I was desperate to get out.

I would still get out into town when I was flush. It was the days of the New Romantics and you had blokes wandering round the bars wearing nail polish without getting a smack in the face. I'd been out with Matty one night when we'd met up with Ham. As Matty got the beers in, Ham stared at me closely.

'John, what the fuck's that on your face?'

'Pan stick,' I replied, trying to make it sound like the most natural thing in the world.

'Pan stick? Why are you wearing fucking pan stick?'

'To hide the lines,' I said indignantly, as Matty came back with the beers.

'Matty, you're not going to believe this!' said Ham, stunned. 'Dava's wearing…' he paused as he got a close look at Matty's face. 'Oh no, not you as well!'

The old pubs of Newcastle were starting to make way for trendy bars such as Tux II, where there were telephones on all the tables to help you pull other people in the bar. Michael Jackson had just released *Thriller* and people were trying to copy his moves on dance floors all over the world. All except me. I'd been doing them for years anyway and there was nothing new that Wacko Jacko could teach me.

Daytime is down time when you're on the dole. If I had no money to wheel and deal, my only real reason to leave the flat would be to sign on once a fortnight. People spend years working, just so they can leave when they get to retirement age and get their lives and their freedom back. When you're on the dole, you have all the time in the world. The downside is that you have fuck all money. So you still don't have a life, it's just an existence. The thing that I found worst of all wasn't so much the lack of money, it was the sheer boredom.

I was in the flat one afternoon, staring blankly at the television when two lads from the estate knocked at the door. They were on their way to a local boxing gym and asked if I fancied going along. They'd tried to persuade me before but I'd never been interested. All I was bothered about was where the next pound note was coming from.

Carol was desperate to get me out of the flat, though, just so she didn't have to look at my face, which was like a smacked arse. Things had been slow with my trading recently and I was a right miserable bastard. Thinking it would do me good to start a hobby, she practically kicked me out the door.

We jumped on a bus and headed to West End Gym, although I was more interested in calling at a couple of second-hand shops close to the gym afterwards. The gym was dank and dark, the equipment ancient. But it produced some good amateur boxers. When we got there, two of them were grunting away on the heavy bags, glistening with sweat.

We messed around on the weights for a bit but I was bored. I wanted to be alone, to have a bit of peace and quiet. I wandered off to the now deserted bags. I picked up a pair of stinking old gloves from the floor and slipped them on. They were wet and sticky inside but I didn't give a fuck.

Alone, I started putting some punches into the bag. I soon settled into my workout, putting in right jabs and left crosses, always leading into a big right hook. I was starting to move a bit now as well, imagining the bag with arms, swinging punches at me like the Fairground Champion. I would duck under one of his big haymakers and slam a punch into where his ribs would be. I was Rocky Balboa! The Italian Stallion! The sweat was starting to run with the exertion, the tension of the last few weeks beginning to flow from my body. I felt relaxed, I felt good.

After a few minutes, a stranger broke my concentration, a man in his mid-fifties wearing a tattered, ill-fitting tracksuit. 'So who do you box for then?' he asked, smiling.

'You what?' I said, trying to get my breath back.

'Who do you box for? Which club?'

'I don't box for anyone,' I said turning away, suspecting that tracksuit man was taking the piss.

But he persisted, seeming genuinely interested. 'You given it up? A lot of people do. Say, how old are you?'

'Twenty-five,' I replied suspiciously. 'Why?'

'It's hard to keep people interested when they get to your age,' he said, shaking his head sadly. 'You're still showing some good touches, though. Not fancy a comeback? I'm Phil Fowler. I coach here and we're always on the look-out for new talent.'

'I've never been a boxer,' I said, now thoroughly confused.

'Never?'

'No. I'm not interested in it. I'm just here to mess around.'

'Do you want to start?' he suddenly asked.

I shook my head, but then a thought dawned on me. 'Do I get paid for it?'

'Er... no,' Phil Fowler replied. 'But you could win some trophies.'

'Trophies?' I said, incredulous, thinking of my current financial plight. 'I need more than just trophies!'

'Give it a go' he said, trying to convince me.

But two of my uncles had been boxers, one amateur and one professionally. It was a mug's game and I had no interest in it.

Fowler tried to make me promise to come along to training

the following week but I had no intention of doing so. I needed to make money, not waste time messing around with boxing.

A couple of months later and things were looking up. I'd scored a couple of times in my dealing and had a little money to go shopping for some home comforts. Every penny went on trying to provide something better for Carol and Kelly. Well, I had a few beers as well but I deserved it! I bought a bed and also a new cabinet for the lounge. I bought it from MFI and, in spite of the instructions that were in the pack, I still managed to build it so it didn't collapse. Unfortunately, the money hadn't stretched as far as buying things to go on it.

'It looks stupid like that,' I said as the two of us stared at the empty cabinet.

'It needs something,' Carol said. 'Why don't we get some wedding photos put in frames?'

'We have wedding photos?'

She didn't see the funny side. 'I could get some nice vases and put flowers in,' she suggested, unperturbed.

'You'll have to wait until I make some more money for that.' Then I had a thought. 'How would you feel if I took up boxing?'

'Boxing? Why on earth would you want to take up boxing?'

'Free trophies,' I replied, thinking back to my chance encounter at West End Gym.

5

NEW KID ON THE BLOCK

*'I always felt good about myself. I was just an
average person. But if an average person makes up their
mind to do something, they can.'*

LARRY HOLMES

At first, people were ripping the piss out of me big style. Taking up boxing at the age of 25! I was being asked if I was going to get a train set for Christmas as well. They also said there'd need to be a change to the Marquis of Queensbury rules before I'd be allowed in a ring, given that my main weapon of choice had always been my forehead connecting with someone else's face at high velocity. But everyone knew what I could do in a street fight. They knew I could handle myself. The main question was whether I could take street fighting into a boxing ring.

I naturally led with my right hand, which made me a 'southpaw' boxer. But I was unusual in that my leading right was also my strongest. Most southpaws would have a bigger left punch instead. At 9 stone, I was classed as a featherweight. I was comfortable with that as I'd spent the last ten years on a diet of beer, pie and chips and there still wasn't a pick of fat on me. At least I'd never struggle to make the weight as so many boxers do!

The training began immediately and it was hard at first, but I loved it. I started jogging for the first time in my life, three miles every morning at a nice gentle pace. I'd be at the boxing club three nights a week, working just on the bags and pads. I would keep on asking Phil when I could fight but he'd tell me to be patient. I had to learn the basics before they'd let me in the ring. Sure, I could punch and I could punch hard, but I needed to work on my upper-body movement, my balance and my footwork. It's amazing how many separate disciplines come together to make a fighting machine.

Phil was also keen to get me moving like an amateur boxer, tagging and evading, scoring points as opposed to looking for the sort of winning punch I normally delivered in the Bigg Market on a Saturday night. Phil's aim was to get me to hit and evade rather than hit but take punishment, which is the professional sport. I knew I would have to adapt my own particular style if I was to be any good. I was only 5ft 5in and my arms were short. Not the classic body design for a successful boxer. Any decent boxer would be able to hold me at bay with a jab if they had a longer reach, which nearly all did. They'd be able to sit back, picking up points by snapping jabs into my face, while I'd be swinging fresh-air shots. So there was only one thing for it. I would have to fight, not box. Fighting and boxing are two completely different things. All I wanted to do was to get in the ring and knock people out.

After just four weeks, Phil deemed me ready to step into the ring for my first sparring session. He was keen to see me put it all together in a real situation so he brought in three of the more experienced club boxers to spar with me, including a local lad called Stevie Bolton who was rumoured to be on the verge of an England call-up.

We were working on two-minute rounds, with my sparring partners rotating after every three rounds. I blasted the first guy, absolutely annihilated him. He was on his arse within 30 seconds and after that he back-pedalled furiously. I was in hot pursuit all the time and it must have been comical to see. Me swinging wildly, intent on caving his head in and him using every trick in the book to duck and dance away from the haymakers I was throwing. This boxing game is easy, I thought. Keep on putting them up and I'll keep on knocking them down.

Phil was less complimentary however. 'Where the fuck you been the last few weeks, Dava? Because you certainly haven't been learning your boxing from me! You looked like you were in a bar-room brawl! Take it easy, this isn't the last bus home on a Saturday night!'

Against my next opponent, I was a little more controlled but, again, I would lose any form of style once I thought I could finish him. Phil had the patience of someone who had seen this many times before, which was a good thing. Again, he called me over. 'You've got to be disciplined, John,' he said quietly. 'You've got to remember your footwork, your movement. Use your jab more. Try to open up your target. If you take your time, the openings will come. But not if you're already on your arse!'

I tried to take the words to heart. Be patient and look for openings. Then it was time for Stevie Bolton, who'd been watching it all with an air of mild amusement. Bolton was a lovely boxer. He was lithe and supple and he moved with the grace and poise of a panther. Watching him shadow box to warm up, I could see instantly that he was good, that he had lightning in his hands. I found myself thinking it was no surprise that he was close to an England vest.

The bell went and I came out slowly, which he hadn't expected. He'd stayed back, waiting for me to dive in, so he could pick holes in my defences. The two of us were standing out of punching range when Phil shouted, 'What the fuck you waiting for? Get it on!'

If this was a Hollywood film, I'd have knocked him clean out. But I didn't. I stayed calm. I stayed disciplined. And I matched him. I held my own for two rounds. To the untrained eye, it was just two guys sparring. But not to Phil. He saw expertly how Stevie tagged and evaded. How I slipped his punches and closed in, hammering big body shots into him. It was a clash of two different styles and, at the end, we were both fucked. Stevie wrapped his arms around me.

'Fuck me, Dava! You caught me with some cracking shots!'

Fowler was standing shaking his head. 'There's no way I can put you in with another novice,' he said, laughing. 'I'll be done for murder!'

It was time to start fighting and I couldn't wait! My plan was to fight close to my opponent, getting inside their defences to fire off my own big punches. I would have to take punches, but I reckoned all I needed to do was catch an opponent once and it would be lights-out time. I would try to control my opponent through sheer aggression. But it was a tall order for an old, inexperienced piss-head just entering the sport. Essentially, my plan would remain the same for the next ten years.

Two weeks later, I had my first amateur fight. It was in the faded surroundings of the Spanish City, the big, old white dome in the seaside resort of Whitley Bay. It was hardly Caesar's Palace but it was a big night for me. I was fighting a guy who'd had 30 amateur fights and won over half. That's a handy record in amateur circles so he was no mug. Usually, there would be no way a novice like me would have his first fight against someone so experienced but Phil was confident and so was I. If he's got a chin, I'm going to find it, I thought to myself.

'Just take your time with him,' Phil told me, as I warmed up in the corner beforehand. 'Keep your discipline. Use your right jab and, if he opens up, clobber him!'

The bell rang and I was out the traps like a greyhound after a rabbit. He tried to back me off with a left jab but I instantly swivelled and let fly with a right body shot straight into his side. Before he even had time to get his balance, I'd steamrollered him into the corner and was blasting him with straight lefts and right hooks into the head. One caught him an absolute beauty and I saw his lips explode. I was coming at him from all angles and he ducked and swung low and left away from me just as I launched a right hook. It flew into fresh air and was so hard it almost swung me around 360 degrees.

My prey was off, already deciding that there was no way he could match me for strength if I got in close. I tried to corner him again and he fired a left-right combination straight into my head. I barely felt them and they didn't stop my progress. Before he'd even had time to step back and get his balance, I'd overpowered him and launched more body shots into his midriff. I felt him deflate and, as he backed against the ropes, I drilled two more right jabs straight through his guard and into his face. He was already desperate to back me off, to slow the onslaught, and he tried to swing a right hook, which fell perfectly into my trap. As a southpaw, he would expect my big punches to come from my left hand. But now his head presented a beautiful target for my strong right. As he swung, he opened up fully and I did exactly as Phil had told me. I sunk a right uppercut straight into his face, right on the button. He was out cold before he even hit the ground.

Phil was ecstatic. 'Go on, son! I knew you were good!' he shouted as he wrapped his arms around me.

I was out of it completely, the adrenalin coursing through my veins, the biggest high of my life. Little did I know it then, but I was already addicted.

By the end of that year, fighting was an obsession. I loved feeling so fit and I loved the thrill of getting in the ring or knowing that, in three weeks, two days, one hour, I'd be back there, hearing the sound of the bell, with another opponent about to feel the Davison hammer. I was fighting pretty much every week and, out of my first eleven fights, I won nine and was also starting to develop a reputation. From my nine wins, seven were with straight knockouts, unusual in amateur boxing circles. One victim had likened getting in the ring with me to being hit by a car.

It sounds great but it was actually having a negative effect. I'd turn up for fights, raring to go, only to find that my opponent hadn't shown. As soon as people heard that they were matched against me, they didn't seem to want to know. I even had some boxing clubs claiming that John Davison was not my real name and that I was really a ringer from Scotland or the south. It was laughable. Even in losing, my reputation as a dangerous opponent had been enhanced. Both my defeats had come to Mo Hanif, an England international who had won the ABA National Title just four years earlier. One defeat was a disqualification for use of the head (old habits die hard!); the other was on a points decision when it was clear to everyone in the hall that I'd given him a kicking. In my mind, Hanif's England vest had been the deciding factor in the judges' decision. The crowd weren't fooled however. They were so incensed that there was a mini riot, with pint glasses and bottles being thrown at the judges from the balcony above. The Shieldfield lads were in that night, although I'm sure it had nothing to do with them! I was pissed off to lose both fights but the signs were there that I maybe had something about me. It was a promising start and Phil Fowler was starting to talk about entering me into bigger competitions. I didn't really care what he did, as long as I could climb into a ring and fight.

For the first time, being on the dole was proving to be a blessing in disguise. I had time on my hands and, now I'd found something to aim for, I really went for it. Part of it was selfish in that I loved what I was doing, the personal challenges it was giving me, the discipline it was teaching me. I'd always been the same in that, if someone challenged me to a fight, I could never back down. Now, here I was with an almost limitless supply of challenges. And I was going to take them all seriously. I was going to take them all personally. There was no way anyone was going to beat me. They would have to fight me like a man with none of this amateur tip-tap crap.

But another part of it was far more serious. I knew that boxing could be dangerous, even more so for me because of my age. I was no spring chicken and I was entering the sport in the aftermath of the death of Johnny Owen, the British and European Bantamweight Champion, who'd died after a World Title fight a few years earlier. The sense of national loss that the whole country had felt at his long, drawn-out death in America had led to the British Medical Association calling for boxing to be banned. I had a wife and baby daughter to think about. I knew that I had to be super-fit and, little did I know it, I was laying the groundwork for everything else that would follow.

JOHN DAVISON: LITTLE MAN, BIG HEART

I'd be out training if I wasn't out dealing. I packed an old canvas bag full of rags and would carry it down the hill to the woods near the flat first thing each morning. I'd hang it from a tree and work on three-minute rounds for as long as I could lift my arms. Then I'd run up and down the hill over and over again until I was blowing out of my arse. I must have looked like a proper nut case. The woods had a small lake on one side and I'd have all these anglers sitting watching me, scratching their heads in wonder as I did sets of press-ups and sits-ups, 300 a time. I even managed to 'inherit' a ghetto blaster from somewhere, a big fuck-off silver beast the size of a house. It was louder than a jumbo jet and I'd pump out some Tom Jones tunes while I worked out. I had to sell it the next time I was skint. The fishermen were delighted, as they'd been shouting for weeks that I was scaring the fish away!

After a year with West End Boys' Club, I moved across to Grainger Park. West End was a good club and Phil Fowler was bringing me on, but I was struggling to get sparring partners who could match me. Grainger Park had some good boxers as well as heavier boxers and, as no featherweight cope with me, I preferred to fight middleweights where I could feel tested. Grainger Park had two excellent coaches in Norman Wright and Billy Melton. I knew that they would keep the fights coming thick and fast.

Norman and Billy left me to develop my own natural style, and that style was violence of an extreme nature. The workouts I was doing had brought my fitness up nicely and I seemed to have bucketloads of stamina. There was a children's park next to the flat and I'd go there and do dips off the climbing frames. I could do 120 per minute, which by my reckoning beat Brian Jacks's *Superstars* record of the time. I seemed to have a natural strength and I was never worried about taking a punch. I'd been fighting meatheads twice my size for years and never been put down. What was a featherweight going to do to me? I'd happily take punches from an opponent, so I could give them back harder and faster. I had a natural power, probably from the years of running away from the police while carrying lumps of lead.

My main weapon was my right hook, which deceived opponents as I was leading with my right hand. They didn't expect me to hit so hard and fast with my leading hand and, in that sense, I was unique. And I was so strong that I needed very little backlift with which to execute a devastating punch. I was wiping people out regularly and Norman decided it was time I had a shot at the ABAs. I'd only been boxing for 15 months.

The ABA tournament is the oldest, most prestigious boxing competition in the world. It's a breeding ground for future professionals and many world-class boxers have fought at both the junior and senior levels. It was in its 105th year and I was setting out to try to follow in the footsteps of British stars such as Frank Bruno, Charlie Magri, Pat Cowdell and John Conteh in winning an ABA title.

It's a long road to the National Finals. The competition starts as a regional one, with the North-East Counties Title at stake. The winner of the North-East Title then fights the winner of the Yorkshire & Humberside Title. From there, that winner meets the North-West Counties Champion and, by that point, the runners and riders have thinned somewhat. The four men left standing from the regional heats go to the All-England Finals and are seen as the top four amateur boxers in England.

The two successful boxers from the All-England Finals go on to the British Semi-Finals, to fight either the Welsh or

Scottish ABA Champion. The two winners then fight for the National ABA Title and the honour of being the best in Britain.

Competition is fierce, as the ABAs are seen as a stepping stone into the professional ranks, with the very best gaining access to the best managers and promoters and also the best purses. So only the best from each region are entered. But, despite only having had the shortest of boxing educations, Norman was confident I could do well in the North-East Area competition.

In my previous two fights, I'd fought two outstanding England internationals in Peter English and Kevin Taylor. Both had beaten me by dodgy points decisions and it was obvious to everyone who'd seen the fights that I'd kicked their arses. I was particularly pissed off by the Taylor result. He was the reigning ABA Champion and, since our fight, had turned professional. I'd well and truly hammered him and he'd been disco dancing like mad to stay out of range in the last round. Yet still the judges had still given a unanimous decision. I was angry but there was nothing I could do.

In those days, the North-East had some top amateur boxers, including local heavyweight Manny Burgo from Blyth, who was on the verge of an England call-up and who had made the national semi-finals the previous year, and Sunderland's Gordon Phillips who had previously made the English semis at light-middleweight. The amateur sport was booming across the country and North-East boxers were expected to perform well that year.

I lifted the North-East Featherweight Title without breaking sweat. Literally! My displays against English and Taylor had been noticed and no one had wanted to fight me. Opponents had literally melted away as the competition got closer and one lone challenger officially withdrew with flu on the morning of the fight. So I won my first title, although I would much rather have fought to win it.

Now I was recognised as the North-East Counties Featherweight Champion, things started to change. At first, it was just little things. I had boxing clubs calling and asking if I'd be their guest of honour on competition nights. I had journalists from the local papers calling to speak to me. There were stories starting to appear about 'Newcastle boxer John Davison'. It was strange seeing my name in print and having complete strangers call and ask me about how my training was going or if I had any ambitions of boxing for England. I'd never given much thought that people might actually be interested in me. All I was doing was a little bit of boxing, a mere hobby, although it was one I was starting to take more and more seriously.

The same people were back on the phone again a couple of weeks later, after I'd smashed through the Yorkshire Champion inside two rounds. The North-East contingent did well that night, with six of their boxers going through to the North-West stage. For me, the win set up another fight; I didn't even know who it was against.

Driving down on the day of the fight, Norman asked me if I knew who I was fighting that night.

'Haven't got a clue,' I replied. 'I don't think you told me.'

'Paul Hodkinson,' he replied.

'Who?'

'Paul Hodkinson,' he said again. 'Do you know who he is?'

'Not really.'

'I'd better tell you then.'

At that time, Hodkinson was England Boxing Team Captain and arguably the finest featherweight in the whole of Europe. He was a similar fighter to Barry McGuigan and he had everything – power, movement, speed and a vast array of clinical and killer punches. He was strong and would wear opponents down through lightning-fast combinations. He was intelligent and could tell when an opponent was starting to tire, when to up the pace. And he had a knock-out punch. Hodkinson had practically lived inside a boxing ring since he was just a kid. He had fought with distinction for Young England in his teens and was a huge name in the amateur world. His home city of Liverpool fully expected that, one day, he would bring home a professional World Title belt. The ABA competition seemed to have thrown up one of the biggest mismatches in history and I was going to be on the wrong end of a hiding.

The fight took place in the old Liverpool Stadium, one of the classic old boxing venues in the country. It was packed to the rafters for our bout, which was the main event of the evening. There were thousands of Hodkinson's supporters making a barrage of catcalls and whistles as I entered the ring. None of them had ever heard of me. They were in a joyous mood having come to see the spilling of my blood and a quick victory for their star man. I was told later that one bookie had put 20 grand on a first-round knock-out. It was like something from a Roman arena, a poor hopeless defenceless Christian sent out to face a lion.

As I got close to the ring, I passed my own small contingent of fans, whose singing had been completely drowned by the home crowd. Carol was there, along with Vaza and all the lads from the gym. A whole coachload had come from Shieldfield and I could hear my brother Davie, who was probably my biggest fan, screaming, 'Come on the Geordie Hammer!' over and over again. Pride welled up inside me and I felt 10ft tall. There's no fucking way he's going to toy with me, I thought. I knew what I could do and I knew how good I'd looked in the gym in the previous few days. I knew that I was good enough to beat him. I wouldn't have got in the ring if I hadn't.

As I was warming up in the ring, Norman was tense. This was one of the biggest fights a Grainger Park boxer had ever had. He was desperate for me to win. I was standing in the corner, rolling my shoulders to keep them supple, focusing on what I was about to do as Norman gave me last-minute instructions. 'Watch his straight right, John, watch his straight right.'

'I'll watch his straight right,' I said, looking over to Hodkinson, who was sitting on his stool listening to some similarly last-gasp tips from his trainer. He was relaxed, but it was just another day at the office for him.

'Watch his straight right, John... he'll try to pick his shots and keep you at range. You've got to watch his straight right.'

'Yeah, Norman,' I said, flicking my head from side to side, relaxing the muscles in my neck. 'I'll watch his straight right.'

The referee beckoned us together for the traditional touching of gloves. I looked into Hodkinson's eyes and he was calm and collected. Not arrogant, just focused and completely aware of his ability and his pedigree. He'd be taking nothing for granted; he was too good for that. The fight meant too much to him. This was all part of his journey. Become ABA Champion. Captain your country. Turn professional. British Title. Commonwealth Title. European Title. Conquer the world.

I walked back to the corner and Norman put my gum shield in. 'Watch his straight right,' he said, looking worriedly at Hodkinson, as the crowd's roar reached a crescendo of anticipation.

'I'll watch his fucking straight right, Norman!' I said,

irritated, biting down hard on the gum shield. 'I just hope someone's warned him about my right hook!'

I turned to face Hodkinson and I felt the power surging through me. No doubt he was feeling the same awesome feeling when you know that, in the next few seconds, you'll be in mortal combat. It's like an elastic band stretching to breaking point. The crowd became so loud I could barely hear myself think. Then the bell pierced the night and Paul Hodkinson, England Captain and European Number One, and John Davison, unknown piss-head from the streets of Newcastle, crashed into one another in the centre of the ring like two runaway trains colliding.

The force of the impact momentarily stunned the crowd to silence. In those first few seconds, Hodkinson unleashed three of the fastest jabs I'd ever seen. Or ever *not* seen, to be perfectly honest. They cut cruelly into the side of my face, momentarily stunning me, more by their speed and accuracy than by their power. By the time I'd fired one back, Hoko had already dipped under it, off to my left, and had launched a body shot straight into my left side. I knew straight away I was fighting in a different league. It was fast and furious but something inside told me I'd been hit harder before. He came close again, clearly looking for a big and early finish and fired another couple of jabs into the top of my head, followed by a combination of hooks and crosses that I only just evaded. The speed was breathtaking and more jabs drilled straight and true, glancing the side of my face, stinging the flesh around my left eye.

As he went for another, I drove into him and fired off a combination of my own. I had to make him worry about me, not the other way round. Fuck his straight right, I thought as I closed him down. He stepped back, let me come forward into range and then fired two more left jabs, designed to back me off. But I refused to go. He looked almost insulted as he drilled another left jab straight down the middle into my chest and tried to follow with his trademark right.

As he swivelled his body to connect, it gave me the opening that I needed. I unleashed a right body shot straight into his midriff and felt him gasp. Before he knew what had hit him, I pushed him back into the ropes and fired off a right hook that connected with his shoulder, making him fall sideways with its ferocity. He steadied himself and, toe to toe, launched a barrage of bombs designed to unbalance me, to push me back me across the ring. They were so fast that all I saw was a haze of red leather. But I felt their stinging impact and, again, all I could think was that I'd been hit harder before. In a perverse way, it actually gave me confidence.

I fired a right cross into the side of his head and pushed him into the ropes, opening up with a combination of my own. Fuck this, I thought. I was going to turn this into a street fight. I grappled with him, throwing him into a corner and drilling body shots into him. He tried to slip right and, again, I used a right-handed body shot. It stopped him dead, but he showed his class by rolling with the punch and cutting left down the ropes and out of danger. The crowd was going crazy. The fight was only 30 seconds old but, already, over 70 punches had been thrown.

I knew that Hodkinson had landed some good punches in the opening exchanges and that he would have been racking up the points. But, to be honest, I didn't give a fuck about the points. I never worried about points when I was fighting. I thought only of knocking my opponent out. After all, it's the best way of knowing for definite that you've won! Nothing is ever certain in boxing, but I did know one thing – Hodkinson hadn't hurt me, but I had hurt him. The first big body shot I'd thrown had been a shock to him.

I went after him and he tried to back me across the ring with some close-quarter combinations. He fired one quick jab and then slammed a right uppercut into my head. I got both arms around him, leaning on to him and pushing him both downwards and backwards. He tried to push me away, to open up some space for some more big shots but he couldn't. It was a test of steel and I was the stronger. I pushed him back again, launching a flurry of punches and catching him with a right uppercut. He backed away leaving me to hold the centre of the ring but I went straight after him, getting inside his guard and slamming some left and right body shots into his torso. It had been a while, if ever, since he'd been hit like that. Again, he'd picked up more points but the England Captain now knew who John Davison was as he danced away hurt.

I was now holding the centre of the ring. Hodkinson came at me again and unloaded a left-right combination, which I slipped and fired a ripping blast of jabs and crosses into his face. He tried to stay and counter-punch and we traded a flurry of punches. Again, he was accurate but I walked through them, catching him with a right uppercut, which seemed visibly to shake him. Again, he backed off and then came back at me, brave as a lion, looking to take back the momentum and control the fight. He got in close and unloaded some body shots. I took them as I dipped to defend myself, before using the natural spring from my legs to angle a left uppercut into his head. I followed up with a right body shot and a straight left.

And then it came. I went for a straight right-and-left combination and Hodkinson slipped it beautifully. As he tried to fire a right hook, he opened up his full profile to my leading right hand. It was only for a fraction of a second but it was just what I needed. I instinctively unleashed my biggest weapon. It went straight into his face and it took him out completely. It was the best punch I'd ever thrown and the England Captain was down for the first time in his career.

The home supporters were stunned. No one in boxing would have expected to see this. Unless Hodkinson could find some sort of miracle, he was about to be on the receiving end of one of the biggest upsets in ABA history.

He dragged himself off the canvas on a count of eight but his legs were gone. The referee looked at him closely before shouting, 'Box on!'

I came steaming out of the neutral corner and straight back in to him. There was no way I was going to give him time to recover either his senses or his composure. The crowd were screaming for him to fight back and he gamely tried to hold the centre of the ring. I attacked him, driving him back on to the ropes with a combination of cruel right hooks and straight lefts. I launched eight, maybe ten unanswered punches in the next two or three seconds, while he desperately tried to defend himself. But he had nothing left. I drove one last right body shot into his ribs and I felt him crumple. As his guard dropped, I fired another left cross and right hook combination that snapped his head back against the ropes. As I did, the referee dived between us. I'd blown away the England Captain within two minutes.

I wasn't really sure what to do. The crowd were almost silent, other than my own fans, all of whom were going absolutely mental off to my left. Stupidly, I suppose, I went to Hoko's corner where he was slumped against the ropes in tears.

'Fuck off! Do you hear me? Fuck off!' his trainer shouted at me.

Charming, I was thinking. I'd only gone across to commiserate with him.

The referee called us both into the centre of the ring. Hodkinson walked over, still stunned. 'I'll have your England vest next,' I said, winking at him.

'Great fight,' he said, wrapping his arms around me, a champion in defeat.

It all pretty much exploded from there. The following week, there was a big photo of my knock-out punch in the national boxing magazine, *Boxing News*. I'd had representatives from the England Amateur Team calling to find out more about me. The England coach, Kevin Hickey, had been in the crowd to see his captain humbled so dramatically. The local newspapers were calling for quotes.

When I returned to training a couple of days later, all the lads were there to give me a standing ovation. There's a camaraderie that exists between fighters, especially those from the same gym. You train together, spar together, help each other get mentally and physically right, and you love it when one of your team has a big win. You can genuinely share in someone else's success. And some of them were going to be pivotal to me keeping on going, because suddenly I was planning on how I could win an ABA title. What did I need to do? How did I have to train? How could I better prepare myself? Suddenly, boxing wasn't a hobby any more – it was a way of life, and I threw myself into it as if my very existence depended on it. In some ways, maybe it did.

The English Semi-Finals were held at Gloucester and I was pitted against another England international, Coventry's Colin Lynch. Same as the Hodkinson fight; I travelled down with Norman, Billy Melton and Billy Armstrong, the head of the club. But things were different to the journey I'd made to

Liverpool a few weeks earlier. The journey down to Liverpool had been mostly in silence, overshadowed by the size of the task in front of me. This time, everyone was laughing and joking. They all seemed totally relaxed and were out to enjoy the occasion. They really believed that I had a chance of winning and that, even if not, I'd certainly acquit myself well. It was a big confidence-booster for me to have people believing in me. My own view was that everyone I got in the ring with had the same equipment as me – two hands to punch with and that was it. And, if I could do that to the England number one, then maybe I wasn't out of my depth after all.

Because I hadn't really expected anything from myself for the Hoko fight, I hadn't really done what you would call any 'pre-fight build-up' for it. I'd just done my usual thing, shopping with the wife and stuff before we had set off for Liverpool. For Lynch, I did things differently. I set my own pre-fight itinerary, and it was rather unique to say the least. It would go on to serve me well all the way through my professional career.

The night before the fight, I wrapped up in three layers of clothes and then skipped three-minute rounds in my kitchen. I'd have the gas cooker on full blast and all the doors and windows shut. The sweat would literally be pissing out of me. Once I'd finished, I'd have a massive lump of steak. I'd sleep like a baby and wake up relaxed and not even thinking about the fight.

It was the most eagerly anticipated ABA fight in years. Lynch was another experienced boxer, who had been a junior ABA finalist and a semi-finalist in the senior competition two years earlier. He had a big reputation for attacking flair and was strong and known to be able to take a punch. He'd been interviewed earlier that week and had said that the Hodkinson result had been a fluke and that he would prove it. 'There's no one can punch as hard as me,' he told anyone who would listen.

The hall was packed and the television cameras were also there, with Harry Carpenter commentating. There was a huge amount of interest in the fight and I was going to be on national television for the first time. Everyone wanted to see the unknown Geordie who'd knocked out the England Captain in one round. Even after my Hodkinson performance, Lynch was still seen as the big favourite. Not in my eyes though. I knew how strong I'd felt against Hodkinson and I was confident I could do even better this time.

Before I went in the ring, someone from the BBC had asked me for a quick word. They wanted to know some details about me – was I married, did I have kids – stuff for the commentary team to use. 'And what do you do for a living?'

'Oh, er... yeah, I'm a brickie,' I said, saying the first thing that came into my head. I didn't want to say that I was on the dole, and 'antiques dealer' sounded a bit too grand for how I actually earned money.

Warming up in the dressing room beforehand, Norman was talking me through how he thought Lynch would fight. 'He'll try to keep you at distance,' he said. 'He'll want to use his skills to outbox you. Try not to give ground to him. Try and dictate the fight. But watch him, he can bang. Don't let him get the space to use his left hook. Stay on him so he can't breathe. Any questions?'

'Yeah,' I replied casually. 'Is my hair OK? I want to look my best for the TV cameras.' We both started pissing ourselves laughing and it took the edge off the tension.

In spite of Lynch's experience and record, I well and truly took him apart. I don't actually think he laid a clean punch on me. I put him down after only 60 seconds, clubbing him with some massive right hooks. He somehow dragged himself up after an eight count and stood frozen in the corner of the ring, his guard locked tight against his head, a sudden realisation spreading across his already blood-splattered face.

I casually walked up to him as he stood transfixed. He was like a mongoose hypnotised by a snake. I weaved slowly left and then right as I smashed yet another right hook straight through his guard. It was so hard that his gloves parted like the Dead Sea and he hit the floor like he'd been shot in the head. It took them ten minutes to bring him round. Of the punch, Harry Carpenter said, 'Davison's right-handed punching has been a revelation this season and we've just witnessed yet another explosion! This is the second major surprise he's caused!'

The next issue of *Boxing News* had a huge headline: 'DAVISON'S A REAL STUNNER!' People were starting to call me 'The Battling Brickie'. I'd never laid a brick in my life, although I'd thrown a few when I was younger!

The Lynch result was the talking point of amateur boxing. Not just the fact that I had won, but that it had been so brutal and so clinical. And it also proved that the Hoko result was not a fluke. The newspapers were calling me the boxing sensation of the year and, being my usual shy, retiring self, I was more than happy to give interviews. John Davison had well and truly arrived!

The National Semi-Finals were held at Preston Guildhall and I was drawn against the Scottish Champion, John Leys. Again, Leys had a strong record at both junior and senior levels and had represented his country on numerous occasions. He was tall and elusive and was known as a counter-puncher. I loved counter-punchers because I knew I could give far more than they could take. Leys was sitting on his arse within two minutes of the first round but managed to hold on until the bell. At the break, I was sat on my stool, with Norman towelling down my back. This is the point where the trainer normally gives some tactical adjustments to his boxer, but Norman was silent.

'Anything you want me to do, Norman? I asked.

'No, no. You just do your thing,' he said casually.

I bounced off the stool and finished the fight within 40 seconds, a big right hook and short uppercut sending Leys sprawling. Counter-punch that!

The final would be held at Wembley Arena, scene of so many classic fights over the years. I was to fight Welsh Champion Floyd Havard, who had beaten Colin McMillan, a future professional World Champion, on a unanimous decision in the other semi. Havard was a ring artist, technically brilliant, and had been Welsh Schoolboy Champion four times, British Schoolboy Champion twice and had won a brace of both Welsh Junior and Senior titles. He could tag and evade all day long, but he lacked power and this would hold him back in the pro ranks, where he notched up 34 wins out of 36 fights without ever getting close to major titles.

Prior to the fight, a boxing magazine ran an article about me. It said that I was just a banger, a street fighter who had no skill. Given that I'd just punched my way through three established internationals, I thought it was as unfair as it was untrue. I'd already sussed that no featherweight had the power to put me down. Conversely, I knew that I could knock anyone if I caught them. So I was boxing to my strengths, going for the kill, not going for points in the traditional amateur style. I'd obviously pissed off some of the snootier amateurs and now I was determined to prove the critics wrong on the biggest stage of all.

In the first round, I looked to box pretty and to match Havard for style. However, he kept on scoring clean points and I wasn't dictating the fight in the way I had in my other ABA bouts. At the end of the first, Norman knew he had to change my tactics.

'What are you doing, Dava?'

'I'm boxing,' I replied.

'Yeah, and you're losing. So stop fucking around and get after him!'

I did just that, pursuing him from pillar to post for the next two rounds. Havard was a brilliant mover. Twice I thought I'd had him, only to find that he disappeared in a puff of smoke. He stopped trying to box and just tagged and evaded. I stopped trying to box a boxer and went back to my normal style of going straight for the kill. It was a brilliant contest and, towards the end, I caught him with a right hook that split his nose across his face. Even then, he somehow found space to evade my finishing punches. We pushed each other all the way to a points decision.

I was convinced that I had it. For two rounds, he'd been like Roadrunner and he was standing in the ring covered in blood, while I didn't have a mark on me. The judges saw it differently, however, giving it to him by two votes to one.

I was upset but I'd surpassed all expectations of me. It showed how far I'd come in just a year-and-a-half of proper coaching. I'd gone from complete unknown to potentially representing my country in the space of just three months. Boxing was now my life. Even in the morning after the final, I was out pounding the streets of London, straight back into my strict training regime.

Kevin Hickey had told me the previous evening that he wanted to speak to me about an England call-up. The sun was rising as I got back to the hotel and I felt glad to be alive. It was a new dawn, in more ways than I could ever dream. John Davison, unknown Geordie piss-head and phantom brickie, was about to go global.

6

FIGHT FOR ENGLAND

'All the time he was boxing, he was thinking.
And all the time he was thinking, I was hitting him.'
JACK DEMPSEY (1895–1983)

The call when it came was sooner than I would have ever dared believe. Just three weeks after my fight against Havard in the ABA Final, I was on the way to the Sixteenth European Amateur Boxing Championships in Budapest as a full England international. The speed of my rise into the England ranks was breathtaking. The England selectors even had to organise an emergency passport for me because I'd never been abroad before in my life.

For competitions, Kevin Hickey would only take boxers whom he truly believed could win medals. He didn't see the point in sending boxers just to make up the numbers. I was one of only three selected, along with the established international flyweight and four-times ABA Champion John Lyons and the Cockney light-heavyweight John Beckles. Lyons was an unbelievable boxer and would go on to win the ABAs a record eight times, earning an OBE for his achievements.

Fighting for your country is the biggest honour an amateur boxer can achieve. It gives you the right to wear your England vest every time you fight, be it in ABAs or even just exhibition bouts. It sets you apart from other boxers, marks you out as one of the best in the country. Pulling one over my head for the first time was a surreal experience. All amateur boxers dream of that moment but few achieve it. I somehow seemed to have done it within two years of taking up the sport.

The England squad trained at Crystal Palace under the watchful eye of Hickey and a superb coach called Ian Urwin. The training for the European Championships involved a two-week training camp prior to the tournament. I was home for just a few days after the ABA Final and then I was off on a plane to Budapest. I wouldn't see my wife and kids for almost a month.

After my first training session, the first thing Hickey did was put me on the scales. 'I don't believe it!' he said. 'You're a bantam!'

'Eh?'

'You're a bantam! You're only 8st 10lb!'

Hickey thought that, with a more careful diet, I could drop down a division and take my power with me, making me an even more devastating opponent. It would mean taking around four to six pounds off my already lean frame, but, given that my diet was not exactly that of an international boxer, careful eating and controlling my liquid intake would mean I wouldn't have too much trouble dropping weight. For the next two years, the bantamweight division would be my home when I fought for England and, other than the booze, I was dedicated, eating nothing but good stuff – chicken, rice, pasta and baked potatoes – in the lead up to fights.

The Eastern Bloc dominated amateur boxing in the Eighties.

FIGHT FOR ENGLAND

The Cold War was still at its height and, in a true reflection of the communist doctrine, boxers fought for their country, not personal enrichment. In Eastern Europe, there was no such thing as professional boxing. The European Championships was a huge occasion and would be covered by over 300 journalists worldwide. Almost 200 boxers were to compete from 20 countries.

I was to fight the East German Klaus Dieter Kirchtein, a renowned international boxer who would have turned professional long ago had he lived in the West. I lost the contest but it was another step in my boxing education. I knew I had a lot to learn to compete with the very best in the world. Overall, Team England did well, with all three of us losing to the eventual gold medal winners in our respective divisions. John Beckles picked up a bronze.

Two months later, and with me now training every weekend with the England Boxing Team at Crystal Palace, I was again selected for England, this time for the TSC Multi-Nations Tournament in East Berlin. This was yet another step up for me as I would get to pit my skills against amateur boxers from all over the world. To win a medal against such opposition was a tall order. England had won only two gold medals since 1969.

It was another competition dominated by the Eastern Bloc. Kirchtein, my opponent in Budapest, had won gold twice running and I was matched against another former Champion, North Korean star Kim Dsi Jon. I punched him from pillar to post for most of the bout. Every time he tried to stand and fight, I forced him back with vicious body punches. In my eyes, I'd taken the Korean in every round but, in an outrageous decision by the judges, he was given a majority verdict. It fucked me off but both my international performances underlined the fact that I was closing the experience gap quickly. The work I was doing with the England coaches was starting to refine the raw aggression I had previously used to win fights. I wasn't giving away as many points with my open style as I came forward. I was more confident I could win fights without looking for a knock-out. I was starting to use my jab more.

My continuing improvement showed when I represented England on home soil for the first time in the following December and I picked up my first international victory. England was taking on Ireland in a home international in Coventry and I was fighting Ireland's up-and-coming star Roy Nash. It was billed as the fight of the tournament, a perfect puncher-versus-boxer confrontation. I'd been wining those all year and did so again, beating Nash easily on points to help clinch a 7–5 win for England. It was coming together nicely, but there was plenty of hard work still ahead.

The local papers were running stories about my exploits every week and I was getting recognised by boxing fans more and more. I'd have weekly invites to boxing shows, where I would be on the top table as a guest of honour. It was free booze so I filled my boots! I would have strangers come up to me in bars and shake my hand. Boxing clubs started asking if they could have one of my England vests for raffle prizes. I was giving them away as quickly as I could win them. I was also getting asked to take boxing classes all over Newcastle.

I started one at the Green Tree pub in Benwell. It was owned by a lad called Downsa and we became good mates. A load of the regulars would come and watch my fights, including Arthur Tams and Tommy Hudson, and it would be free beers all night for me after I'd won.

But representing England was a double-edged sword. When

I was signing on, I had to be 'available for work' and that didn't mean fighting Koreans behind the Iron Curtain. So my dole money would be stopped every time I left the country. It was a ridiculous situation because I had a family to feed and I was a sporting ambassador for my country. I had to rely on small grants from Sport Newcastle and the North-East Boxing Board, as well as the generosity of friends and family. Amateur boxers don't get paid for representing their country. They can claim expenses, but 'expenses' doesn't include lost salary. We were all fighting simply for the love of getting in the ring.

On one occasion, I got a job at the Vickers armaments factory, close to where I'd been born. Just a month later, I was called up for an international tournament. I hadn't been at Vickers long enough to be paid while I was away and I couldn't claim anything from the Government. The lads in the factory had a whipround for me, raising nearly 300 quid, which covered the money I would lose while I was away.

At boxing tournaments in this country, the organisers would often ask, 'Do you want the trophy or the money?' I'd already filled the MFI cabinet to bursting point, so I'd always take the cash instead.

Although it was a world of new experiences, I hated being away from the family. It was hard for Carol, having to look after a toddler and a baby single-handed. My son Aaron had been born in the January of that year. Just one look at him and I knew he would grow up to be a battler like his dad. He's lucky I didn't win the arguments with Carol over what he would be called. I wanted to call him 'Spartacus' after the famous gladiator, but Carol would have packed her bags if I'd got my way. But Carol supported me every step of the way and would attend every fight she could. The lack of money meant that she couldn't come to the international tournaments but it was something we both just had to get used to.

At that time, the England squad was full of future professional stars. As well as John Lyons, the finest amateur boxer in history, there was Hoko, Colin McMillan, Ritchie Woodhall, Nigel Benn, Henry Akinwande and James Oyebola. All would go on to lift World Titles in the professional game. There were also local stars such as Manny Burgo, who was an excellent heavyweight with lightning-fast hands. He would never get real recognition when he turned professional, even though he had a great record of 13 wins from 15 fights.

The training was always competitive. It was a battle to see who was the fittest, the fastest. We'd be blasting each other to bits in the ring, with Hickey desperately trying to rein us in. Because of my style of fighting, based on work-rate, I had to be super-fit and I was a fanatical trainer. I could hold my own easily in such exalted company.

1986 arrived and the ABAs kicked off again, although this time I was one of the favourites for the National Featherweight Title. It had been an explosive 12 months for me as I'd gone from unknown to fighting and almost beating some of the best amateurs in the world. Although fighting for England at bantam, I stepped back up to featherweight for the National Championships. I cruised through the North-East and Yorkshire stages to once again face my main rival Hoko in the All-England Semis. But it wasn't just a place in the British Semis that was at stake.

Just four weeks later, Team England was to travel to Reno, Nevada, for the Boxing World Championships. Hoko and me were seen as the only two contenders for the England vest at featherweight. Our match was billed as a winner-takes-all battle, or so it seemed. Kevin Hickey had already stated he would pick the one he felt was the better boxer.

Hoko was well prepared for me this time. He'd worked hard in training to try to counteract my aggressive front-foot style and big right hook. He tried to counter-punch me away and stop me getting off my biggest bombs, but I came at him over and over again, hurting him and making him dance. This time, I couldn't find the knock-out punch so it went all the way to the judges. They gave the decision to Hoko by one point.

However, the following day, Kevin Hickey called me and told me that, irrespective of the previous night's result, it would be me who was given the honour of representing his country in America. It was clear who Hickey thought had won the fight.

The World Championships were the big one, eclipsed only by the Olympics in a boxer's wish list. Again, Hickey chose to send only those he believed could win medals. I was one of a three-man squad, along with John Beckles and a young lightweight from Lancashire called Neil Foran. We trained at a special camp in Bristol prior to heading off for America where we would be competing against the Eastern Europeans, as well as the Cubans, who had a reputation for the finest boxing coaches on earth. The best boxers from North America would also be there. A young Lennox Lewis would win gold for Canada as part of his own journey to the top of the world.

America was a different experience to my previous trips abroad, which always seemed to be to Eastern Europe. We flew from London to San Francisco and then on to Reno. It was warm, it was sunny and I was there for three whole weeks and determined to develop my first proper suntan.

We had time to acclimatise to the heat before I stepped into the ring against the East German Rene Breithbart, another gold medallist from Budapest and a big international star. I was well prepared, having watched videos of him fighting back in Bristol. Again, I came close to upsetting the form book, before losing on a majority decision. It was the third major international name that I'd pushed to the very limit. It was clear that I was getting closer to taking a huge scalp, despite my natural style not being suited to the 'tag and move' ways of amateur boxing.

The upside of losing was that I had almost a week-and-a-half of 'playtime'. Team England went straight on the piss. We spent most of our time in Las Vegas, in the various casinos on the mile-long 'strip'. The casinos all dished out free food and free booze to gamblers and we would pretend to be playing on the slot machines then fill our glasses and our faces. It was my first experience of American 'supersize' portions. The food was served on plates the size of tractor wheels. Ask for a salad and you got a field of vegetables. The steaks were the size of a house. John Beckles would be sitting shaking his head and saying, 'How can one person eat this much?' just as I was clearing my plate and moving on to finish his! I went out to America a featherweight and came back a heavyweight.

When I wasn't boxing, I was still dealing as often as possible and I bought some weird and wonderful things. As well as the standard pottery and porcelain, I came home with a skeleton one day, like you see in laboratories in old films.

'That's not coming in the house!' Carol shrieked when she saw it.

'Why not?' I asked. 'It's not like he can do you any harm. He's dead.' I had to sell it the following day just to keep the peace.

My reputation continued to grow both within and outside boxing. A friend approached me one day because he was in some trouble. He'd fallen out with the wrong people and had heard that a local hardman called Viv Graham had been paid a grand to do him over. He asked if I could help. I wasn't sure what I could do as I'd never even met Graham before, but I said I'd do my best to sort it out.

Graham had a fearsome reputation. Along with his friend and associate Rob Armstrong, he worked the doors in Newcastle, controlling teams of doorman all over the city centre. He was a bodybuilder and he worked hard at it, developing an unbelievable physique as he topped the scales at around 20 stone. In later years, he would reputedly control the whole of the city centre and, at that time, his influence was growing. Although he had a reputation for being both fair and generous, he was not the sort of bloke you wanted knocking on your door if you'd crossed him.

He could usually be found on the door at a nightclub called Tuxedo Junction. I had a wander down there one night and walked up to the team of doormen. 'Which one of you is Viv Graham?' I'm sure he'd heard that question asked many times before.

'I am,' he said, stepping forward.

'I've come to ask a favour.'

It turned out that Graham was a boxing fanatic who'd fought as an amateur many times. He knew of me and my England exploits and I suppose it was a mutual-respect thing. Over a couple of drinks, I explained the delicate situation. He wouldn't confirm or deny that he had been paid to do anything, for obvious reasons, but he did say that he was sure nothing would come of it. I took him at his word and it was good. My mate remained untouched.

After that, each time I was out, I'd go and see him and he'd always be generous, getting me beers and talking about boxing and training in general. I knew the pubs and clubs he looked after and I never had to queue to get into them. He was a great lad, as was his mate Rob. At one point, he asked what I did for money, as he'd read the stories in the local papers about me getting grants because I was on the dole.

'A bit of this, a bit of that...' I said. 'I'd sell my granny if I thought I could make a profit.'

'I'll sponsor you,' he said generously. 'Let me know when your fights are and I'll make sure you're OK.'

In November, I was again selected for England at the Felix Stamm International Trophy in Warsaw. By now, I'd crossed the thin line between success and failure on the European stage. I demolished both the West German and Polish Champions to reach the final. As I was leaving the ring after my semi-final victory, my opponent in the final, Yuri Alexandrov from the USSR, caught my eye. He sneered and slowly drew an imaginary dagger across his throat, to signify what he was going to do to me. I laughed in his face.

But the final was a bridge too far. Alexandrov was a highly experienced boxer and the very best the USSR had to offer. I was matching him all the way when he caught me with a heavy slashing hook which opened up a cut above my left eye towards the end of Round Two. The referee immediately stopped the fight, with me standing in the ring incredulous, shouting at him, 'There's nothing wrong with me! Look! There's nothing fucking wrong with me!'

It wasn't even like it was a bad cut. There's nothing a boxer can do about losing if he gets a cut and, although it was a pisser to lose a major tournament in such a way, I had the consolation of a silver medal and an enhanced reputation.

A month later, I captained England for the first time in a home international against the Scots in Dundee. I was now classed as England Number One and I would go on to captain the National Team eight times in the next 18 months. I beat a Scottish bantam called Mike Devaney, stopping him in the second round of our fight.

Afterwards, the ABA English Secretary came to congratulate me, saying, 'You gave him a hell of a boxing lesson there.'

Little did I know it, but Devaney's fate and mine would be interlinked over the next 18 months.

I was out in town one night and called into one of Viv's bars. I was having a few drinks, talking about boxing in general, when I suggested we do some training together so he could see first-hand what he was getting for his money. He loved boxing, loved the gym and it would be a bit of a laugh.

I started meeting him at the gym he usually trained at in Longbenton. He'd fought with distinction as an amateur boxer there in the past. It was run by a lovely bloke called Norman Fawcett who was a professional trainer and promoter. If it had been a real fight, it would never have been sanctioned because of the difference in weight. Viv was huge, at least 20 stone, and he was easily the strongest bloke I'd ever seen. He could bench 200kg and had the physique of a professional bodybuilder. But he also knew exactly how to punch after years of working out on the bags and pads and also the doors of Newcastle. It must have been some sight, watching a featherweight taking on someone who would have been in the heavyweight division. He was twice my size and had a punch like a mule.

He surprised me just how quick he was for such a big man, but I suppose in his line of work he had to be. We started training together regularly and, after one session, he said, laughing, 'You're the hardest little bastard I've ever met! It's lucky there's not 14st of you!'

I used to irritate the fuck out of him because I was so fast and light on my feet. He used to compare me to a bee, slipping in to sting him then out of the way before he could swat me. But his muscle hadn't slowed down his hand speed or even his movement across the ring. After one sparring session, I called in to see Ham with a real shiner.

'What happened to your eye, Dava?' he asked.

'I've been sparring with Viv,' I replied. 'I hit him 55 times, he hit me once and we were even.'

Entering 1987, and boxing dominated my life completely. I had local competitions and dinners to attend. My third tilt at the ABA national title was about to begin with me in better shape and with better skills than at any time before. I had training, international matches and European competitions to look forward to with the England National Team, which I was now captaining regularly. And I'd also found out that I'd been selected for the Great Britain Olympic squad as all eyes started to fix on the up-and-coming Olympics, less than 18 months away.

I cruised through to the quarter-finals of the ABAs, again to face the North-West Champion. Paul Hodkinson had moved on into the professional ranks and the new kid on the block was another Scouser called Ritchie Wenton. He was expected to follow in Hoko's footsteps and had a similar pedigree. He was as hard as they come and would later fight Marco Antonio Barrera in Atlantic City for the World Super Bantamweight Title. But, compared to my last visit to Liverpool, the tables were well and truly turned. The last time the city had seen me I was a complete unknown, but now I returned as firm favourite to win the fight and also as England Captain.

In the same stadium in which I'd beaten Hoko just two years earlier, I showed just why I was England Number One. My fitness levels were now at the point that my body was operating on just a 30-second recovery period, from hardcore fighting back to resting pulse rate. The fitness and strength I possessed was one of my major weapons, as crucial as my ability to punch, and the Ritchie Wenton fight was a perfect example of what I was capable of.

Fighting in my England vest, I took Wenton apart in the first round. He came at me with a big crowd behind him, looking to use combinations to open me up, but I simply broke apart his attacks with massive body shots. He gamely tried to come forward but I stopped him dead every time, pushing him on to the ropes where I could punish him with right hooks to the head. It was a methodical beating as I worked his head and body. By the end of the first round, he looked like he'd done 12 rounds with Tyson and he was already gasping for breath. I'd barely broken sweat.

Wenton came out for the second round, looking to pressure me, to snatch back the momentum of the fight. But I could fight at 200mph and I increased the pace yet further, lashing him with a confusing blur of hooks and uppercuts and then coming in close to bully him. I whirled around him, hitting him from all directions and using my strength to push him into the ropes, where I could open up the smallest of gaps between us and smash shots into his ribs. Still he tried to fight, but I ate at his stamina, leaning on him and pushing him around. When a shot to the head fired his gum shield across the ring, I knew he wasn't going to last much longer. He was exhausted, simply unable to cope with the speed of my punching and the damage it was doing.

I finished him seconds later. I pushed him on to the ropes again and opened up with another barrage that left him defenceless as he took shots from places he could no longer see. The referee dived in to stop the slaughter. I went straight to his corner to commiserate with him, to show him respect for his efforts. He was a hard little bastard.

Into the British Semi-Final and I faced Scotland's Mike Devaney, whom I'd steamrollered through in the England v Scotland International a few months earlier. Given that victory, I was a firm favourite to beat him again but I wasn't complacent. No two fights are the same and my preparations were meticulous. Devaney knew what to expect this time but I was still cruising when I was given a public warning after our heads had clashed and the referee had felt I was the perpetrator. It wasn't the case as Devaney was a taller opponent, so the way I piled in would always leave the risk of heads clashing. The public warning effectively gave him the bout and passage to the ABA National Final, even though I'd completely outfought him. It was a result that would come back to haunt me.

As 1987 closed, life was good as my boxing career went from strength to strength. I was England Number One and now regarded as one of the best amateur featherweights in Europe. I was fit and had avoided any major injuries or cuts that would slow down my rise further up the ranks of amateur boxing. I knew that age was against me but, luckily, the big one was just around the corner. The Olympics, the biggest amateur sporting event in the world, was just nine months away. I'd already been selected to attend elite training weekends with the Great Britain squad. If there was any rhyme or reason as to why I'd fallen into boxing, then I felt that could be it. An unlikely Olympic hero? Maybe. Like athletes the world over, I dreamed the Olympic dream on the long weekends away from my family.

7

FOOL'S GOLD

'The thrill of competing carries with it the thrill of a gold medal.
One wants to win to prove himself the best.'

JESSE OWENS (1913–80),
QUADRUPLE OLYMPIC GOLD MEDALLIST, BERLIN 1936

The 24th Modern Olympics, to be held in Seoul in 1988, was to be the biggest sporting occasion the world had ever seen. After the politics of the previous two games, where boycotts by both the USA and the Eastern Bloc had devalued the Olympic ideals, the global Olympic family was to join once more for a celebration of sporting brilliance. A record 10,000 athletes from 160 countries would compete that September for the right to be called an Olympic Champion. Over 2.7 billion people were expected to watch the drama unfold on television and, as England Captain, I was expecting to join in the party.

Boxing had been a good medal earner for Great Britain in the past, although no boxer had struck gold since middleweight Chris Finnegan in Mexico City in 1968. However, professional stars such as Alan Minter and Pat Cowdell had both brought home bronze medals from previous games. Minter had gone on to win the unified WBC and WBA

Titles in 1980 before bowing to 'Marvellous' Marvin Hagler. Cowdell had lost to the great Azumah Nelson in his own World Title quest, but had lifted both British and European Titles. To emulate such professional stars on the amateur stage would be unheard of for someone like me who had come into the sport so late.

But my hopes were not without firm foundation. In the previous two seasons, I'd established myself as England Captain and one of the best bantamweights in Europe. As well as my ABA exploits, I'd been a mainstay of the England Team in the home international competitions, beating the best the other home nations had to offer. The days of 'surprise package' John Davison were long gone. I now had a strong international pedigree. My style was one of constant work-rate and constant pressure, and I had to be fit to maintain it from the first bell to the last. I was one of the fittest men in boxing and I'd well and truly caught the Olympic bug.

But chasing your dreams doesn't come without a price. I barely saw Carol and the kids and it was hard for us all. I trained each and every weekend with either England or the Great Britain boxing squad, both of which were coached by Kevin Hickey, who well knew my capabilities. It meant that there was very little quality time simply to enjoy being a family. I missed them terribly and there were times I wondered what the fuck I was doing.

The training camp for Great Britain was also based at Crystal Palace and I was usually on the Clipper bus from Newcastle on a Friday night, getting to London just in time to fall straight into bed. We had a punishing training regime, similar to the England squad. Hickey had us training seven times a day, which was an absolute killer, but it had to be done. In boxing, preparation is everything. The Great Britain squad also had elite training weeks once every three months. It was more of the same, for a more sustained period of time and it lifted your fitness levels still further.

Competition in the squad was fierce, be it for a timed run or number of press-ups you could do in 60 seconds. Everyone had one aim, one goal – to secure a ticket on the plane to Seoul. But, for me, it was even more imperative that I maintain my high standards all the way to selection. The Olympics would be the biggest sporting occasion of my life and I knew that I only had one chance. At 34, I would be considered far too old for the Great Britain squad for Barcelona '92. Seoul was a once-in-a-lifetime opportunity.

Mornings began with a 7.00am jog around Crystal Palace, which alternated between three and five miles. Once I got back, I'd have a freezing-cold shower to spark me up for the day and then a light breakfast of scrambled egg and toast. At 10.00am, training began in earnest. We'd be in the gym, working on the heavy bags and hook and jab pads under the guidance of Kevin Hickey and Steve Urwin. We'd work on our technical skills, as there's always something a boxer can improve on. Hickey had accepted now that there was no way he would ever turn me into a jab-and-slip mover, tagging and evading my opponent. He recognised where my strengths lay, in brutally overpowering an opponent, wearing him down with an avalanche of punches and then finishing him as soon as the opportunity arose. When the others worked on the bags, working on combinations such as jab, left, right, hook, I would just go and slug the bag to pieces with hook, hook, hook... It wasn't the most graceful, but it was efficient and it won me lots and lots of fights.

In one session, Hickey was trying to get me to back off from an opponent once I'd hit them with a jab. I had no real interest in what he was saying, because, every time he told me to back off, I'd question it.

'Back, back, back, John.'

'Back? Why? I'm wearing him down.'

'But he'll get a clean hit on you. You'll take shots.'

'Yeah, but I'll knock him out.'

Eventually, he got the message. When the squad were working on slipping and moving, he'd tell me simply to 'fuck off and kill a bag'.

We'd finish the morning session with work on the treadmills and then have an hour off. After a lunch of chicken, vegetables and potatoes, we'd be straight back into it, moving into the ring for sparring sessions, where we all used to blast each other to bits.

The final two sessions of the day were working on the two complementary disciplines of strength and dexterity. Too much weight training and your body gains strength but becomes too rigid and you lose speed. Too little and you couldn't knock the skin off a rice pudding. So, to complement each, we did a full range of stretching exercises. In many ways, the training was years ahead of its time compared to other sports. It would be ten years before footballers started to understand the importance of these sorts of training techniques.

Come Saturday night, we were let loose in London. It wasn't like we were schoolboys, so there was no curfew. In my younger days, I would have taken full advantage of this opportunity by finding the nearest pub and getting legless. Invariably, someone would have started a fight with me and I would have been battling in the street, before staggering off to bed with double pie and chips. But things were different now. They had to be. First, because everyone was absolutely fucked after a full day's hard training; but, second, I recognised the opportunity that I had. Sure, I still had a few beers in the lead up to a big fight and, when not in hard training, I could party with the best. But I tried to keep myself in check when in serious training. After fights, however, I would usually go out into Newcastle and get absolutely mortal, completely off my tits. I'd get it all out my system, be carried home and then go back to taking everything in moderation.

I was still juggling to make money any way I could. I was in the pub one day when this lad came over and asked me if I wanted to buy some designer T-shirts. He opened up a big holdall and it was stuffed full of logos – Adidas, Nike, Reebok. He was knocking them out for a couple of quid a go and they were obviously snide.

'How much if I buy them in bulk?' I asked.

'Depends on how many you want.'

'A couple of hundred.'

And so yet another new enterprise started. I was buying them for a quid a go and knocking them out for three quid. My main approach was to drive to building sites or road works. I'd pull up and shout to the lads to come and look at my wares. I was knocking out hundreds of them.

It soon went from there. I was getting my hands on shell suits, polo shirts, watches and I was selling them faster than I could buy them in. It kept food on the table and me in the ring. Even when I was working it didn't stop. I got a job working at Newcastle United's ground on the redevelopment of the West Stand. I was knocking out snide Newcastle shirts and jackets to the lads I worked with and making an absolute fortune as I went.

The media interest surrounding my Olympics bid was constant and everyone now knew I was in with a good shout. The local papers were full of 'DAVISON FOR SEOUL' stories and, by now, pretty much everyone knew who I was. There were still some poor unfortunates that found out the hard way though.

I was standing pissed in a taxi queue in the Bigg Market one Friday night. As always, the queue had been massive and the taxis few, but eventually I was second in the queue behind four lads who were obviously as pissed as me. We waited and waited and, eventually, they decided to fuck off. They'd only got about ten yards away when a taxi pulled up and I opened the door.

'Fuck off, you!' one of the lads shouted as they ran towards me. 'That's ours!'

'No, it's not. You've left the queue.' I climbed into the back seat, but they were having none of it.

The back doors flew open and one of the lads started to try to drag me out. One punch and he fell backwards into the road. The other three, having seen their friend get a smack, now meant business. One of them opened the other back door and jumped in, trying to get me in a headlock. I held him down with my left hand and started smacking him with my right. While I was busy, one of the others climbed in behind me and started to put punches into the back of my head. I slammed my head backwards, catching him beautifully, splitting his lips and stunning him, as I finished off his mate who was now trying desperately to get out. The taxi driver had jumped out of the cab and was standing helpless as it all kicked off in the back of his motor. The lad I was punching broke free and fell out on to the road so I turned my attentions to the one I'd nutted. I spun round, slamming a left hook straight into his already battered face and he, too, lost any stomach for a fight. But now I'd really lost it. I scrambled back across the seat of the taxi and out into the road, shouting that I was going to kill the four of them. They were off like rabbits! I ran up the street for maybe 30 yards, knowing that no one else in the queue would be stupid enough to nick my taxi after what they'd just seen. The Gang of Four were faster runners than they were punchers and they disappeared into the night. I bet they weren't telling that story in their local the following day as they nursed their broken noses.

Viv was still giving me sponsor money regularly and, one night, I thought I'd see what else he might be able to do to help.

'Why don't you give me a couple of doors to run?' I asked.

'John,' he said patiently, 'the idea of being on the door is to protect people. Even when they're pissed and being arseholes, you still have to show restraint. It's a different way of using your head to the way that you're used to! You'd be knocking out anyone who even looked at you the wrong way. The bar would be fucking empty.'

I would go to the door where he was working and he would usually have some money waiting for me. One night, he passed it over and, as we stood talking, I started to count it, the natural suspicions of a wheeler-dealer I guess.

'I'm fucking giving it to you,' he said, raising his eyes to the heavens. 'I'm hardly then going to fucking rip you off!'

I suppose old habits die hard!

I was still trading at antiques fairs and car boot sales and I drove Carol mad with some of the things I brought home. Although the skeleton was a forgotten memory, I turned up at the house on day with a cheetah skin, complete with head and claws.

'What is that?' she asked.

'It's a cheetah,' I said defensively. 'Fastest land animal in the world.'

'That one obviously wasn't.'

I also had a lucrative sideline in ginger jars. I was buying boxes of them from a cash and carry and I'd rub mud on them to make them look old. Each one cost me three quid but, every time I rocked up at an antiques fair, they were one of the first thing to get any interest on my stall.

'Not sure what it is,' I'd lie. 'I picked it up in a house clearance a few weeks ago. Never seen one like it before in my life. It's totally unique.' I'd sell one for 20 quid and wait half-an-hour before I took another one from the box I had under my table. I made an absolute killing.

Even at home, training dominated my waking thoughts. By now, I'd moved again, this time to West Denton Boxing Club, just a few minutes from my home. The coaches Billy Melton and Frankie Kernan were great on pad work and they really started to bring the best out of me. I now felt that I could box with the best if I wanted to, although I remained an all-out brawler out of choice. Boxing and fitness was my thing. If I was bored, out would come the skipping rope or we'd have friends round and I'd be knocking out a couple of hundred press-ups. I was obsessed.

While I was at West Denton, I was asked to coach the Army at Albemarle Barracks, for their up-and-coming tournament against the Royal Navy. They hadn't won a match in ages and real pride was at stake. The army boxers were good and brave, but they used to pile straight in, a bit like me in my early amateur days. I worked on their technical skills, using jabs and combinations to open up opponents and they went on to beat the Navy in style. For a celebration, me and a promising young club mate, a lad called Frankie Foster, said we'd do a three-round exhibition bout at the barracks. We entered the ring in silence and, at the end of the first round, you could have heard a pin drop. No excitement, nothing. I gestured for Frankie to join me in the middle of the ring and whispered, 'We must have been fucking awful there, mate. We'd better pick it up a bit.'

We did, going for it and lashing each other with some good shots. Again, the crowd remained totally impassive, like they were in church more than a boxing match. Again, I called Frankie over. 'Fuck me, we're going to have to really go for it here!'

Frankie nodded, and we both came out all guns blazing, fighting like there was an ABA title on the line. I caught him with a body shot that put him down on one knee and, as he stood up, I heard someone shout, 'Permission to cheer, sir?'

'Granted,' came the reply.

'Come on, chaps!' The place exploded into life as Frankie and I blasted each other for the rest of the round.

January 1988 was to be my moment of destiny. England faced Scotland in an international contest and I was fighting the only man who could steal my Olympic place. It was generally accepted that there were only two possible contenders for the bantamweight vest in the shape of Mike Devaney and myself. It was one-all in our rivalry, although he knew that he hadn't really beaten me in our last fight. Either way, it was clear. Beat Devaney and the place would be mine. Lose, and my Olympic dream would be shattered. I didn't say a word to anyone but I knew that there would be nothing for me to aim for if I lost. The Olympics was the highest level of achievement for anyone in sport, and defeat could mean only one thing – retirement.

As if I needed any further motivation, the international was to be held at Gateshead Stadium just a stone's throw from my house. I was also selected as Captain again, for the eighth time. The Davison clan would be out in force for the event, as would hundreds of friends and supporters from the amateur circuit who would pack the venue, and the highlights were to be beamed to the nation on *Grandstand* the following day. It was to be the biggest international contest since the previous Olympic Games.

I knew I had my destiny completely within my own hands. I trained like I'd never trained before, which is saying something! Every single day for two months, I did a full training session. Every single day, I sparred with Frankie Foster. It was pure, single-minded determination. I would not lose to Devaney. There was no way I could lose. Three rounds, just nine minutes, separated me from the ultimate goal and my dream of pitching myself against the very best in amateur boxing, in the breeding ground of future professional World Champions.

Four days before the big night, I found myself in the shit. I had pushed myself so hard with all the extra training that I'd miscalculated completely. My body had peaked and was on its way back down. I was in trouble, big style. I called Kevin Hickey, who ordered me to rest completely for two days, to not so much as lift a finger. So there I was, sitting in the house with Carol waiting on me hand and foot. It was every man's dream but I was burning up inside. How could I have been so fucking stupid? I went back to the gym the day before the fight for a light session and that was it. Just like Christmas Eve once the shops close, you know there's nothing more you can do. It was just a question of sitting and waiting.

From the first bell, Mike Devaney never knew what had hit him. I set the tone for the contest in the first few seconds, smashing a perfect right uppercut straight into his head. As he tried to backtrack, I hounded him into the ropes, smashing him with hooks and uppercuts all the way. Rebounding from the ropes straight into my killing zone, I opened up on him with a combination of uppercuts and hooks, clubbing into the side of his head, wiping out his senses. The contest was only

30 seconds old when the referee dived in to give him a standing count. He was rocking but I knew that he was hard. There was no way I would underestimate him. The referee waved us on and he went into survival mode, looking to tag and evade me. I slipped his jabs and hammered a body shot into him, feeling him wince. At the end of the first, the crowd was going absolutely mental. It was all going to plan.

Round Two and I knew that he would have to come after me, as the standing count alone was enough to win me the decision. I could hear his coach shouting at him to attack and he came bravely forward. I changed tactics completely, staying back and letting him come on to me. My switch to intelligent, defensive boxing was a perfect ploy. He tried to close tight, but always being wary of my body shots. I picked at him with short-range jabs and crosses. It became almost a textbook amateur boxing match, me using the skills I'd learned training with the very best in Britain. I knew I could do it all day if I wanted. Devaney had to make something happen and he was running out of time. He kept coming at full tilt, trying to pressure me on to the back foot but I refused to let him dominate. He would fire two punches into my raised guard. I would smash four into his face. Every time he went for a body shot, I covered up and broke him with vicious counter-punching.

The third and final round and Devaney now needed a knock-out to beat me. I simply needed to stay on my feet as our Olympic ambitions came down to just three minutes. They may as well have thrown the Great Britain vest in the middle and shouted, 'Last man standing!'

He came out looking to put me down, knowing he had no choice. Again, I boxed intelligently, with my guard held high. Every time he came to attack, he would punch straight into my guard, welded tight to my head, then I would systematically break him up. He would throw two punches, I would throw four. He would throw four, I would throw eight. And on and on and on. About a minute into the round, Devaney's work-rate started to subside. He had given all that he had and he had punched himself to exhaustion against my rock-solid defences, while I had sapped his energy with cruel, clinical counter-punching. And now I opened up once more.

Bang! A right hook almost took him clean out and he instantly switched back to survival mode. I closed him down, pushing him into the ropes, grappling and leaning on him to take away those last precious reserves of strength. Then I unleashed yet more big punches. His guard was starting to fragment and a straight left split it in two, connecting with his face with vicious intention. He was hurting now and another clubbing left took away any fight that he had left. He scuttled away, trying vainly to defend himself against another onslaught as the final bell went.

Harry Carpenter, commentating, was ecstatic. 'What a performance from the England Number One. Absolutely fantastic!' I was jumping up and down like a maniac. I'd absolutely smashed him and even the following day's newspapers were calling it a decisive victory.

The judge's decision was unanimous and reflected how easy I'd made it look. Pictures of my delighted family were broadcast to the whole nation. It was clear what the victory meant. The dream was still alive. There was no way that I would not be selected. It wasn't as if the fight had even been close. Although Devaney had managed to compete for part of the second round, he'd been blown apart in both the first and third. I'd been stronger, faster, more intelligent, everything. Victory does not come any sweeter.

Interviewed afterwards, I'd said to the reporters, 'The Olympics is my target and it would have been difficult to keep going if I'd blown my chances here. I've boxed the best in the world and, believe me, I know I can bring a medal home with me.'

The headlines – 'DAVISON ON THE WAY TO SEOUL' – appeared in the local newspapers and it was hard not to agree. It would take an absolute disaster now to prevent me from realising my dream and I truly believed I could win a medal. I didn't think anyone in the world was capable of beating me because of the way I fought, the way I trained. Everything was 100 per cent, all the time. I could punch, my hands were like lightning. And I was work-rate personified. Constant punching. Constant forward pressure. People just couldn't live with me.

I believed I didn't have to be a great stylist to win fights. I just had to work hard and make stylists brawl. I had a good chance of beating anyone. It's a boxer's psyche, it was my psyche. All boxers need confidence, bordering on arrogance. But when you could back up that confidence with the sort of performances I was delivering…

My winning run continued into the ABAs yet again. The North-East Divisional Title was again taken easily and Ritchie Wenton was again demolished in two rounds in the English Semis. Coming into the British Semi-Final in the April, however, I'd been ill with 'flu and hadn't trained for over a week. I was struggling to make the weight and so took a load of water tablets, trying to lose as much water as possible prior to the fight. My opponent was the Army's Keith Howlett, who was a cracking boxer and he beat me on points. It was a blow, as I'd been the firm favourite for that year's title, but you can't account for illness and he'd beaten me fair and square. He underlined his quality by going on to win the National Title that year. Worse was to follow, however.

Four weeks later, I received a letter from the Great Britain Selection Committee. It told me that, regrettably, I had not been selected for the final Great Britain Olympic squad. It was the first time I'd ever been floored in boxing. I couldn't understand what had happened, but I was absolutely devastated. The answers came a few days later when the squad was announced.

The Olympic boxing squad is picked by selectors from the English, Scottish and Welsh ABAs. Obviously, all are keen on their own fighters making the squad and will try their best to make sure of their inclusion. This makes for the possibility of a certain amount of horse-trading. For the Seoul Games, the English selectors were keen that Ritchie Woodhall would be picked. The Scottish selectors would agree only if their man got the bantamweight vest. And that was that. I was out and Mike Devaney was in.

Ritchie Woodhall would later turn professional. He always looked upon selection for the Olympics, and the bronze medal that he won in Seoul, as confirmation that he could do well in the professional game. It gave him the courage to take the gamble and step into the pro ranks. He would win a World Title, as would another of the squad of eight, Henry Akinwande, who would one day be a World Heavyweight Champion. But for Woodhall especially, it was the watershed moment of his life. It was also mine.

Kevin Hickey called me a few days later to commiserate and to offer me a place in the England Team competing in the Acropolis Cup. 'You're still the best bantamweight in the country,' he told me. 'You can still make your mark at the Commonwealth Games or World Championships.'

While I appreciated what he said, it just didn't ignite that same spark of desire. How could it? And, anyway, who's to say I would still be able to make the teams then anyway? I was 29. One bad injury could finish me. I'd been ready. I knew I could have won a medal. All those weekends, all the pain of being away from my family. The struggle to find jobs, the living on the breadline. There was only one decision a man with any pride in himself could make.

I fought one last time against Frankie Foster at a social-club night in Newcastle. Gone now was fighting in big public stadiums in front of thousands. Gone was testing myself against the best in Europe and, indeed, the world. Gone was the England vest. I was back where I'd started just five years earlier, among friends, at the grass roots of boxing. I beat Frankie on points and, in doing so, I won the 'Best Boxer of the Night' award. It felt like the most precious thing I'd ever won because I knew it would be the last.

It was over and I never wanted to see the inside of a boxing ring again as long as I lived.

8

SMALL TIME, BIG TIME

Pugilist – pyoo-juh-list
Definition: One who fights with the fists, especially
a professional prizefighter; a boxer.
OXFORD ENGLISH DICTIONARY

Towards the end of that summer, the pressure was building. Tommy Conroy, a local professional boxing trainer and manager, had called me several times. 'Why throw it all away, John?' he'd ask over and over again. 'You've got so much left inside you, there's so much you can still achieve.'

Conroy was an experienced trainer who had originally worked in the North-East with a local promoter called Frankie Deans in the early 1980s, before taking the gamble of going it alone. He tried over and over again to convince me that my natural style would translate well to the professional game. At the time, his stable included a local lad called Harry Escott, who had been the first apprentice professional and who was earmarked for great things. 'You might even get a British Title shot,' he said, although I doubted it myself.

In my heart of hearts, I'd never considered turning

professional. The idea of fighting for money was completely alien to me. I was no more a professional sportsman than the famous Geordie cartoon character Andy Capp. Boxing had started as a hobby, albeit a time-consuming one. And then I'd had the buzz of pulling on an England vest, of representing my country, and I could think of no higher accolade. I'd given my all, sacrificed everything to represent Great Britain at the Olympics, only to have it snatched away. I'd lost out on weekends with my family, decent jobs, all in the name of British boxing. I was still gutted by what I felt was a betrayal.

Like a hundred million others, I'd watched Ian Taylor, the Great Britain men's hockey 'keeper as he'd carried the Union Jack at the head of the GB Team at the opening ceremony in Seoul. Every single member of the GB Team was beaming with pride and, although I'd been glad for my friends who'd made it, I'd watched with tears in my eyes. I felt cheated, used and I had no interest in carrying on fighting.

I visited Tommy at his makeshift gym at Barnes School in Sunderland. He was a nice guy and he had a reputation for looking after his fighters. There was a natural bond between us. Tommy had been a good amateur and, like me, had started boxing at the late age of 25. His ethos, which he tried to instil into all his fighters, was that boxing was as easy as A-B-C – Attitude, Bottle and Character. He was looking to expand his stable and, as well as me, he was also in talks with my club mates Frankie Foster and Shaun Kernan, as well as another promising amateur called Terry French from Swallwell.

Tommy was confident that I could make the grade and it took him three months of persuasion before I took the plunge. I was conscious that time was not on my side. I was just weeks from my 30th birthday which, for featherweights, is usually a milestone for all the wrong reasons. The battleships in the heavyweight division might be able to continue well into their thirties or even forties, but their boxing was more about power than speed. Lower down the scale at featherweight, a fighter is usually shot before he hits 30. The fitness simply disappears and you can no longer match the pace of younger men. Barry McGuigan, the most successful featherweight in recent history, had retired burned out at only 28. That, in itself, was particularly ominous.

The physical demands of professional boxing are so different from those of amateurs that they might well be classified as different sports. The most I'd ever had to box in my amateur career was four three-minute rounds, 12 minutes in all. In the pros, I might well have to do 12 rounds. It might not sound like a huge difference, but try it sometime on a punch bag. See how effective your punching is, your co-ordination, your footwork, by round eight, when your arms are burning so badly you can barely lift them. And then imagine someone smashing punches into your head and body, far harder than anything you have experienced before, for those eight rounds. Making you bleed, stealing your breath. Taking away your energy, your will to win, and your will even to survive. And then try to do another four rounds. Because that's the very minimum of what it takes.

In amateurs, the referee will give a standing count if you take a big punch; you don't have to be put down. But in professional boxing, it's all about how much punishment you can take, how much heart you have. A brilliant amateur might make a mediocre professional if they can't get up to speed quickly. If… it's the biggest word of all in boxing, and no one would know if I could bridge so big a gap until I was in the ring and either hurting someone or getting very badly hurt.

But there were some positive signs. Earlier that year, I'd been hired as a sparring partner for local star Billy Hardy, while he prepared for his British Bantamweight Title fight against the southpaw John Hyland. Hardy's trainer, Geordie Bowes, offered me 40 quid for a week's work. It was welcome money for the Davison household and I readily accepted.

I travelled down to Hartlepool for the training, but Bowes paid me up at the end of the first day, after I'd continuously hammered Hardy on the ropes. And it wasn't because he was having difficulty with my southpaw style. 'You're just too strong for him,' Bowes had told me as he handed over the cash.

It was true. In each round, I'd simply counter-punched him on to the ropes and then let fly with big hooks and body shots. Hardy couldn't cope. Each session had been interspersed with Bowes screaming at his man to get his hands up to try to protect himself from the onslaught. Though Billy would later become a rival, I had nothing but respect for him and what he did in his own quest for a World Title.

I'd also sparred with Tommy's rising star, Harry Escott, at West Denton Social Club one afternoon and, despite his record of ten wins from ten pro fights, I'd made him look distinctly ordinary. Again, I'd used my strength to dominate the centre of the ring despite his undoubted pedigree. Professional boxing might just suit me, I thought.

So yet again, I had a choice to make. I can honestly say that, if I'd been picked for the Olympic Team, I would never have turned professional. But now, I had something to prove, especially to the people who'd betrayed me. And I felt fresh, I felt strong. At the end of a sparring session that Tommy had arranged to have a look at me, he was laughing. 'Aged 30 but boxes like he's 20! Come on, son, you can't say no to me after a performance like that!'

I had other approaches, notably from Terry Lawless, one of Mickey Duff's representatives. At the time, Duff was one of the biggest names in British boxing as both a promoter and a manager and he was renowned for bringing through World Champions. I think he ended up with 20 World Champions in all, a phenomenal achievement. Although I was flattered that they were interested, I would have had to move to London and, with a young family and no friends down there, it was never going to be an option.

So, after giving it some thought, I called Tommy. 'Let's do it,' I said. 'But I need to fight as soon as possible. I'm on the bones of my arse and I've got kids to feed.'

'What are you doing for work, John?' Tommy asked.

'I write my name twice a week at Newburn Job Centre,' I replied.

'I know someone who's looking for a labourer for a few weeks. It'll help out a bit. I'll get you sorted.'

He duly did and, suddenly, after years of having no job, I now had two! Within a couple of weeks, my life consisted of roadwork each morning, followed by a shift as a scaffolder which Tommy arranged for me. I'd be back at the gym each night, covered in grime and still in my work boots. As in the amateurs, I channelled everything I had into this single opportunity and something clicked, something came together. I'd always loved tear-ups, real, extreme violence where you take it in spades but give it back in buckets. In the amateurs, the refereeing was far stricter and it was unlikely to get to that stage. But now I was discovering a whole new world. I was watching videos of exponents of boxing in its most brutal form – Marvin Hagler, Roberto Duran and Sugar Ray. I was learning from the masters as I went, studying their style of attacking, explosive boxing and looking to take the best of their moves and add them to my own vicious armoury. I discovered that boxing was about being truly tested, having the desire to win, which would make you get off your stool exhausted and hurt and go out again to meet your foe, to finish the job. It's the point where strength of body meets strength of mind, an iron will, and a refusal to be beaten no matter what. It was the art of fighting in its purist form and I couldn't wait to get started.

Money was tight as ever and I needed new kit, which didn't come cheap. I'd spoken to Viv a few times since I'd been kicked out of the Great Britain squad and he'd always said the same thing. 'Just let me know what you want to do and I'll see if I can help.' I was bouncing off the walls of the house early one Sunday morning so I thought I'd give him a call.

'Fuck me, Dava, you pick your times!'

'I'm turning pro.'

'You what?'

'I'm turning pro. It's all sorted. Tommy Conroy's going to train me and he's lined up a promoter from Glasgow. I'm going up to see him next week.'

'I'm surprised.'

'So am I.'

'What do you need?'

'I haven't really given it much thought,' I said. 'It's all happened so fast.'

'Go and buy whatever kit you need,' he said. 'Gloves, tracksuits, anything. Rob and me will cover it. The money's here.' He paused. 'Good luck. Now fuck off, I'm going back to sleep.'

The following week, I got £1,000 in an envelope by way of sponsorship, which paid for everything I needed.

Professional boxing is not necessarily the two best fighters being pitted against each other in noble combat. Far from it. A fight will only happen if the money is right. And, in boxing, it's television that generates the cash. Sure, ticket sales are important, but it's a television contract that brings home the bacon and enables a fight to take place. If a fighter and his team can't generate interest from television, you'll never get a title shot at any level, no matter how good you are.

In the 1980s, Mickey Duff dominated boxing because he had the BBC on an exclusive contract. This meant it was difficult to bring a fighter through unless you made a deal with Duff, which effectively meant that you were always negotiating from a position of weakness as to what your purse would be.

Tommy had other ideas, though. He had worked with a Glasgow promoter, Tommy Gilmour, on a number of occasions, taking his lads north of the border to fight on dinners promoted by the St Andrew's Sporting Club and televised on BBC Scotland. Gilmour was an associate of Barry Hearns, who had been a major force in snooker with his Matchroom organisation, before moving into boxing in the mid-1980s. He made the call and, next thing, I was sitting in his office in the middle of Glasgow. The businessman (Gilmour) looked the 'athlete' (me) up and down with mild amusement. 'What do you want from boxing, Davison?'

'Money,' I replied.

He threw me out of his office and back into the reception. A little while later, I was called back in.

'I'll ask you again. What do you want from boxing, Davison?'

'I want the money,' I repeated, confused.

Again, I was thrown into the corridor where I told Tommy what had happened.

'You can't fucking say that!' Tommy shouted at me. 'You've got to tell him what he wants to hear. Don't fuck this up, John. You might not get another chance.'

JOHN DAVISON: LITTLE MAN, BIG HEART

I was called back one last time. 'What do you want from boxing, Davison?'

'I want to be a champion,' I lied.

'Good, I knew we'd get there eventually.'

'And I want the money,' I said, winking at Gilmour, who exploded with laughter.

At the time, though, money was my dominating thought. Although my dealing gave us a little spare cash sometimes, it was in no way enough to buy any luxuries. I was desperate for my first fight, and I'd already decided how I was going to spend the money I earned from it. First, I fancied a diamond-encrusted Rolex and I was also going to buy some nice Armani suits in keeping with my new status as a professional boxer. I also fancied a big white snow leopard, which I was going to walk around the streets on a gold chain to scare the shit out of the neighbours. Yeah, fuckin' right!

Anyone who thinks that boxing is all luxury hotel suites, limousines and the crown jewels is sadly mistaken. People think of boxers at the top of their profession when they picture such riches. Tyson and his $30 million fights, Eubank and his American trucks. But on the bottom rung, getting smacked in the face for 12 rounds is a pretty shitty way of making a living.

The deal I signed would make me 400 quid a fight. I'd be boxing on the under-cards of local sports dinners, or maybe regional title fights. From that amount, Tommy would get 25 per cent, which was standard for a manager's fee, although he waived his fees on my first five fights because I was fighting for fuck all anyway. But the taxman would have to be paid, taking his 20 per cent. Once I was up and running, I would lose almost half my purse before I even swung a punch. But this was the standard deal for professional boxers and it was the one area where my amateur pedigree made no difference. It didn't leave a lot to live on between fights. Once the scaffolding job finished, I was back to signing on. There simply were no other jobs. The country's unemployed had been told by one Government minister, Norman Tebbit, to get on their bikes and look for work. This had started a mini crime wave where I lived, as the only chance the unemployed had of getting on a bike was if they nicked one.

So it was up to me from the start. Stay on the bottom rung and starve or start moving up quickly. It was a no-brainer. I was going to have to take the fights as fast as they would come and hope I could keep winning, to build a decent purse. Tommy was in agreement, especially given my age. My boxing career was going to be a race against time. I was going to be a man in a hurry. And I fucking relished the thought.

In those days, to register as a professional boxer, you had to satisfy the British Boxing Board of Control's regulatory procedures. First, you had to complete an application form. No problems there, I got the wife to do it for me. I then had to complete a medical examination from a board doctor, all the standard stuff, such as eye tests. All professional boxers must have a licensed manager, which ensured that only people who could actually box could sign up as professionals. No manager would waste his time and money with someone who couldn't and, anyway, it's bad for business to have your local pub nutter pulling on gloves, thinking they can actually win a boxing match against a pro. But that was it. It was long before the days of MRA brain scans and HIV tests. After that, all I needed to do was attend an interview with my local Area Council, where I had to be on my best behaviour and not swear, and – hey presto! – I was a fully fledged professional boxer.

At the interview, I was told that the Board monitored each licensed boxer, to ensure that at all times their conduct did not reflect badly on the sport. As if! I'd long since given up fighting in Newcastle City Centre and had instead settled for the far more sedate arena of the professional boxing ring.

My first fight was confirmed at the Premier Sporting Club in Newcastle on Thursday, 22 September 1988, just one week after the Olympics' closing ceremony. This was a new club, to be launched that night by football pundit Jimmy Hill and Britain's former World Lightweight Champion Jim Watt. Both Harry Escott and myself were asked to be involved in the publicity and a photo of the two of us, with the legendary Scottish fighter, was used for the newspapers. It was a black-tie dinner club, with boxing taking place during the meal itself. This always made for a slightly surreal atmosphere, two people beating seven colours of shit out of each other in the middle of a room, hazy with blue cigar smoke, and to the backdrop of tinkling cutlery and polite dinner-table chatter.

My training had gone well and I'd found it easy to build up stamina to go the eight rounds I would be required to box, although the round length would be over a shorter two minutes. As a gentle reminder that I was starting out at the very bottom of the sport, I had to get the bus to the Newcastle Civic Centre, where the event was to be held. It was a lovely, late-summer evening as I stood at the bus stop, my boxing gloves tied theatrically around my neck.

'Where you going?' the driver asked as I'd climbed on board.

'I'm off to work,' I'd said, smiling.

My first professional fight was to be against super-featherweight Steve Pollard from Hull. It would be the top billing of four fights that night, all involving boxers from Tommy's stable. However, when Pollard pulled out, a boxer called Des Gargano was put up in his place. Gargano usually fought at bantam and was vastly experienced, having had over

30 bouts. Although he'd only won nine, he was an extremely tricky opponent who would go on to share a ring with Naseem Hamed in 1994 and have an amazing 122 professional fights in a 15-year career. He was a 'journeyman' who was, yet again, filling a vacancy at short notice. The bloke was boxing practically every week! All his defeats had been on points and he'd never been on his arse, due to his back-foot style, which meant that he was harder to catch than Linford Christie. The sport of boxing takes in all waifs and strays and our fight summed that up perfectly. I'd drifted into the sport because I had no money for ornaments. Des was a keen angler and had wanted money to buy a new fishing rod. Just a couple of years earlier, he had been ranked number eight in Britain for both his bantamweight boxing skills and fly fishing!

The term 'journeyman' should not be used lightly to describe Gargano, however. Although he was a master of not being hit, if you'd put him in a boxing ring with your average pub hardman, Gargano would have punched holes in him.

So I found myself sitting in a room with Frankie Foster, Shaun Kernan and Harry Escott. We were all fighting on the same bill, ready to smash someone's face in to put food on the table, to pay the mortgage, to buy shoes for the kids. I'd never been nervous in the past and I can honestly say I wasn't for my first professional fight. Everyone was laughing and joking, taking the piss and breaking the tension. But as the time got closer, as with all boxers, I started to zone in, to think about the task ahead. That's the time that you want to be alone, to focus your mind. There isn't any point in worrying about a fight because it just wastes your energy. I was content to let my opponent worry about me.

I always liked to kick back and chill with some music, a great way of relaxing. Later in my career, I got so good at it I could just fall asleep and Tommy would have to come and wake me up! I lay listening to my Walkman, cocooned from the world for half-an-hour by the sounds of Tom Jones, a man guaranteed to get me in the mood for either loving or fighting! Then it was time to get changed and do my stuff.

I'd promised myself a bottle of red wine if I won, adopting the 'carrot and donkey' philosophy of motivation. I was calm, I was collected, and I was focused. It was time to start getting ready. It was time to go to work. It's time to go to war, I thought, as I stepped into the banqueting suite, seeing the punters for the first time. It's time to go to war. I felt the hairs on the back of my neck prickle. It would remain my last thought before I left my changing room for every fight I had, other than kissing the Bible that I brought with me.

I was someone with a pedigree now and wanted to look the part, to look like a former England Captain. Now that I wasn't wearing an England vest, it had opened up a whole new world of fashion to me! I had a snazzy new pair of shorts, white with a dark-blue trim. They were the latest in ring fashion and, although they hadn't come from the same tailor as Iron Mike's, I looked fucking great in them. Well, I thought so anyway! I used the latest super-strength hairspray to fashion the biggest quiff I could muster. My official weight for the match was 8st 12lb, but my official height was 7ft 3in.

And then I saw Gargano, my first professional boxing opponent, and I could tell instantly that the man was a veteran of the ring. He'd somehow managed to outdo me, possibly using a mixture of superglue and cement, and had created a quiff so large it scraped off the ceiling. If he'd tilted his head forwards, he could've taken someone's eye out in the upper balcony. I entered the ring knowing that my opponent already had the psychological advantage, having taken first blood in the Battle of the Hairstyles. It was a big blow to my confidence but I was just going to have to deal with it in my own 'special' way.

The first round was all about Gargano trying to suss me out and me trying to knock him out. I hadn't really bothered asking Tommy what he knew about Gargano's style. It didn't really matter how he fought. Irrespective, I would fight the same way I'd always done. In his face, coming forward, hurting, punishing, non-stop pressure. A war of attrition. He would have no choice but to fight my type of fight so what was the point of studying his style? If I dominated the fight, the centre of the ring, he'd have no 'style', he'd be sucked into a brawl and he'd just be trying to survive.

In the opening round, Gargano was fast and really moved around the ring, and for the first two minutes it was pretty much me coming forward and him backing off away from danger. I caught him with a couple of uppercuts and he took them well. He used his jab a lot, which was never going to hurt me. It would be interesting to see what happened when the fight opened up.

But when the second round started exactly the same way, I realised that Gargano wasn't there to fight. He was there to jab and move, tag me, get out of the way and pick up his cheque at the end of the night. He was a runner, who would disappear as soon as there was the first scent of trouble, only to reappear again on the other side of the ring as if by magic. And he could do that for eight rounds if you let him, in the hope of scoring enough clean strikes to win on points. No wonder he'd never been put down! But I knew I would catch up with him at some point and I had a big box of tricks up my sleeve for when I did.

Towards the end of the second round, Gargano shot a couple of left jabs into my head. Neither hurt, but I backed off anyway. He didn't follow. I closed the gap to him and he jabbed again. Again I danced away but it wasn't in his game plan to pursue me. The third time, as he went to jab, I ducked low and fast and opened up with a brutal combination, everything I had, body shots, left-right combos, the works. It was as if someone had set off a firework inside the ring; someone had lit the blue touch paper on my arse.

Gargano got the shock of his life. He immediately went into reverse gear, desperately jabbing to try to keep me at bay, but there was no way his jabs could hurt me. I stayed with him, taking his shots with ease, pushing him into the ropes and blasting him with cruel body punches, aimed at snapping his ribs. I slammed a right hook into his head for good measure, but, as I went for another, he ducked left for all he was worth, shooting away down the ropes. The assault had lasted only a few seconds, but Des Gargano was rocking.

The crowd had instantly reacted and I started to inch forward on my front foot, now fully switched into hunting mode. I'd been given a good reception anyway, as this was my hometown and I had a big reputation. But now, the etiquette of the night had been broken. People on the tables were starting to shout, cheer even. I heard one person close by screaming, 'Go on, Dava, kill the bastard!' as I looked to get Gargano back in my sights. Step by step, I closed the ground between us, him using his footwork to try to maintain the space, moving first left then right, trying to keep me off balance and on the move. He was an expert at this and it showed as he weaved to and fro, never staying still, looking to regain his composure.

Again, he was in for a surprise. He had no concept of just how fast I could move across a boxing ring, how quickly I could trap him. I was an ex-England Number One, for fuck's sake! I worked to close him down, step by step, patiently cutting off his escape routes. It was like a game of cat and mouse. He slipped towards a corner, trying to maintain distance between us, looking again to shoot off down the ropes. But this was exactly where I wanted him and I was on him in a flash, nailing him good and proper with one big right hook. Now he was well and truly in the shit, trapped in his own corner, with Mr John Davison Esq in Terminator mode.

I hammered him with a right uppercut. It wasn't as clean as I'd wanted, taking both his head and gloves, but the sheer ferocity and blinding power staggered him. One left cross blew his guard clean apart and my trademark right hook flew like an Exocet missile straight into his head. Gargano was down instantly, rolling on to all fours where he stayed, shaking his head, as if trying to clear the mist that had so suddenly descended upon him. He struggled up on a count of eight, still unsteady on his feet. The referee checked him for vital signs and, for a moment, I honestly thought that he was going to stop it there and then. But instead he shouted, 'Box on!' I was moving in for 'the kill' when Gargano was, in time-honoured tradition, saved by the bell.

I strutted back to the corner where Tommy was waiting for me. He looked stunned as he pulled my gum shield.

'See that fucking punch, Tommy!' I said excitedly. 'What a fucking cracker! I think part of his face is embedded in my glove!'

'What are you doing, you stupid bastard?' he shouted back incredulously.

'Eh?'

'What are you doing?' he repeated, near panic. 'If you knock him out, no one else in the country will come near you!'

It was my turn to be stunned. 'I didn't think the idea of professional boxing was not to try and beat your opponent.'

'Of course you'll fucking beat him.'

'Yeah, and if I do it quickly, we can catch last orders at the bar,' I said flippantly.

'Do you want another fight or not? Don't go for the knock-out, John!' he said almost begging. 'You'll be a marked man if you do.'

'OK, OK...'

'And don't, I repeat – DON'T – cut him!'

And so my first fight, the Battle of the Hairstyles, turned into something of an exhibition match for me. I kept on going forward, looking to punish him but not finish him and he kept in reverse gear, just trying to survive. He did cause me problems however, of a completely unforeseen nature. Under the ring lights and amidst the heat of battle, my hairspray, mixed with sweat, started to run in my eyes. It was stinging like fuck and I was finishing each round like Luke Skywalker, having to use the force to find my prey. It went all the way to points but everyone in the room knew I'd creamed him. The referee, Arnold Bryson gave me a maximum 80 score, which only served to underline my total dominance.

I was lying in bed the following day, basking in the glory of my first victory, when the phone rang. It was Tommy.

'How are you feeling?'

'Champ!' I replied laughing. 'It's "How are you feeling, Champ?"' I said, kicking back and stretching.

'Maybe. I've got you another fight but it's pretty short notice.'

'How much?' I asked, wanting to know the most important detail first.

'Four hundred.'

'When?'

'Next week.'

'Where?'

Above: Me (*second from left*), with brother Thomas, sister Alison and mother Margaret, in the Shieldfield years.

Below: The Davison clan (*left to right*): Alison, Thomas, grandmother Frances, sister-in-law Christine, father John, brother David, me, mum and Margaret.

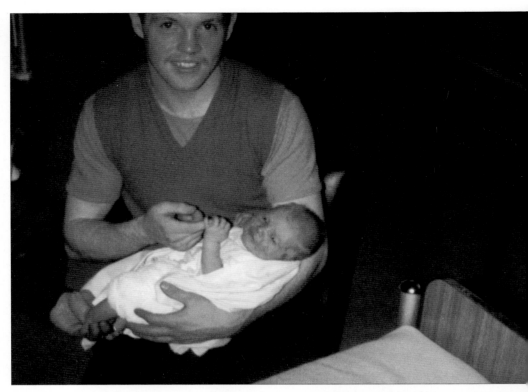

Above: A proud father, with my daughter Kelly, March 1983.

Below: Starting my boxing career, aged 25.

Above: A family man, with my wife Carol, daughter Kelly and newly arrived son Aaron, 1985.

Below: Flying to Berlin for the TSC Multi-Nations Tournament. The squad included eight time ABA winner and amateur boxing legend John Lyons O.B.E., 1985 (*far right*).

Above: John Leys in my ABA Semi Final in Preston, 1985. Leys was the third home international I stopped on my way to the final. I was a complete unknown when the competition began.

Below: Mike Devaney – I would beat him twice, but he took my place for the Seoul Olympics.

Left: England boxing captain, just four years after I stepped into the ring for the first time.

Below: With commentator and boxing legend Jim Watt and stablemate Harry Escott as part of the publicity build-up to one of my early professional fights in 1989.

Above: 'Million Dollar Punch' – no one gave me a chance against Narachawat but I KO'd him in five, Hartlepool Borough Hall, March 1990.   © Dirk van der Werff

Below: About to defend my international title for the first time against Bangsaen Yodmuaydong, South Shields, May 1990

With mum and Carol after I stopped Bangsaen in five rounds.

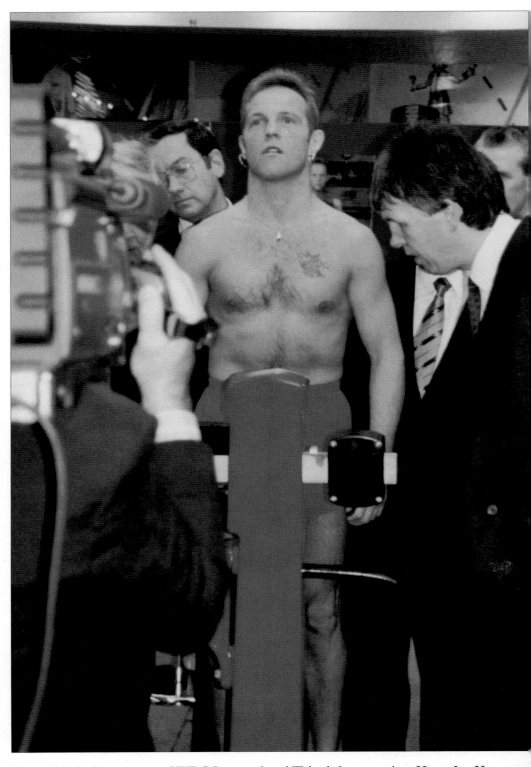

The weigh-in for my second WBC International Title defence against Hyun Jae Hwang, Hartlepool Borough Hall, November 1990. My third successive fifth-round win saw me win the belt outright.

In action against Sakda Sorpakdee, Hartlepool Borough Hall, October 1991. Sorpakdee would break my jaw, but I would break his heart.

Showing off the WBC International Featherweight belt on the St James' Park pitch. I did the same in Sunderland and received a great reception from both sets of fans.

Above: Receiving the Newcastle Sports Personality of the Year award, 1992.

Below: Matching Pair! The first man to win two WBC International Titles, with kids Aaron and Kelly.

Above: British Title fight against Tim Driscoll, Crowtree Leisure Centre, Sunderland, September 1992.

Below: Celebrating with my mum as the new British Champion.

Top: Steve Robinson on the back foot in our World Title clash, April 1993

Left: At the end of the fourth it was slipping away and I knew I had to do something to turn it around.

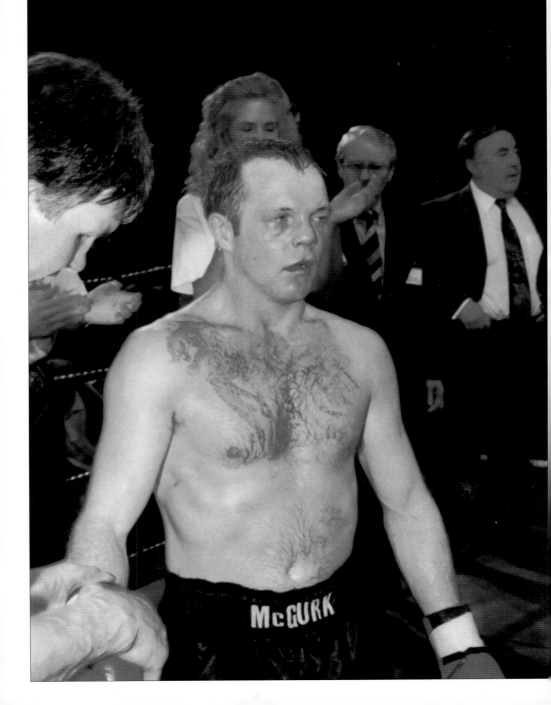

Awaiting the decision of the biggest fight of my life. I'd given everything to save my World Title dream...would it be enough?

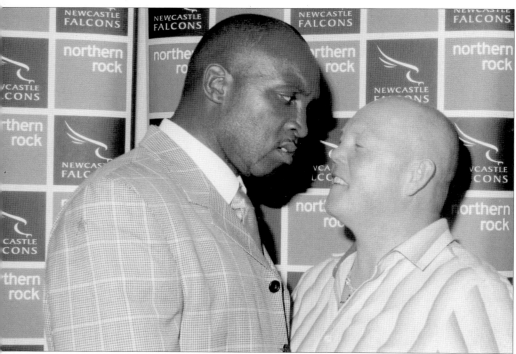

Above: With Lennox Lewis before the Palacio fiasco.

Below: The Dark Destroyer and the Geordie Hammer – with two times world champion Nigel Benn.

Today, with my girlfriend Caroline and her sons Dominic and Patrick.

'Sunderland. Crowtree Leisure Centre. The support match to Billy Hardy's European Title warm-up.'

'Yeah, fine with me.' I said, thinking of the unexpected cash windfall.

'Don't you want to know who it's against?'

'Does it matter?'

'Not really.'

'Keep it as a nice surprise for me then.'

It didn't bother me fighting twice in a week. I was super-fit and also, although the Gargano fight had been a nice workout, he hadn't really tested me at all. It had felt more like eight rounds sparring and, anyway, another 400 quid in the Davison Christmas kitty was not to be sniffed at.

The venue was something to be worried about, though. Crowtree Leisure Centre was right in the middle of Sunderland and Billy Hardy was a legend in the city. At that time, he was British Bantamweight Champion and his European Title tilt was seen as the hopeful next step to bringing a World Title belt back to his hometown. The place would be packed with a partisan crowd, which would usually be great for a fighter from just ten miles up the road. But at the time, there were serious problems between Sunderland and Newcastle caused by their respective football teams.

Football creates local rivalries, pure and simple. But in the North-East in those days, it was on another level altogether. There had historically been so much violence when the two teams played that the local police had ordered kick-off times to be at midday on a Sunday to stop people getting a skinful before the game. It was the only local derby in the country where that had had to happen. The 'away' fans' trains were regularly pelted with bricks from bridges and every game had mass punch-ups on the terracing. A game at St James' Park was almost abandoned when Newcastle fans invaded the pitch and tried to pull the goals down. It wasn't just local rivalry between the two clubs and their supporters – it was pure hatred. To go to Sunderland wearing a black-and-white top was to write your own suicide note and I doubted a red-and-white shirt had been seen in Newcastle City Centre for 20 years. Tommy was Sunderland born and bred and I looked upon myself as fighting for the whole region. However, it would be important that I was accepted by the local crowd, and that there was no trouble with my own supporters from Newcastle.

The day before the fight, Tommy told me that, yet again, my opponent had pulled out. 'You'll be reacquainting yourself with an old friend instead.'

I pissed myself laughing when he told me who it was.

I did my lucky routine of kitchen skipping and a massive steak Again, I was raring to go, although I already knew that there would be one battle that night that I had already lost.

The referee gestured to bring us both together for the start of the first round. As we touched gloves, Des Gargano smiled ruefully. 'Not fucking you again,' he said, shaking his head.

I could only stand and marvel at his hair, which had grown at least another 2ft taller in the seven days since I'd last seen him. What a fucking pro, I thought.

The fight was practically a carbon copy of our earlier bout. Even though Gargano tried to frustrate me, I stayed calm, remembering lessons learned from my first sparring sessions. An angry boxer is a bad boxer. Take your time. Be patient. I had him doubled up in the third round with a beautiful body shot that severely winded him and, twice, I steamrollered through his own jabs to smash big right hooks into his head with a sickening thud. It was forward, forward, forward all the time. At one point, the crowd had the comical sight of me opening up into a sprint to try to catch him. At the end, I jumped on the ropes, punching the air in a victory salute and I was suddenly aware that the crowd was going mental. I'd been accepted all right! They'd loved every minute of it and clearly respected the heart I'd shown in trying to entertain them. As I saluted them, they started singing, 'Dava! Dava! Dava!' over and over again. It was a beautiful moment for me and, just as importantly, it was two wins out of two.

Tommy was lining up the fights thick and fast. Just one month later, I had my first pro fight outside the North-East, against Gary Maxwell in Nottingham. Maxwell was a step up in class from Gargano. He'd been a pro since 1985 and had just been rated in the top ten super-featherweights in Britain, having won nine of his last ten fights. That one defeat had been for a Midlands Area Title and he was looking for a win in front of his own supporters to bounce back quickly.

We travelled down in Tommy's car on the morning of the fight to save on expenses. Again, I was getting 400 quid for the fight. The way things were going, I would only need another 20 fights to get my Rolex!

In front of his own supporters, Maxwell was well fancied and started off like a runaway train, driving forward into me, blasting off a combination of jabs and hooks. We traded punches in the centre of the ring, fast and furious, just how I like it. There was no fucking way I was moving from there and, after a few seconds, he backed off.

I was just thinking that I could now settle in, when he came back for more. So I hit him. Then I hit him again. And, within seconds, I was clubbing him all over the ring. He tried to rally but I caught him with another beauty, a right jab that seemed to dim his lights before – surprise, surprise! – a right hook put them out for the night. He was on his arse within two minutes of the first bell. He crawled to his feet on a count of eight, but, even as the referee was checking him over, he fell back into the ropes as he gamely tried to raise his guard. The referee shook his head and waved it over, aware that he was making a hugely unpopular decision. But it was the right one. Make no mistakes, I would have been back in there to finish him with more of the same and I could have done him some real damage.

Again, I was up on the ropes in a victory salute, only this time, the crowd weren't celebrating with me.

'Did you have to do it so quickly?' Tommy complained.

'It wasn't my fault, Tommy,' I replied, the picture of false innocence. 'All I did was swing a punch. He walked straight on to it! Anyway, it means we can catch last orders. And you're buying!'

I was begging Tommy for more fights and he kept on finding them anywhere he could. My fourth fight in two months came at the back end of October, against the future Welsh Super-Featherweight Champion James Hunter. I'd only accepted the fight at lunchtime that day, being told I might have to concede some weight to my opponent. Hunter was 11 years my junior and over half a stone heavier, but he simply could not live with the pace of the fight. He spent most of the time trapped against the ropes as I came at him from all angles. The result was another easy night's work for me.

And so to the final fight of the year, my fifth fight in only ten weeks. Unbelievably, I was looking for five wins out of five, beyond my wildest dreams, when I was booked to return to Nottingham for a rematch with Gary Maxwell. Robin Hood must have been there that night because I was well and truly robbed, the referee awarding the decision to Maxwell by one point. It was a disgraceful decision in favour of the home fighter, when it was clear to everyone in the room that I'd easily beaten him. The fight had been over two-minute rounds, which meant it had been harder for me to do my normal thing and close him down, but even so I'd given him a pasting. My supporters kicked off and there was a mini riot in the hall. Pint glasses showered the judges, fists were flying, and bouncers were piling in all over the place. It was better entertainment than some of the boxing!

I was severely pissed off to lose my 100 per cent record. But surprisingly, Tommy wasn't too downbeat. 'Before this,' he told me, 'no featherweight in the country that I approached wanted to fight you. At least now they'll think you're beatable, that your run is over.'

I hated the smell of defeat and, when the judges had given the decision, I would have happily gone another eight rounds with Maxwell there and then. I don't think I was even out of breath. Maxwell went on to lose eight of his next ten fights and retired. I now had a blemish on my record, a stain, and I knew that I would have to be faster, fitter, stronger to avoid ever having to rely on a judges' decision again.

9

HEAD AND SHOULDERS

'It's just a job. Grass grows, birds fly, waves
pound the sand. I beat people up.'
MUHAMMAD ALI

Christmas Day 1988 was a joyous affair in the Davison household. For the first time, I could really spoil the kids and I went to town big style. To the backdrop of Cliff Richard's 'Mistletoe and Wine' and Kylie and Jason's 'Especially for You', I watched them ripping open their presents with shrieks of delight. It was a brilliant feeling, seeing their faces light up, feeling their arms around me as they hugged their dad. It reminded me why I was a professional boxer, why I was in the hurting game. For the first time I could treat them to nice things, a feeling that other parents probably took for granted. It was a reminder of the reason why I'd turned professional in the first place.

After all the hard work of the previous few months, I had a well-earned rest and a few nights on the beer. But going out was starting to feel different now. I was more aware of what was going on around me, especially on nights in Newcastle, where I was getting recognised more and more. I didn't want to get too pissed, get into a fight, where I could maybe break a hand or something and screw up my new career. My hair-trigger temper was more under control now. Well, most of the time! A boxer only gets paid when he gets in the ring and I needed to fight as many times as possible in the coming year.

Newcastle City Centre was still a war zone most weekends, but the atmosphere was even more volatile than in the past. The New Romantic age was well and truly dead and a new type of music was starting to find its way into the bars and clubs. Rave music was changing the way people approached their night out. In the past, you went out and got as drunk as possible as quickly as possible but, by the late 1980s, people were starting to rediscover drugs in a big way, especially Ecstasy, speed and acid.

After the years of economic depression, things were looking up again. You had the comedian Harry Enfield with his 'Loadsamoney' character flashing wads of cash and yuppies in red braces. People had a bit of spare cash again and were determined to enjoy it. Half the city were pissed out of their brains at weekends, while the other half were high as kites, rubbing themselves in Vicks VapoRub, or sneaking pills into clubs shoved up their arses. Most of the clubs and pubs from my youth had changed; the Dolce Vita was now Walker's Nightclub. It became so mental there they had to install a metal detector at the entrance, like the ones used at airports, to check people for concealed weapons. The Oxford had been chromed up into the Studio. The Mayfair was still the Mayfair but it was now the home of Goths. It was also starting to do all-night raves called 'Resurrection' which would develop into massive all-nighters. I personally thought rave was crap – all fucking car horns and cats meowing. No wonder people had to get off their heads before they could dance to it. But its emergence made for a raw atmosphere as the two cultures clashed, which was made worse as rival drug-dealers began turf wars to protect their lucrative new businesses.

It was around this time that I met Steve Carey, known as 'Keza', and his mate 'Bubbla'. They were both huge boxing fans and came to all my fights. They were both big lads; Keza would have topped the scales at 20 stone and at 6ft 4in was a seriously imposing figure. Keza and Bubbla both had big reputations. On a night out, both squads of doormen and punters in bars seemed to part like waves when they walked in. We started going out regularly and, suddenly, I started hearing all these stories that people were saying that I now had bouncers! Like I needed bouncers! They were mates, top lads, and we'd get in some right states together.

I was in Macey's Bar in the Bigg Market one Friday night when some random kid pushed past me at the bar, spilling my drink all down my shirt. In the old days, I would have hit first and then asked questions later. But this was the new me.

'Watch what you're doing, son.'

He looked me up and down, his eyes vacant. It was clear that he was off his nut. 'Fuck off, you little prick... I'll bite your fucking nose off.' Nice.

I grabbed him by the throat and held him against the wall. Bouncers came running from all directions. 'Take him outside,' I said to one of the doormen as I relaxed my grip on him.

The lad was having none of it, though. 'Come on! You and me outside! Think you're hard?'

'You really don't want to do that,' said one of the bouncers. 'That's John Davison. If he hits you, he'll fucking kill you.'

There was a flicker of recognition on his face. 'Go on, fuck off,' I said, turning away.

JOHN DAVISON: LITTLE MAN, BIG HEART

He sprinted through the bar as fast as his legs could carry him. Everyone was pissing themselves laughing at him.

I also started knocking round with Tony Minett, otherwise known as 'Aka'. He owns a taxi firm in Newcastle now, and I used to do a bit of training with him. He could punch so hard my hands would be shaking afterwards. I'd use two sets of pads with wood in the middle but it never made any difference.

Early in the New Year, me and Tommy sat down to set our plans for the year. He thought I was good enough to get a shot at the British Featherweight Title, which was held by Hoko. But, to do so, I needed to increase my profile. The plan, if that's what you could call it, was pretty simple. Keep on fighting. Keep on winning. Keep on building the record and hope that the exposure I needed for a British Title shot would come. I was a man in a hurry.

And so it was that I found myself one of the only blokes in the country that wasn't getting shit off his wife for not taking her out on Valentine's night. As the rest of the country settled down to candlelit dinners and soft, slow music, I found myself at Crowtree Leisure Centre, looking deeply and meaningfully into Tommy's eyes.

'He's a hard fucker, John. He doesn't go down easily. And he won't dance like a Gargano. He'll stay with you and go punch for punch. You've got to keep moving, keep drawing him on to your right and see if you can finish him.'

'No bother. I'll just smack him and put the lights out.'

'It won't be that easy, John. He can take a punch. This is your hardest fight so far. You'll have to be patient. Remember, you can be forgiven one loss. But two in a row and it could be over before it's even begun.'

My opponent was Nigel Senior, another experienced pro who'd had 37 fights, winning 11 and drawing 4. Like

Gargano however, his record did not tell the true story. Of his 22 defeats, 20 had been on points. And he had a reputation as a fighter who could take punishment and he was very rarely put down.

I was fighting in front of yet another packed crowd, who had come to see Billy Hardy defend his British bantamweight crown against Glasgow's Ronnie Carroll. The atmosphere for the fight fans was all the more electric for knowing that Britain's own Frank Bruno would step into the ring in Las Vegas just four days later to fight Mike Tyson.

It was my second fight in Sunderland and there was a carnival atmosphere. As I entered the ring to the sound of *Rocky* pumping out, the whole hall erupted, chanting my name over and over again. It felt fucking brilliant.

As it turned out, Tommy was right. Senior took punches that night I doubt many other boxers would have survived. By the second round, he was having to grapple and hold, leaning on me, pushing downwards to try to frustrate. Even though I was conceding almost five pounds in weight, I was still the stronger and, as the referee pushed us apart, I came back at him and clipped him with a cracking right that made him slip straight to his knees, his eyes momentarily vacant. He got up though, shaking his head to clear away the mist. Senior was still competing hard until the sixth round, when I cut him with a slashing left. I tried to finish it there and then but still he stayed with me, taking punishment on the ropes until the bell.

In the seventh, my superior fitness started to tell and his work-rate dropped dramatically. I was dictating the fight now, completely in control, coming forward all the time as he tried to spoil and clinch, his breathing short and laboured. Going into the eighth and final round, I was well ahead on points and Tommy wanted me to stick out of trouble just in case. But I knew that he was exhausted. His body punches, which earlier in the fight had slowed my advance, were now a mere irritation as I looked to come forward to finish him. I was walking through everything he had, sinking some hard and spiteful shots into him. Twenty seconds into the round and roared on by the crowd, I caught him again with a huge right hook that snapped his head back and put him flat on his back. That's it, I thought, game over, as I watched him scrabbling around on the floor. But he somehow stumbled to his feet and the referee waved to box on. I piled straight back in, merciless in my onslaught, the crowd a baying mob screaming me forward into the kill. I smashed him across the ring, catching him with four, five, six, seven left and right hooks that had him stumbling backwards, completely gone. He bounced back off the ropes and into yet another massive right hook, which completely took him out. He was down for the third time, lying flat on his stomach, his arms outstretched with his face to the canvas. There was no fucking way he was getting up. I was already walking back to the corner, pulling at my gloves when I heard the referee shout, 'Box on!'

Unbelievably, but very bravely, Senior was back up on his feet and ready for more. I was miles ahead on points and there were maybe 15 seconds left. I could have stood on the spot and blown kisses to the crowd as I waited for the final bell. But it's just not in my instinct to do that. Senior still wanted to fight to the last so he deserved my very best out of respect. There's nothing harder than trying to go the distance when all you have left to fight for is pride. But another barrage and Senior's guard was down. He fell backwards into the ropes where I clinically set about dismantling him, piece by piece. Body, body, head, body, body, head, body, body, head... It was like trying to fell a giant redwood. As he finally started to go, blood pouring down his face, the referee threw himself between us and pushed me away, cocooning him in a protective embrace.

The record would show that I stopped him with just two seconds remaining. It was another win, another step in the right direction and, after being cheated in Nottingham, it felt like I had washed away the stain of that 'defeat'. The performance would also add to the Davison reputation that was building in professional boxing circles. I was a ring warrior, an all-out action man, someone who never took a step backwards. Someone who went to war every time he fought. Both Newcastle and Sunderland fans were standing as one, chanting over and over, 'Dava! Dava! Dava!' It would become my anthem and it would bring a lump to my throat every time I heard it.

Then came the biggest chance of my career so far. To make it in boxing at that time, you had to get exposure. To have exposure, you had to work with one of the big promoters. If you did, it was usually on their terms so the money you got paid was less favourable unless you were already part of their stable, or unless they negotiated an option whereby they took a financial interest in you if you beat one of their own fighters. And just after the Senior fight, it looked like I'd hit the jackpot.

In the late 1980s, Britain had a wealth of riches coming through the professional ranks in a number of divisions, but especially at middleweight – Nigel Benn, The Dark Destroyer, who was a former England Team colleague and an explosive power puncher from East London; Chris Eubank, the flamboyant technician with a granite jaw, who'd begun his career fighting in America; and Michael Watson, a modest yet silky ring magician, who was the housewives' favourite. All three were seen as World Champions in waiting. All three were expected to dominate boxing at the very highest level. But the scene was too big for two of them at that time and sometime, somewhere, swords had to cross.

They were to do so on Saturday, 21 May 1989 in one of the most hyped boxing matches of the decade. Benn, the man with a perfect 22 fights, 22 knock-outs record, was to defend his Commonwealth Middleweight Title against Watson, whose statistics were almost equally as impressive. It was huge and was to be shown at primetime on ITV in Britain, but also worldwide. There was particular interest in America, as the expected victory would give Benn a multi-million-dollar showdown with their IBF Middleweight Champion Michael 'Second To' Nunn. The event, promoted by Frank Warren, was to take place in a huge tent in Finsbury Park and I was going to be there, in the ring, doing my stuff!

We'd been contacted a few weeks earlier asking if I would fight London's Colin 'Sweet C' McMillan on the under-card. It would put me in the spotlight for the first time as the fight was being televised all over the world. You bet your fucking life I would!

McMillan had been an amateur at the same time as me and had made the ABA semi-final the same year I got to the final. Floyd Havard, the man who had beaten me by a half point, had stopped him in two rounds. I'd sparred with him a number of times at Crystal Palace and I knew I could beat him because I was simply too strong. McMillan was a great boxer, a stylist, but he lacked power. He simply wouldn't have been able to compete now that we were away from the more protective amateurs.

I kicked off training six weeks before the fight. It was a massive chance to explode into professional boxing as I had done in amateur boxing just four years earlier. But someone, somewhere, didn't want McMillan facing me in the ring. It would be his fourth professional fight but he'd already had one banana skin in the form of an average boxer from Watford called Alan McKay, who'd stopped him in the third round in his last fight. Did he really want to take the risk of that second straight defeat, that second straight knock-out? Especially against a Geordie banger with a reputation for putting people well and truly on their arse? The answer was 'no'.

No manager wants their bright young thing to get beaten up. They want them to take their time, not be rushed, and carefully managed towards a big title. Getting chinned by me would not be beneficial to McMillan's career at this delicate time and I was far too dangerous an animal to take a risk with. He was pulled out just 24 hours before the fight. The official reason was a shoulder injury but I doubted it, given the number of fighters who suddenly seemed to get injured just before they got in the ring to face me.

I was fucking raging. I'd lost the chance to show what I could do on a massive stage. It was a complete waste of time and, also, training didn't pay the bills. I had to find fights somewhere to earn the money my family needed to live.

Tommy kept on trying to line them up but they fell by the wayside as quickly as he could make them. It was a nightmare. I was signing on each week at Newburn Job Centre and I'm sure they thought I was taking the piss.

'So you've earned no money in the past fortnight, Mr Davison?' the spotty halfwit behind the desk would enquire.

'Not a penny,' I'd say, thinking of the vase I'd just flogged for 50 quid more than I'd paid for it.

'And are you actively looking for work?'

'Of course I'm actively looking for work!' I'd say

indignantly. 'I've got a whole team of people trying to get me work.' Tommy Gilmour and Tommy Conroy were practically setting their ears alight on the phone, casting their net far and wide to get me back in the ring.

'And are you able to work?'

'If someone gets me an opponent I am.'

'And what sort of employment are you looking for?' he'd ask sarcastically.

'I can take you outside and demonstrate,' I'd offer with a wink.

My time was spent in the gym, just keeping myself ticking over. A fight could come at any time and I was ready day or night to jump on a train or in a car if need be. It fucked everything up. I was practically on call 24 hours a day.

After months of inaction, my frustrations were finally eased in August when Tommy rang. 'You're fighting in two weeks in Nottingham. Bit short notice but better than nothing. It's against another old friend.'

'What? Maxwell?' I shouted down the phone, the very thought of my loss the previous year stinging me.

'Colin Lynch.'

'Game on,' I said, smiling.

Lynch had sworn revenge ever since I'd wiped him out in one round in the ABAs a few years earlier. After the fight, he'd told everyone and anyone that would listen that it had been a fluke punch, which was bullshit, bearing in mind what I'd already done to Hoko and also what I'd gone on to achieve in both the ABAs and with England. He'd turned pro two years earlier and had won the Midlands Area Featherweight Title within 12 months. His last fight had been in Salerno, Italy, where he'd been unlucky to lose a decision to Freddy Cruz, a man who would himself fight three times for World Titles. Now Lynch was hell bent on putting the record straight and, to him, I was no longer a surprise package. He would right the wrong, equal the score, gain his revenge.

That's what they all thought!

I'm always at my best when I'm at my most determined, when I've got something to prove. And that night, I had something to prove both to Lynch and the Nottingham fight fans, who had laughed and sang as I'd been robbed against Maxwell. Harnessing my aggression, I was hyped up as I left the changing room. As I walked through the crowd to the sound of the *Rocky* anthem, I was smashing my gloves together, shouting, 'Come on!' in defiance at the crowd, who were getting behind their man by screaming abuse at me. Not that I gave a shit. I was John Davison, ex-England Captain. I was the best and Colin Lynch was going to get both barrels, everything I had, from the first bell. He wouldn't know what had hit him.

He didn't, although I'm sure someone told him afterwards.

In the first, he was cautious, tucking up tight with his guard welded to his face, peeping round from behind it to launch short left hooks. They didn't trouble me so I stayed close, drilling right jabs into his gloves and then bringing in a left body shot from under to catch him every time. I kept it nice and patient and, at the end of the first, the crowd cheered enthusiastically. They could see an even contest developing. It was going to be a good fight.

Lynch must have thought the same, because he came out in the second looking like he meant business. He picked it up a notch, looking to control the fight and put me under pressure. His main weapon was a stinging left hook and he started to back off from me, trying to find the space and opportunity to get it going. He opened up, but, every time he went to use it, he left himself crucially exposed to my leading right hand. It made it easy for me. As a target, his head was so perfectly placed I could have hit it blindfolded.

Lynch went to launch a big left and I stopped him dead with a short right hook into the side of his head. He went down like a sack of shit, falling sideways to the floor. It was so fast, the crowd initially thought that he'd slipped. They were howling indignantly as the referee indicated a knock-down to the judges. But as Lynch clambered to his feet unsteadily, he knew the score. It was his worst nightmare all over again. He was in the ring with John Davison, the Geordie Hammer, and John Davison was going to give him a kicking. The referee gave him an eight count and then urged us back into battle so I nailed him again, driving him into the corner and opening up with a cruel barrage of head and body shots that put him straight back on the floor.

The crowd were silenced now, knowing that one of their own was being systematically destroyed before their eyes. I had barely broken sweat as Lynch struggled to his feet, his legs wobbling wildly. Blood was pouring from his mouth and a large welt had appeared over his left eye. He was already finished, but he had obviously decided to go down fighting.

As I steamed into him again, driving him hopelessly against the ropes and smashing a final right uppercut into his head, his corner launched their towel into the ring. I'd done him in just 90 seconds of Round Two.

Interviewed afterwards, I was buzzing. 'I can win the British Title,' I said to the reporters. 'There's no stronger featherweight in the country than me. You've seen what I've just done. Tommy is going to push the British Boxing Board to get me an eliminator as soon as possible.'

Boxing News joined in the following week with the headline

HEAD AND SHOULDERS

'DEVASTATING DAVISON EYES UP TITLE'. I was desperate to get Hodkinson back in the ring. But he was now being carefully orchestrated towards a future World Title shot by Barney Eastwood, who had managed Barry McGuigan at his brilliant best. There was no way on earth that Eastwood would have put his man in the ring with me, in case I ruined all his carefully laid plans.

Hodkinson was still to make a decision on the Lonsdale Belt. He also held the European Featherweight Title and had just defended both against Welshman Peter Harris. But it looked like his hand was about to be forced by the European Boxing Union, who had told him he had to make a mandatory defence of that title against the Italian Salvatore Bottigliari within four months. If he did so, he would have to relinquish his Lonsdale Belt. In preparation, the British Boxing Board of Control issued a new set of rankings which put me behind Sean Murphy from St Albans, Rochdale's Kevin Taylor and Harris. I was now officially the fourth best featherweight boxer in Britain, with Harris ranked at number one. It looked as though the four of us would be expected to slug it out if Hoko vacated his British crown. I would meet Harris in an eliminator, while Murphy and Taylor would do likewise. The winners would battle it out for the vacant belt. But I wasn't being arrogant when I'd said I was the strongest of the four contenders. I'd sparred Harris before his fight with Hodkinson and punched him all over the ring. And I'd sparred Murphy a number of times at Crystal Palace while training with the England squad. I'd given him a hiding every time.

Tommy's other idea was to switch targets and go for a Commonwealth Title instead. He wrote to the Board to request a sanction for me to fight the Champion, Ghana's Oblitey Commey. Suddenly, my name was being linked with titles. It was accepted throughout the whole of boxing that I'd bridged the gap between the amateur and professional sports in spectacular style. Just 12 months into my professional career, the title chase was now on.

In the meantime, I kept up the momentum with yet another victory in Glasgow, against the previously unbeaten Andre Seymour from the Bahamas. Seymour was a stable mate of Ray Minus Junior, who was in Glasgow to defend his Commonwealth Bantamweight Title against Scotsman Ronnie Carroll. Seymour was a good fighter, who had the pedigree of having fought at two Olympics, and he was sharp from sparring with the Commonwealth Champion. He was also about 8ft 3in and had arms long enough to wrap around the ring. It was going to be like fighting an octopus!

Beforehand, I was told that a member of the Board had travelled to Scotland especially to see me in action. If he had been wondering what I was all about before the fight, he soon realised. The Glasgow crowd got behind me from the first bell, which I expected as there's always been a natural affinity between Glaswegians and Geordies. I went to work methodically, getting under Seymour's long reach and smashing him with left and right body shots. Every time he tried to back off, I hunted him down. It set the pattern for the whole fight. The last three rounds involved him desperately hanging on to me, blood pouring from his nose and mouth. The result was an easy points win, but more was to come. The highlights of the night were to be shown on BBC Scotland, the first time I'd appeared on television as a professional. I had entertained the crowd so well that they showed the whole of my fight, every single second of it that night. It would go on to win Scottish Fight of the Year and I created a little bit of history by being the first English boxer to win that accolade.

HEAD AND SHOULDERS

In Seymour's corner that night, as part of the Bahamian delegation, was the 82-year-old Chris Dundee, older brother of the legendary Angelo Dundee, the man who had coached Muhammad Ali. Dundee had been Ali's promoter and had brought him to Britain to fight Henry Cooper in 1966. What he didn't know about boxing wasn't worth knowing. Not that it made any difference to the result. After the fight, Seymour told reporters, 'I've sparred with some of the best in the world and I can say that John Davison is in that league.'

Tommy was still struggling to find opponents for me to blast through. More and more fighters seemed to want to stay in and wash their hair on the night that they were supposed to climb in the ring with me. December saw another victory, this time against Birmingham's Karl Taylor in Leicester. However, I hadn't been scheduled to fight. Desperate to maintain my momentum after two more collapsed fights, I was a late replacement. I only found out about the fight at 3.00pm when Tommy called me at the house.

'Can you fight tonight?'

I'd actually had a bit of a session the previous night and not got to bed 'til half-four, but what the hell. 'How much?'

Tommy and I jumped straight on a train, getting there just half-an-hour before I was due in the ring. Taylor, who, years later, would fight eventual World Champion Ricky Hatton for the British Lightweight Title, ended the fight a bloody mess, his face looking like he'd been hit with a sledgehammer. I suppose in a way it had.

In just 15 months, I'd fought nine times and had five cancelled fights. I had eight wins, one robbery and the talk in the press was of title shots. But, unless I could get an opening at British Title level, the future would be pretty bleak.

I was not at the glamour end of boxing. There were no flash

hotels, no casinos, no photo shoots or magazine covers. It was just life on the road, running here, there and everywhere just to get another fight. The money was getting better, but only just. I was still spending long periods signing on, just so the family could survive. I was like so many other fighters on the circuit, desperately trying to make ends meet, just another boxer trying to get a break. The best I could hope for was a British Title eliminator in 1990, which would be a 'must win' fight for me. A defeat there and I'd be back to fighting for a few hundred quid. The title talk would be over.

But my record was good and in the North-East I was packing them in every time I fought. People wanted to watch me because I was so entertaining. Someone had once said to me that I looked terrible in the ring. I came forward with no finesse, no guile. But I didn't need that. It wasn't my style. I walked through punches to land bigger ones of my own, turning every fight into a slugging match. So I was no Sugar Ray Leonard, but so fucking what? The fans loved it and I'd already gained a reputation as one of the best-value fighters around. I gave people what they wanted, a proper all-action, non-stop battle.

It was a double-edged sword. People were desperate to see me fight, but opponents weren't too keen to be on the receiving end. True, a ticket seller gets noticed. But, in boxing, the common denominator every single time was money, and, if another boxer was going to take a risk with me, they would have to be very well paid to do so in case it was their last payday. The worry was that, in the game of chess that was the title belts, other boxers such as Hodkinson had control of the Board and the piggy bank that came with it. They could pick and choose, take their time. But time was the one thing I didn't have. I needed checkmate and I needed it quickly.

10

MILLION-DOLLAR GEORDIE

'The greatest danger is not that we aim too high
and we miss, but that we aim too low and we hit.'
MICHELANGELO (1475–1564)

The New Year started off as the old one had ended, with the frustration of a cancelled fight. Hoko's manager and promoter Barney Eastwood tried to get me to London, this time to fight Tomas Arguelles of Panama as top billing at one of his sports club dinners. Arguelles had previously drawn with Hodkinson in Panama before losing a rematch in Belfast four months later.

Tommy and I jumped straight on a train and headed south, to the Grosvenor Hotel in Mayfair. But, when we got there, we found out that Arguelles had bulked up since his Hoko battles. At the weigh-in, I was asked to concede 6lb in weight, a ridiculous amount at featherweight, given the difference the added bulk can make to the power of your opponent's punching. But they were willing to pay me a grand for my troubles and I reckoned that, given the sheer size of some of the opponents I sparred with, 6lb wouldn't cause me too much trouble. I would just have to turn it into a bar-room brawl.

Tommy was adamant, however. There was no way he was going to get me softened up on a mere black-tie sporting-club night. My stable mate Paul Charters, who would later fight for a European Title and who had come along for the ride, stepped in as a replacement and was unlucky to lose the points decision. I was left fuming in the bar, with a spare plate of beef and Yorkshire pudding. It was scant consolation for the wasted journey and for losing a grand.

Just as it was starting to look bleak, Hoko relinquished his British Title and all the manoeuvring of the four main contenders came to fruition. Tommy Gilmour called to confirm he'd negotiated my much-awaited British Title Eliminator for 19 February against Peter Harris and the venue was a nice surprise. After my recent swashbuckling performance against Andre Seymour, I was going back to Glasgow by popular demand! Again, the fight was to be shown on BBC Scotland.

It looked as if Tommy Conroy's original idea to try to break into the big time through Scotland was going to pay dividends. Win, and I would get a crack at the British Title against the other main challenger, Sean Murphy. The initial plan was to bring that to the North-East, which would have guaranteed a sell-out crowd. I held my breath and hoped that nothing would go wrong.

Two weeks later, the fight was off. Harris's camp pulled him out, claiming injury. It looked as if we would have to start all over again, trying to get Murphy in the ring instead. I could only sit and shake my head in disbelief. Given that I was already in a race against time, it looked as if I'd never get a chance to make the next step up.

And then it came. Local boxing manager and businessman Gus Robinson had recently entered the promotion game and he contacted Tommy Conroy to offer me the chance of a lifetime. Robinson had strong links with Charlie Atkinson, a professional trainer and manager from Liverpool. Atkinson had been in Thailand for the last few years, working with a number of top-quality fighters and had trained a number of World Champions. Now, yet another of his boxers, Srikoon Narachawat, had struck gold, winning the WBC International Featherweight Title.

This was a junior world title, aimed at boxers outside the top ten world rankings who were struggling to negotiate fights with those within the top ten for whatever reason, although it was usually lack of financial muscle. The International Title carried with it a mandatory right for a shot at the senior WBC World Title, held at the time by the Australian Jeff Fenech. Britain already had one WBC International Champion in the form of Chris Eubank, who had won the middleweight version just two weeks earlier in London. He would defend it twice before challenging Nigel Benn for his world middleweight crown.

The International Title was a short cut from all the domestic politics surrounding the British and European belts. In later years, Naseem Hamed would win and defend it seven times as a platform for his own full World Title bid. If I could win the fight, it would open doors that would otherwise be bolted shut. It was a once-in-a-lifetime opportunity.

It was going to be a tough task, however. Narachawat was a truly class act. He'd won all 12 of his professional fights and was also a Thai boxing champion. While I had been kicking a football about or stripping old houses in my schooldays, he had been training with some of the best Thai-boxing coaches in the world. Thai boxing, which involves fists, feet, knees and elbows, is an amazing way to teach your body to absorb punishment as well as developing big punching power. Narachawat was hard. He was not the sort of bloke you wanted catching you in bed with his wife.

The Thai had won the title in the bear pit of the old Lumpinee Stadium, Bangkok, where he'd beaten the holder, Argentinean Miguel Angel Francia, stopping him in the final round. Francia was a huge scalp for the Thai to have taken, as he was the South American Featherweight Champion at the time. It was a remarkable victory that had underlined Narachawat's pedigree as a top featherweight and an extremely dangerous opponent. He was a national hero and the Thai government had given him a beautiful house and a limousine to honour him for his achievement. Narachawat would be supremely motivated, as he would lose those luxuries if he lost his title.

He trained with stable mate Sot Chitalada, the two-times World Flyweight Champion who had beaten Charlie Magri in London four years earlier and was on the verge of breaking into the top ten world rankings. His future looked bright. All boxers have to go where the money is and Narachawat was keen to fight in Britain, where the financial returns were infinitely better than in his homeland, while Atkinson carefully managed him towards a full World Title shot. It was going to be a massive step up in class for me.

Negotiations carried on until the early hours but, eventually, a deal was reached. Gus Robinson had a three-fight deal agreed with ITV's *Fight Night*, the legendary boxing programme, which was watched by over 11 million viewers at the time. But he needed a good British name to pit against Atkinson's new champion. He needed someone who could generate publicity, someone who would sell tickets. And I was identified as the man.

The fight would be staged in the North-East, where a sell-out crowd would be guaranteed. It would also be shown on delayed transmission on ITV. For the first time, millions of people would see me do my stuff.

I was to be paid just £4,000 for the fight, which doesn't sound much, but was far more than I'd earned from a boxing match before. No one gave me a hope of beating the big-punching Thai but, if I did, Gus Robinson would have an option on my next two fights, which would be televised title defences. Narachawat's camp also wanted a guaranteed rematch in Thailand if their man lost. They promised that we could fly in a month before the fight, stay in the best hotels and be treated like kings.

But Tommy wasn't keen and neither was I. Once you travel abroad, you risk dodgy judges' decisions and the only way to be sure of winning is to knock your opponent out. Being robbed in some shit-pit in Bangkok just didn't really appeal to me. Conroy played hardball, insisting that any rematch would have to take place in the UK or he would pull me from the fight. Eventually, Narachawat's camp relented and the contracts were signed for 20 March 1990.

The fight marked a departure from Tommy Gilmour's original strategy of fighting in Scotland to build my profile, but it was simply too good an opportunity to miss. The latest world rankings had just been announced and I had just broken into the top 30 for the first time. It was impressive, but there was a long way to go to the summit and that's where I wanted to be. Why be in the sport in the first place unless you had the desire to be the best? It was like a game of snakes and ladders and I needed a ladder quickly. Beating Narachawat would catapult me way up the rankings, ahead of my main rival Hoko, the American Featherweight Champion Ricardo Capedo and even the Mexican Marco Villasana. As the icing on the cake, I was told that John Morris, Secretary of the British Boxing Board of Control, was going to be at ringside. It was almost too good to be true. The boxing pundits said I didn't stand a chance, though, and the Thai was instantly installed as the bookies' favourite.

I now found myself in a sticky situation. I was already contracted to fight in Glasgow in what was supposed to have been my British Title Eliminator. This had now been downgraded to a 'warm-up' fight against a late replacement, the American Bruce Flippins. It was due to take place just a month before the International Title fight. The risk was that a cut or bad defeat could delay the title bout or even lose me the title fight completely. I suppose I could have pulled out, feigned injury, but that just wasn't my style. I had no intention of ducking out. I'd have happily fought them one after the other and got two paydays! My plan would be to steamroller Flippins and hope for an early finish. I told the press, 'It's a gamble… I know it's a gamble. But it's one I'm willing to take. I could get injured or cut sparring in the gym. I need a fight. In fact, I'd hate to go in against Narachawat without one.'

Flippins, from Denver Colorado, was no mug. He had just lost a bout to another American featherweight, the 'Flushing Flash' Kevin Kelley in New York. He'd acquitted himself well against Kelley, the man who would go on to win the WBC, WBO and WBU Featherweight Titles and who would destroy Prince Naseem Hamed's aura of invincibility by flooring the Brit three times in Madison Square Garden. Twice, Flippins had stung Kelley, before getting stopped in the fourth round. One thing for certain was that Bruce Flippins was no warm-up man.

Because of the interest that had been generated since the title fight had been confirmed, I was asked to do some publicity for the Glasgow event. Both Harry Escott and I were scheduled to fight and the papers dressed us up in tartan suits and had us standing holding life-sized cardboard cut-outs of Andy Roxburgh, the then Scottish football manager, and his captain Richard Gough. Neither of us was too sure what exactly that had to do with the up-and-coming boxing night, but we went along with it anyway. Pictures of us looking like proper dickheads were splashed all over the papers the following day, but we had a laugh.

Nothing was going to stop my bandwagon. Even though I had a heavy cold and couldn't train in the days leading up to the match, the fight was a one-sided affair. Flippins had both height and reach advantage and used his long left jab to try to keep me at bay. But it didn't matter. I took his punches without blinking and went to work on the inside, breaking him up. As early as the second round, he was clinging to me, blood pouring from cuts over both eyes as I dismantled his failing defences at will.

In the third, the American tried to make a fight of it, going toe-to-toe with me in the middle of the ring. It was a feat that no other fighter had managed for any sustained period of time. Over a 30-second period, we slugged it out, trading blow for blow. He took some massive left and right combinations that clearly hurt him. After that, any stomach he had for a fight was gone. He clung and spoiled, wrapping his long arms around me in what seemed like a lover's embrace. The referee had to warn him constantly for leaning on me, but, every time he let go, I poured more big punches into him. He was trying to survive, pure and simple.

In the sixth round, I finally got the space I needed, just for a split second. I opened him up with massive body shots and he visibly crumpled. It was too much for him and, as his guard went down, he was left cruelly exposed. I finished him with a clinical right hook just as the referee was diving in to save him further punishment.

The following day I went straight into training for the International Title fight. I was having to prepare on only a four-week build-up because of the Flippins fight but it didn't particularly bother me. I must have been the fittest man in Britain because I could just go on and on. I felt like an old-time fighter in that I could have fought 20 or 30 rounds if I needed to and not been tired. And there was something inside that told me I could win, that there was an unstoppable force pushing me forwards, deeper and deeper into professional boxing. The four weeks flew and suddenly it was D-day – Davison Day!

The weigh-in was a new experience. It was my first major press conference and it was there that I met my opponent for the first time. Narachawat was very quiet, almost painfully shy. In broken English, he said that he was delighted to come to Britain and that he hoped he would please the fans and give a good performance. Looks were deceiving, though. I'd seen a tape of his title win against Francia and it was clear that he was a fearsome warrior. In a brilliant display of attacking boxing, he'd cut the Argentinean so badly it looked like half his face was hanging off. I was asked what I thought the result would be.

'I'm going to knock him out,' I said simply.

The official weights were confirmed with him a mere half-a-pound heavier than me. We did the traditional camera shot for the press, standing almost nose-to-nose, eyeballing each other. He had the faintest of smiles on his face, almost as if the flashing cameras and the shouted questions from the media embarrassed him. But it wasn't that. He was drinking it all in, sizing me up, and he clearly liked what he saw.

It was a huge time for North-East boxing, the region being almost knee-deep in title fights. Billy Hardy had just lost an IBF bantamweight clash to the Texan Orlando Canizales and Glen McCrory was due to defend his IBF cruiserweight crown against Jeff Lamkin just two days later. The importance of my fight against Narachawat was underlined by the attendance of the Presidents of both the WBC and IBF, who had flown in to be at ringside. I hadn't known they were John Davison fans until then!

It was always a special feeling for me when I stepped out to walk the walk, but a fighter's first title fight is something special. The TV cameras, the fans, T-shirts, banners... they supercharged every emotion in my body. 'Let's do it, come on, let's do it...' I was repeating over and over again, psyching myself up. Tommy never really spoke to me in the last few minutes leading up to a big fight. He knew I was prepared. He knew there was nothing more he could say or do at that point that would have an effect on the result. He respected the fact that it was all down to me and that I was out on my own.

I can honestly say that I remember very little of those times, from any of my fights. There was always a feeling of 'let's get it done'. But sometimes, I just didn't think at all. I just switched off completely. I no longer had the feelings of a man. I was a machine; all thoughts and feelings locked away deep inside, pure determination racing through my veins. I wanted to win, but it was more than that. The very nature of how I fought meant that I went out looking to destroy my opponent.

That's not to say I felt malice towards them. Some boxers feed on hatred, but I can honestly say I've never hated anyone in my life. The way I looked at it, the men standing opposite me in the ring were in my way and had to be removed as quickly as possible. I would always have bought them a pint after I'd knocked them out.

Borough Hall, Hartlepool, was the venue for my biggest fight so far and it was packed to the rafters to see me take on the pride of Thailand. There were hundreds of people milling around outside, desperately trying to buy a ticket so as not to miss what promised to be an explosive encounter. Paul Lister and Manny Burgo were going to be on the same bill so it was a massive night for North-East boxing. Hundreds of extra police had been drafted in to deal with the crowd and coaches had been escorted all the way down from Newcastle. The burning question was whether I could overcome the odds against so powerful an opponent. I'd never had to go 12 rounds before, something Narachawat's camp were well aware of. The Thai's manager was supremely confident.

'We'll be taking the belt home with us, that I can promise,' he said when interviewed about his charge. 'He's never been down, never been hurt. He's too strong. He will not lose to Davison.'

Tommy was also in a bullish mood however, telling the press, 'I've got immense faith in John. I've seen a massive change in him since his amateur days and even in the last year. He's tightened up, he's stronger and he's meaner than ever. He'll win the fight. But I expect him to get even better. He's 31 but he fights like he's 21. There's no way he's reached his peak yet.'

In spite of Tommy's confidence, not many people gave me a chance of causing what would be a massive upset. But I knew I could win; I wouldn't have got in the ring otherwise. My preparations had mentally prepared me for the task ahead. It was all about self-belief. I was John Davison and Narachawat could not hurt me. No one could hurt me – well, except maybe the wife! But Narachawat would not just be fighting me. I'd have thousands of fans urging me forward. I'd personally sold about 200 tickets, just to family and friends. There was no way I'd let them down.

Standing in the ring, 'Blaydon Races' echoing round the hall, I looked over at Narachawat, who was warming up, oblivious to the intimidating atmosphere. He was calm and looked slick and also huge compared to the weigh-in the previous day.

Most Thai boxers prepare in the same way, boiling down for the weigh-in and then bulking up again on fluids prior to the fight. The effect can be dramatic, up to half-a-stone in weight.

'Is that the same bloke?' I asked Tommy in disbelief.

'I think he's sent his big brother,' Tommy replied raising his eyebrows. He gave me his last instructions, reiterating what we'd planned and worked on in the gym for the last month. 'Remember, John, you've got to pace yourself. You've got to be patient. This could go a full 12 rounds and you need to make sure you don't run out of steam.'

'Yeah,' I said, nodding.

'Stay close to him. Stop him getting off those combinations. Don't go piling in. You'll take punches. They'll sap your energy, tire you out. Don't go looking to take his head off. Remember, this lad can punch.'

'No worries,' I said.

My senses were fine-tuned, the tension at breaking point. At long last, this was it. After all the disappointments, I knew that, if I won, the tables would finally be turned. I'd have a queue of up-and-coming fighters wanting to take me on. I'd never struggle to get a fight again.

'Remember, John... pace yourself,' Tommy warned me one last time.

And then the bell rang and I flew out of the corner like a rocket, Tommy's instructions already forgotten.

In the first minute, I hit him with everything I had, determined to unsettle him. I looked to knock him out of his rhythm or even just knock him out, I wasn't fussy. He tried to back out of danger but I drove into him, throwing him against the ropes and hammering him with body shots. He tried to shoot right, away from the blows, but I nailed him with a beautiful right hook and I saw surprise on his face as he realised just how hard I could punch. He backed away again, looking to keep distance between us, trying to buy some time, but I stalked him, cutting off his space and firing punches into his body.

The pace was absolutely frantic as I went forward over and over again. It was the high-tempo attacking boxing I loved and I came at him from all angles. It blew him away. Just before the end of the round, I smashed another right hook straight into his face and he wobbled momentarily. The crowd exploded again, the noise so deafening that no one heard the bell and the referee, Larry O'Connell, physically had to drag me off him. As we parted, I gave him one more smack in the face just for good measure and I saw the shock in his eyes. Round One to me.

'Jesus, John! I thought you had him there!'

'He'll go, Tommy,' I said. 'He isn't that strong.'

The second round started at the same pace as Narachawat tried to match me for work-rate. We slugged it out in the centre of the ring, neither of us willing to take a step backwards. It was a war of attrition, the sort of tear-up I loved. We both unleashed a furious barrage of punches, taking and giving big shots. I caught him with another right hook and then followed up with a straight left which exploded into his face, splitting his lips and smearing his face with blood. He backed away and tried to pick me off with his left jab, smashing three into my face in quick succession. But I was so hyped up I didn't even feel them and I drove him into the ropes with some body shots, before slipping right and clubbing him in the side of the head with another right hook. Every time I connected, it seemed that the roar of the crowd got louder. It was clear that the Champion was going to have to do something spectacular, because there was no way he could continue to take this sort of punishment.

At the beginning of the third, Reg Gutteridge, commentating, said it was time to see if Narachawat had weathered the early storm. But it was no 'early storm'. It was me, it was the way I fought and I knew I could keep it up for 12 rounds if I had to. I had no intention of easing the pressure and the third and fourth rounds went exactly the same way, with me hunting him round the ring, closing him down and then smashing shots into him. His own attacks had pretty much ceased as he desperately tried to keep me at bay with left jabs. But I simply took them full on and then hammered big shots into his body. There was nothing he could do to stop me hurting him.

'How are you feeling, John?' Tommy asked at the end of the fourth.

'I feel great.'

'You're out-punching him every time. Just keep on enjoying yourself. Try to keep your right hand coming over the top. That's where you'll get him.'

Into the fifth and the relentless pressure was starting to take its toll on Narachawat. He was struggling big style. I was tormenting him, pushing him around, leaning on him to sap his energy, snapping at him with short-range left and right crosses. I was bullying him and there was nothing he could do.

As he tried to back away, I sent yet another right hook exploding into his face and I felt him stagger. I tried to nail him again but he ducked away out of range. I closed into him, and he went to jab again, to push me back. I wouldn't go, though, so he clung to me. The referee pulled us apart and, as he did so, Narachawat went to fire a left hook. In the blink of an eye, I unleashed a short right hook over his swinging left arm. It was so fast I doubt anyone in the hall saw it. It hit him with a sickening thud, snapping his head back, lifting him off his feet. He crashed to the floor where he lay crumpled like a rag doll.

It was one of the hardest punches I'd ever thrown, maybe only bettered by Hoko's. The hall erupted, people were standing on seats, throwing glasses, and it was absolutely mental. He was lying, flat on his back, arms outstretched, completely motionless as the referee counted him out. I was up on the ropes, punching the air as officials and doctors invaded the ring.

Narachawat's manager was stunned. He could never have imagined that his Champion could be beaten in such a manner. 'I've never seen anything like it,' he said, shaking his head in disbelief at the reporters. 'It was a million-dollar punch.'

Back in the changing room, I was mobbed by well-wishers. No one could believe I'd actually done it. I'd just cracked open a can of lager when there was a knock at the door and in walked the ex-Champion, come to congratulate me. He looked wistfully at the belt, which was hanging over my shoulder. He couldn't believe how hard I'd hit him and asked me how I got so much power behind my punches.

'Through this!' I said, taking a huge gulp of lager.

We got talking about technique and he started demonstrating his defence.

'What the fuck's he doing?' Ham asked as he burst through the door.

'Showing me how to use my defence,' I replied, deadpan.

'Fuck off, pal!' he said laughing. 'He's just knocked you out!'

John Morris from the British Boxing Board also came in to congratulate me. 'That's one of the best knock-out punches I've ever seen!'

'I've done better,' I said modestly. 'Does this mean you'll give me a shot at the British Title?'

The effect such a result might have on my future could not be underestimated. Over 10 million people had seen the punch and boxing legend Jim Watt, who was commentating, had described it as a 'meteoric victory'. 'On that showing, Davison could take on anyone in the world,' he told the millions of viewers.

At first, I didn't appreciate how my life was going to change. The following day, I was standing in a shop in Newcastle City Centre when I noticed four lads staring at me.

'What the fuck are you looking at?' I said with my most menacing sneer. They almost shit a brick.

'I'm really sorry, mate,' one of them started babbling, 'I saw you on the telly last night. You're the boxer... I was just wondering if you'll sign this.' He offered me a piece of paper and a pen, his hands trembling.

Suddenly, I had people knocking at the house asking for autographs. I started getting letters from fans all over the world asking for signed photos. Tommy had to organise to get a proper picture taken with me wearing my newly won belt. I always took the time to reply to them in person. I suppose, having come from nothing, I appreciated it far more than someone who thinks it's their destiny. One fan, a lovely bloke called Jimmy Stanley, even paid for a two-week holiday in Tenerife for me and the family, just to say well done. It was the first time I'd gone abroad without having to take my boxing gloves.

JOHN DAVISON: LITTLE MAN, BIG HEART

The holiday was brilliant, the first time I'd ever been away with Carol and the kids. We'd sit on our balcony drinking sangria as the sun went down. There was also a brilliant bar in the hotel that was full of Brits on the piss. There was always entertainment on and one night they were running a 'Best Dressed Woman' competition. Only it wasn't for women, it was for men. A quick trip to the room and I emerged wearing some of Carol's clothes, a knee-length skirt and a crop top. I'd even done my make-up. I was gorgeous! I'd really gone for it and was even wearing one of her thongs and a pair of her shoes. I tottered down to the bar where the other contestants had gathered. But there was only going to be one winner and I was duly crowned Best Dressed Woman, despite my skinhead! I was on a roll! It was my second title win in a month. I wanted to go downtown dressed like that to celebrate but the other lads bottled it.

On the last night of the holiday, I'd gone to a club with some lads from the hotel for a final few beers. I noticed a couple of the locals staring at me and I knew they weren't thinking, 'Is that the Geordie Hammer?' I didn't want any trouble so I thought I might as well go back to the hotel and get an early night, but to do so I had to walk back across the beach.

On the way back, I was aware instantly that I was being followed. They obviously thought they could turn me over and nick my wallet. I walked slowly, pretending to stagger a little so they thought I was pissed up and would not offer much resistance. The attack came quickly. One of them tried to grab my arms from behind, while the other came round in front of me to smack me in the face. I fired my head back quickly and violently, smashing the first bloke's nose. He went straight down, letting go of my arms as he slid on to the sand. So that left it nice and even now, a one on one. A left jab spread his nose across his face and then my right hook sang him lullabies.

172

Back home, I'd get phone calls from reporters asking what my future plans were. 'Keep on fighting,' I would tell them. 'Keep on winning.'

Nike agreed to sponsor me but it was no million-pound deal. I was invited down to the factory in Hartlepool. 'Just grab yourself whatever you want,' I was told. 'You can always come back again in a couple of months.'

I packed Tommy's car with luminous shell suits, T-shirts, trainers, the works.

'Why are they all different sizes?' he asked.

I didn't answer but, by the following week, half of Byker was kitted out in brand-new sports gear and I had a nice wad of cash in my wallet.

Everyone thought that now I'd won the International Title I'd be a millionaire. I had neighbours saying to me, 'You'll be moving out now you've won the title. You'll be moving to Darras Hall where all the footballers live.' Everyone actually seemed to believe that the punch had earned me a million dollars, not four grand less fees. Fucking idiots!

'Why would I want to do that? I'm still the same person inside. The money's not going to change me!' I'd reply, and it was true. I'd be eligible to sign on again in a month! I never even thought of myself as being remotely famous. I just wanted to fight and have a good drink.

The weekend after I won the title, I was on my stall at a car boot sale in Blaydon. I was mobbed for autographs, but I ended up gutted because I spent so much time signing my name I never got a chance to offload the crate of fake Ming vases I'd been hoping to shift.

11

ALL IN THE DEFENCE

'When you actually go in the ring, it's a very lonely and scary place. It's just you and the other guy. Boxing has to be the toughest and loneliest sport in the world.'

FRANK BRUNO

I had a couple of mammoth sessions in the Bigg Market to celebrate my title win. I'd be out with Keza and Bubbla or maybe Ham and Matty and I'd have complete strangers coming over to me and offering to buy me drinks. There's a limit to how much someone can drink though, so, when people asked, I used to say cheekily, 'Just give me the money instead.' They did! I could go out on the piss with 50 quid on my hip and come back with 90 and absolutely steaming. When I walked into a bar, you could tell the change in atmosphere. People would be pointing over at me or waving. Later on in the night, everywhere I went I would be met with a chorus of 'Dava! Dava! Dava!' It was brilliant and I couldn't even begin to imagine the reaction of fans if I went on to bigger and better things.

I was also invited by both Newcastle United and Sunderland Football Club to go out on to the pitch at half-time for a lap of honour with the belt. In all, over 50,000 people applauded my victory. I never thought I would have been on either pitch unless I was involved in a riot! To do so as a professional sportsman was like something from *Roy of the Rovers*. St James' Park was especially symbolic. I'd helped build the new stand just three years earlier when I was still harbouring hopes of an Olympic medal. It was like coming full circle.

I met all the players after the game and had a few beers with them. Micky Quinn, the star centre-forward of the time and still a legend in Newcastle, was a larger-than-life character. He started jumping around with my belt round his waist shouting, 'Sumo! Sumo!' which was his own nickname with the Geordie faithful.

Gus Robinson made an instant offer of a title defence and I jumped at the chance. I was tied to him now for my next two fights, but that wasn't a bad thing. First, he knew how to put on a show and generate interest in boxing matches but, also, the money would be better anyway because I was the man in possession of a belt. It was important to keep the momentum going, but I had to make up for lost time financially. Tommy reckoned that I could fight again within three months, but I wanted it as soon as possible. Within a few days, Charlie Atkinson, upset at losing his grip on the International Title, agreed to send another of his Thai champions over to fight in the lion's den. He chose another hardman, the southpaw Bangsean Yodmuaydang, as the man to avenge Narachawat's defeat and restore Thailand's wounded pride. The fight was scheduled for May 1990 and would again be in my North-East heartland, this time at Temple Park, South Shields. Again, it would be shown on *Fight Night*, thus keeping my name up in lights.

Yodmuaydang, a southpaw like me, was another power puncher who had won 12 of his 13 professional fights. He'd wiped out nine opponents by the fifth round, including the current WBC International Super-Bantamweight Champion, Paquito Openo. The only man to beat him was Ruben Palacio, a hugely experienced Colombian featherweight. Even he had bowed to the Thai's power punching initially. In the first round of their bout, in sweltering Thai heat, Palacio had been floored by an uppercut that had almost sliced him in half. He'd somehow staggered to his feet and held on, but had been forced to use every ounce of skill to scrape home with a split decision.

Eight years younger than me, Yodmuaydang was ranked 14th in the world and everything was in place to make him a champion. As well as power and skill, he had a hugely experienced team behind him. He was guided by a Buddhist monk called Sudchia Sappelek, the man who had unleashed the Galaxy twins on an unsuspecting world in the early 1980s. Those two brothers had dominated their respective divisions for years. Kaokor Galaxy had lifted the WBA Bantamweight Title and lost only two of his 26 fights. But his brother Kaosai was even more impressive, winning the WBA Super-Flyweight Title in 1984 and going on to defend it 14 times, and he showed no sign of relinquishing his crown.

Boxing News summed it up perfectly with the headline 'DANGER TIME FOR DAVISON' in the week before the fight. It said that I'd fought way above myself in demolishing Narachawat and that it was hard to make a sensible prediction of how the fight might go. It underlined just how dangerous Yodmuaydang was. I suppose, for me, it was just another throw of the dice.

After only having had a month to prepare for the Narachawat fight, I wanted to do things properly. I trained most days anyway because boxing was my religion, but I kicked off pre-fight training in earnest six weeks before the big night. I had a set programme to have my body peak for the fight itself. The first week would be at a steady pace, gym work, sparring, weights and stretches. But then, for the second week, the pace would drop right down. Everything in moderation, everything slower. It would increase again in week three, drop down again in week four and then we'd blast away in week five, with me giving it everything I had. The sparring sessions in this week were absolutely brutal and I treated them almost like the fight itself. I was like a caged animal, desperate for fight night, and my sparring partners bore the full brunt of my desperation to be back in the ring and fighting for real. I worked with Harry Escott, Frankie Foster and Paul Charters, the solid team spirit of the boys bringing out the very best in me.

For the week of the fight, the pace changed again. I just honed my body and mind, completing my final preparations. I relaxed, slept and switched off from the hysteria around me. I didn't want to burn up energy thinking about the fight and I had the mental strength to put it to the back of my mind. I just got on with life. I played with the kids, mowed the lawn and went to the supermarket. I knew that, when I needed to, when I was sitting on my own in that lonely hour before I was called to action stations, I could flick the switch and the hunger would be there.

The changing tempo was designed to ensure that my body could be pushed to the limit in the fight itself. I knew I had to dictate the fight. I had to be fitter than Yodmuaydang, if I was to stand a chance. As always, the training was fanatical and I worked hard on developing my punching power even further. Tommy bought a 'drunken sailor' for the gym, which I worked on every day. It was a brilliant bit of kit, resembling a head on a pole. When you hit it, it would fire backwards and forwards and from side to side. You could use it for your punching accuracy as well as slipping. The trick was to be able to smack it when it was bouncing around, over and over again. It worked your power, your co-ordination and your timing.

I developed still further the ability to launch a hook or uppercut with very little back lift. I'd been doing it for years anyway, but now my punching moved into a different stratosphere. It became so hard and so fast I could hit the drunken sailor to make him recoil all the way to the floor, and I could do it over and over and over again. By the time I stepped in the ring, I knew I would be in the best condition of my life. Yodmuaydang had said he loved pain in training. I resolved to dish it out in buckets to see how much he really liked it.

Again, the region went big-fight crazy. Everywhere I went there were T-shirts with my face on, people driving past me tooting their horns and waving. I couldn't walk down the street without people coming up and patting me on the back, asking for autographs, wishing me luck. There was an overwhelming expectation from the fans, which belied the size of the task in front of me. But again, I was confident in my own abilities. Asked how I thought the fight would go, I replied, 'He'll go when I hit him.'

My supporters would be coming from all over the North to Temple Park in what looked to be yet another sell-out. I sold almost seven grand's worth of tickets myself. The phone was ringing at all hours of the day with people desperately asking if I could beg, borrow or steal them a ticket from somewhere.

'There must be tickets left.'

'There's not,' I would insist. 'Every single seat has gone.'

'There must be a space somewhere.'

'There'll be a big square in the middle if you want to bring your own seat and sit in there, but I wouldn't recommend it.'

JOHN DAVISON: LITTLE MAN, BIG HEART

It was going to be a carnival atmosphere as my place was confirmed as one of the biggest ticket-sellers in British boxing. People were so desperate to see the fight that tickets changed hands for four or five times their face value in the streets around Temple Park. Anyone who was anyone wanted to be there to see me do my stuff, which was to smash Yodmuaydang to a bloody pulp.

Lying in my dressing room, eyes closed, I could hear the chanting of the crowd, my name booming out over and over again. I was aware for the first time of the weight of expectation on my shoulders. All these people were here to see me, John Davison, piss-head and former street fighter. From the sound of it, they were already soaked in booze, ready for a massive party. All I had to do was deliver the required victory to kick-start everyone's night out.

But Yodmuaydang was a natural fighter, groomed from an early age for a life in boxing. Like Narachawat before him, he was also an international Thai boxer. He usually fought at super-bantam, but had already proved that he could step up a weight and bring his power with him. Yet, even though I'd only climbed in the ring a few years earlier and should already be retired according to the normal laws of boxing, I was expected to beat him and beat him well.

If I won, there was talk of a fight in America against Mexican World Champion Jorge Paez. The flamboyant Paez, who usually fought in Bermuda shorts and celebrated each victory with a show of acrobatics in the ring, had said he would fight in the North-East if the money was right. More realistically, there was talk of fighting the winner of the up-and-coming WBC Featherweight Title clash between another Mexican, Marcos Villasana, and my old mate Hoko. John Morris had already stated that the British Boxing Board would back a Hodkinson versus Davison World Title clash if we both won our up-and-coming fights. People were already speculating on the size of the payday I could expect. I might make 50 grand! 100 grand! Beating Yodmuaydang could move me into the big league for the first time.

But it was all just talk. The road to glory in boxing is littered with men who lost that one vital fight and fell just short of their one big shot at immortality. Between my own chances of a World Title fight stood a hard-as-nails Thai who hadn't come to Britain for a tickle fight.

For the first time, I had something to lose. For the first time, the thousands who packed into the hall expected a performance in keeping with my reputation for hardcore, extreme boxing violence. Some boxers get nervous before a big fight, but I always thought they were soft as shite. It's a job; you've done your preparations, now get out and do it!

When I was called from my dressing room, I practically ran into the ring.

My tactics were the same as always, all the way back to my first amateur fight in Whitley Bay. Hurt him as soon as possible, control the fight completely, close down his space so he has nowhere to go, throw leather until he's hurting, bewildered and exhausted, and smash him so hard that he falls over and doesn't get back up. As game plans go, it was pretty simple but it was very, very effective. It was also the only way I knew.

Just like my fight against Narachawat, I was into Yodmuaydang from the first bell, never giving him time to settle into his own rhythm or use his longer reach to keep me at bay. I tried to bully him, lean on him, push him around. We traded punches and he stung me with a couple of right hooks. Jesus, he could punch! I hit him back with some from the same bucket and we went into 'all-out war' mode within the first 20 seconds. He seemed happy to stay close and trade with me blow for blow, which surprised me given what I'd done to his countryman. It was a war of attrition and it was important for me not to back away, as I wanted to show him that I was stronger than he was.

I maintained a blinding pace, attacking him constantly, never letting him pause for breath and, towards the end of the first round, I caught him with an absolute beauty. As he drilled a right cross into my head, I took it crouching, at the same time smashing a powerful left hook flush on the side of his face. I felt him shake as the full impact rippled through his body, sending aftershocks into his legs. But still he came back, straight into my face, gripping me in a vice-like hold with his left arm as he tried to smash blows into my ribs with his right.

Sitting on my stool at the end of the round, Tommy asked, 'Can he punch?'

'Oh, yeah, he can bang!' I said with no pun intended. 'He can take one as well.'

The second round went the same way, the frenzied crowd baying for his blood. It was clear that there was no way that the pace of the fight could be maintained. Again, we clubbed each other in the middle of the ring, all the style and finesse of Sugar Ray long gone. It was a slugging match, pure and simple, and it was my type of fight. There'll only be one winner, I thought as I launched assault after assault with grim determination 'and that'll be me.'

Yodmuaydang was strong and brave and had clearly come to fight. But he was stupid to take me on at my own game. He hadn't realised that I was John Davison and that no one could hurt me.

In the middle of the third, I smashed another left uppercut

into his head, opening up a gash above his right eye. Blood was seeping down his face from a thick, red jagged split that shimmered under the ring lights. He was taken to his corner to be checked by the doctor and, for a few seconds, I thought the fight would be stopped there and then.

I paced the ring, backwards and forwards, adrenalin pumping, seeing nothing but Bangsean Yodmuaydang. I stared at him the way a sniper must look at his victim down the barrel of his gun. I knew I was completely in control. Yodmuaydang was cleared to resume hostilities and he attacked with a new resolve. He drove straight into me, trying desperately to break me there and then. He let fly with two lightning jabs that flew straight into my face and then smashed a low blow into my nuts. Bastard! Larry O'Connell instantly broke the two of us apart, giving him a warning and deducting a point, which would effectively cost him the round 10–8. Two can play at that game, I thought, as I tried to get my breath back. As the referee was gesturing us to box on, I fired a straight left, which drove straight into his left eye, splitting the wound still further, and then smashed him around the ring with some massive hooks and uppercuts that he simply couldn't answer.

At the bell, there was no release of tension, the doctor spending the whole time in Yodmuaydang's corner examining his eye. Again, it looked like the fight was going to be stopped. The crowd was on a knife edge, pumped up in their own personal war against the Thai, ready to explode in celebration. But again, Yodmuaydang was cleared to continue.

'How are you feeling?' asked Tommy.

'I feel fucking great,' I said as I stared at the Thai's blood on my gloves. 'Am I winning?'

'Every round.'

In the fourth, Yodmuaydang, knowing the cut was getting worse, sought to cover up and protect his right side. He stopped coming forward, looking to use his left jab more and more, to see if he could slow the pace of the fight. But I wouldn't let him. I chased him around the ring, catching him with good strong body shots designed to crack his ribs. And then I nearly blew it. As I caught him on the ropes, smashing more body shots into him, he ducked down into a ball, closing his guard tight to protect himself from the pounding. I hooked him in the head and instantly felt my hand explode. It was agony. I backed away, hitting him with a left cross as I went. Yodmuaydang was in no mood to come after me. By now, he was suffering badly but I was also in trouble.

At the bell, I told Tommy. 'I think my knuckle's broken.' It was an injury I'd had before.

'How bad is it'?

'Well, I can feel it,' I said, the master of understatement as I gritted my teeth against the throbbing pain.

'Can you carry on?'

'You'll have to carry me out in a coffin.'

'He's tiring fast, John, but he's still going to be dangerous.'

'You're telling me! He's like a fucking mule!'

'You're getting some big shots in now. Try to work his body again.'

'Yeah, I know, Tommy. Then right hand over the top!'

At the start of the fifth, Yodmuaydang came out and went for broke. Obviously, his corner had told him he was not going to last the fight with the cut still bleeding so badly. He went for gold, swinging big haymakers in an attempt to catch me with one big hammer blow that would instantly reverse his fortunes and win him the fight. I boxed intelligently, slipping and moving, evading the worst of his blows and then I nailed him from the outside with two jabs that went straight through his guard. It finally seemed to break his will. He was exhausted, blown out, unable to cope with the 100mph pace I was setting for him to match. As his attacks started to fade, I practically picked him up and threw him into the ropes, smashing a left and then a right hook into his face. His balance went completely. As he staggered backwards, I opened up again with everything I had, throwing caution to the wind as I launched punch after unanswered punch into his face, the screaming of the crowd driving me on. In those few seconds, I became a punching machine, smashing more and more unanswered blows into the exhausted Thai.

He was going! Yodmuaydang tried desperately to clinch but I threw his arms away and started yet another barrage, ripping punches into his face over and over again as he tried to cover up and block the onslaught. He was going! I caught him with another big right and his guard dropped down by his side as his senses started to dull. He was going! Three more punches into his head and he fell against the ropes, his eyes glazing over, and his mouth hanging loose and open. He was gone! Larry O'Connell dived between us, waving his arms as the crowd exploded. The official time would be one minute and twelve seconds of Round Five. But, in reality, it had been over since the left hook I'd smashed into him at the end of the first round.

The newspapers the following day made good reading – 'MASTERFUL DAVISON STOPS THAI IN FIVE'... 'DAVISON CLOSES IN ON WORLD TITLE SHOT'... 'BACK STREET FIGHTER DAVISON'S TITLE CRACK'. Even Jim Watt said, 'This could well propel Davison to a World Title shot after such a performance.'

About 40 people headed back to the house after the fight. I'd bought crates of lager and dozens of bottles of spirits. By midnight, the party was in full swing. It didn't finish until the sun was rising. I ended up dancing in the front garden with my title belt wrapped around my waist.

The phone rang all the following day. As well as the usual well-wishers, I had reporters calling to see what my plans were next. The World Title chase was now on!

'Paez is a real possibility,' I told reporters. 'He's a showman, a beautiful boxer. But I think a banger like me would find him out! He won't be doing many back-flips by the time I've finished with him.'

Tommy Conroy and Gus were in touch with Paez's people in America constantly as they tried to negotiate a deal that would bring the Mexican Champion to the North-East. ITV had already said they would be keen to take the fight.

'But the one I really want is Hoko,' I said, yet again making my intentions clear. 'If he beats Villasana, I want to be the next person in the ring against him and I intend to be at ringside in Manchester to press my claims.'

It all seemed to be coming together. Hodkinson was the firm favourite to beat the Mexican in front of his own supporters and it seemed likely that, if he won, the WBC would press my claim for a full title shot as their own International Champion. A Hodkinson v Davison fight would be huge, with one of the big North-East football stadiums the planned venue for the occasion.

Tommy had already said, 'If Hoko wins, I'll be talking to Barney Eastwood, although I doubt very much that he'll fancy taking on John.'

Although I was now the International Champion, I still needed a break, something that would really make my name nationally. Things were still hard financially. Although I'd now defended my title, the money I was making was still small in comparison to the riches that some British boxers were earning. True, my profile was building and I was the biggest ticket-seller in the domestic game. But I needed more national exposure to start to earn real cash. South of Hartlepool, the Great British public wouldn't have had a clue who I was, unless they were boxing fans. My name had not transcended the sport, as Nigel Benn's or Chris Eubank's or even Hodkinson's had. The house we lived in was still rented from the council. I couldn't afford a car. It wasn't exactly celebrity status. Even winning my first defence wouldn't keep me from the dole queue for more than a few weeks. We were living on hope.

Just one month after Yodmuaydang, Tommy and I travelled to the G-Mex Leisure Centre in Manchester for Hodkinson's clash with Villasana. It was the biggest fight of Hoko's life and he was expected to fulfil his destiny, by winning a world crown in front of his own adoring supporters. Even though I was seen as a future title challenger, I was snubbed by the promoters, having to pay for my ringside seat. It didn't bother me; I wasn't going to shed tears over it. 'I'll pay now,' I told Tommy. 'He'll pay when I get him back in the ring.'

Before the fight, I was asked if I would do an interview for television. 'How would you go about beating Villasana?' the reporter asked.

'The only way to beat him is to knock him out,' I replied on primetime television.

'But no one can do that!' he said incredulously.

Villasana had twice contested the WBC World Title against the legendary Azumah Nelson, losing both to close decisions.

'Paul throws that many shots he might well get a points decision, especially here in Manchester,' I replied. 'But I can take someone out with one punch. That's how I would beat Villasana.'

Tommy and I were hoping for a Hoko victory. The two of us in the same ring would be the biggest fight of the year in Britain, the fight that everyone would want to see. The television companies were ready to put the money up. The promoters were ready to roll with purse offers. The British Boxing Board wanted it. Even the WBC would be keen to see a clash of steel between their respective featherweight champions. The fight was so close I could almost reach out and touch it. But the best-laid plans of mice and men sometimes get well and truly fucked up. Villasana had not just come to make up the numbers. Although Hoko was on top from pretty much the first bell, smoothly boxing his way to his destiny, the Mexican showed unbelievable strength and bravery to hang on. In the eighth, having taken severe punishment and way behind on points, Villasana suddenly came to life, stunning the home crowd by smashing a sweet left hook straight into Hoko's head. The referee stopped the fight just seconds later, with the Mexican systematically dismantling a wiped-out Hodkinson against the ropes. It was a classic mugging and it was not the result I'd either wanted or expected.

Tommy was on the phone to the Mexicans the following Monday to see if they fancied a quick payday in the North-East. The answer from Villasana's camp was that he would not have to make a defence of his newly won crown for six months, but that they would consider a defence in Britain if the money could be found. My team set to work, trying to structure a deal that would make it worth Villasana's while to risk his title in a fight against me. Although he'd come here to fight Hodkinson for the vacant title, now he'd won, he had the right to pick and choose both his opponents and his venues. A few weeks later, any chance of fighting him in 1990 was dead when his first defence was announced for September, in Mexico, against Javier Marquez, the then Mexican Featherweight Champion.

Just a few days later, the Jorge Paez door was also slammed shut in my face. He had decided to step up in weight, to challenge the American Tony Lopez for his IBF Super-Featherweight Title. The fight was to be in Sacramento also in September. That would leave me with no prospective World Title fight until at least January of the following year. In the meantime, I would have to keep fighting just to pay the bills.

My options were now severely limited. Hoko had not relinquished his European Title when he'd fought Villasana, so there was still a chance I could get him in the ring to contest the European crown. But it was less likely now than ever before after his defeat to Villasana. Barney Eastwood now had the task of carefully moving him back into contention for another World Title shot. Hoko had slid down a snake and now needed another ladder. Another defeat, especially to a banger like me, who would be hurting him from the first bell, could well spell the end of his promising career.

Eastwood said all the right things in print, confirming that Hoko would meet me if the money was right. But Tommy also spoke through the press, saying, 'Barney Eastwood knows my telephone number... all he has to do is get in touch. We can sit round a table, face to face, and thrash out a deal. It's the fight that everyone wants to see.'

The call never came. There was no way Hoko would be climbing in a ring with me.

There was, however, the matter of my own International Title. I would have to make a voluntary defence no later than November or risk being stripped by the WBC. Charlie Atkinson still fancied his chances of regaining control of it, if he could just send one more Asiatic hardman to finally turn me over. But the added motivation for me was that, to defend it successfully again, would mean that I would keep the belt outright.

It was around this time that my world was blown apart. My dad had been unwell for a while and doctors had been running tests. When the results came back, it was the worst possible news. He was diagnosed with cancer. At first, doctors thought that they could operate but, when they got him into theatre, they discovered it had spread and that there was nothing they could do. It's difficult to comprehend something like that, as you always think that your parents are immortal. It hit my mother hard and the whole family had to play the most painful of waiting games.

The third fight of my International Title trilogy was confirmed for 13 November 1990. This time it was Hyung-Jae Hwang, the Korean Super-Bantamweight Champion, who came to Britain to rip the International Title from my grasp. Hwang was a fighter as opposed to a boxer and the fight was going to be on his 24th birthday. A little while earlier, he'd taken Choi Youn-Kap, the world-ranked number six, to a points decision. On the back of that performance, every other top Korean featherweight had avoided fighting him. He was the Korean version of me!

I returned to Hartlepool Borough Hall for the ensuing battle and, as always, there was a fine line between success and failure. Win, and a crack against Villasana could be mine in the New Year. Lose, and at 32 I would struggle ever to get another fight at the top level.

The pre-fight build-up went like clockwork, and I approached the fight in some style as I was picked up and taken to the weigh-in in a Rolls-Royce. Hwang could only stare as my 'entourage' and I emerged from the car. But the assembled 'Davison posse' was not your usual collection of bad-ass rappers, the type that Iron Mike Tyson surrounded himself with. It was Carol and the kids, although they were probably louder than Iron Mike's tribe could ever be.

Quite a few superstitious punters put their hard-earned cash on yet another fifth-round stoppage, thinking that history would repeat itself yet again. Even *Boxing News* predicted a six-round emphatic victory for me. Yet again, my preparations had been 100 per cent on the button. I was on a roll and I knew it.

I had Hwang's birthday present waiting for him as the first bell went. Unfortunately for him, it was wrapped in red leather and it smacked him straight in the face. I hit him from all angles in the first minute or so, instantly bringing the crowd to fever pitch. The stunned Korean was on the back foot instantly, as I attacked him in the fashion of a man on a mission. I don't think he even knew what time zone he was in by the end of the first round, especially after I'd clocked him with a beautiful right jab that had buckled his legs and split his lips. Jim Watt, commentating, remarked, 'Davison is doing a classic softening-up job here! There's no sign of age with him. He's 32 and fights like he's 22 and, make no mistake, he can maintain this sort of pace all night if he has to.'

It was comfortable. You know when it's flowing. You know when you've got 'The Power'. It was like one of those perfect fights when everything you do comes off. Hwang tried to stand and trade punches, so it meant that I didn't even have to chase him around the ring! But he was resilient, taking an absolute pounding from me in the first three rounds. I was hitting him so hard that three times I punched his gum shield straight out of his mouth. His eye was cut, his nose was spread across his face and he had stopped being any real attacking threat. But he was grimly hanging on as I threw everything at him but the kitchen sink. He was still standing up in front of me, still game, still in the fight. But he was hurt and it was only going to be a matter of time.

I made sure I was careful and got everything right. As the bell rang for the fifth, there was a roar of expectation as the crowd thought of its betting coupons. Could I get yet another fifth-round stoppage? Closing down Hwang's space, I caught him with a flurry of jabs that pushed him into a corner. I opened up with increasing power and venom, lashing punch after punch into him. A powerful uppercut opened him up and sent him spinning on to the ropes. Having breached his defences yet again, I powered in for the kill, slamming more punches into him. He offered no defence and Larry O'Connell again dived in to save one of my opponents. It was becoming a hobby for him and another win in my favourite fifth round sent the bookies home in tears!

It was an emotional moment retaining the title and knowing that the belt was mine to keep. It had been my easiest and toughest fights all rolled into one. Hwang hadn't put much pressure on me when he attacked, but he'd taken everything I could throw, far more than any other boxer ever had. Even the partisan 'Dava!' crowd applauded him as he left the ring. He'd won a lot of friends in the crowd and rightly so.

Interviewed in the ring, my arms around my mother and Carol, the sweat and blood of battle running down my face, I dedicated the performance to my dad, who was now too ill to come to the fight, as well as my school friend, Jeffrey Robinson, who had died a few days earlier. Jeffrey had been a fine piano player and, when we were out on the town in our younger days, he'd always jump on a piano in a bar and knock out some tunes. It was a tragic waste of life.

A few weeks later, Tommy and I were invited to a boxing dinner in Sheffield. It was a black-tie event, with a local club providing the entertainment. As part of the night, they introduced all the names in the room and it came to me. 'Ladies and gentlemen, please give a round of applause to Mr John Davison, WBC International Featherweight Champion!'

Afterwards, I was introduced to a local boxing trainer, a guy called Brendan Ingle, and one of his young future hopefuls, a teenager who appeared very small and slight for his age.

'Can I have your autograph mate?' the young lad asked.

'Of course you can, son,' I said, the magnanimous boxing Champion. I took his notebook and pen and scribbled my name.

'You've got a rock-hard punch.'

I burst out laughing. 'Yeah, a few people have told me that,' I said. 'Normally as they're being brought round.'

'One day I'm going to be like you,' he said fiercely, a flash of determination in his eyes. 'I'm going to be a champion.'

I patted him on the head. 'Course you will, son,' I said, sympathetically. 'Course you will'.

I wandered off to the bar in search of 'refreshment', while a young Naseem Hamed, one day destined to be a Prince, stood by, looking star-struck.

12

FRENCH CONNECTION

'Words cannot describe that feeling ... of being a man,
of being a gladiator, of being a warrior. It's irreplaceable.'

SUGAR RAY LEONARD

My fourth international defence was scheduled for March 1991 against Ghana's former Commonwealth and African Featherweight Champion Percy Commey. As far as I was concerned, it was just another payday, as I didn't expect Commey seriously to test me. But, just after the dates were fixed, I had the best news since I'd entered boxing.

Just two weeks after my demolition of Hwang, I was nominated as number-one contender for the European Featherweight Title. After all my failed attempts to get Hoko in the ring, the European Boxing Union ordered him to defend his crown against me within six months. Hoko had just beaten Guy Bellehique, the French Featherweight Champion, with a third-round knock-out, to retain his European belt. It looked impressive, but Barney Eastwood had carefully chosen Bellehique for Hoko's first fight since Villasana. The Frenchman had not been expected to win.

195

But, as always, fate conspired to throw a spanner in the works. Towards the end of January, with my preparations just beginning, I received what at the time seemed a completely innocuous injury while sparring. But hospital tests showed that I'd ruptured a small vein leading from my eye to my nose. The medical advice was to have three weeks off from sparring. It was a pain in the arse but I was still confident I could squeeze together the preparations needed to beat Commey. But the British Boxing Board of Control medical team, in their infinite wisdom, banned me from fighting for three months!

This wouldn't just fuck up my International Title defence. It would also ruin any chance of finally getting Hodkinson back in the ring. The contracts had already been signed and the fight had to take place no later than 30 April. It was scheduled to take place at the King's Hall in Barney Eastwood's native Belfast. Eastwood had won the purse offer to stage the fight, and had chosen Belfast in the hope that his home city would get behind his fighter and provide such an intimidating atmosphere that it would affect my performance. Some fucking chance!

Tommy appealed the Board's decision and the ban was shortened. I could now start sparring from 1 April. My International Title defence was cancelled, and it didn't give me a huge amount of time to prepare for Hoko, but I was confident that it would be enough. It wasn't like I was going to forget how to hit someone in the space of two months!

But boxing was suddenly put on the back burner on 26 February, when a tragedy of national proportions engulfed the whole country, touching the Davison family in the process.

Sergeant Tom Davison, my baby brother, was in charge of A Platoon, 3rd Royal Regiment of Fusiliers, as it snaked its way through the Iraqi desert in its Warrior armoured personnel carriers. Coalition forces had been at war with Iraq since 17 January, when a massive aerial bombing campaign had been launched.

For families of those troops in the land force, awaiting the order to attack, the hope was that they would never be used. But, on Sunday, 24 February, the Allies launched a combined air, ground and sea offensive and my brother went to war. It had promised to be the 'Mother of All Battles' and the worry at first was that British casualties were going to be huge. It was an awful time for the families of anyone serving in the armed forces.

But Iraqi forces were smashed within days and it was clear that the war would end within hours. And then, in an incident that was reported all over the world and which coined the phrase 'friendly fire', death rained down on an unsuspecting British convoy from the skies above, from American 'tank-buster' jets. The 3rd Royal Regiment of Fusiliers didn't stand a chance. Tom was spared but nine soldiers in his command were killed in those few moments.

The conflicting emotions for the families of those who survived are hard to put into words. Obviously, there is a feeling of huge relief that he was not injured or killed. But it was still an awful situation for any member of your family to be involved in and your first reaction is that you want to protect them, to punish those guilty for taking so many lives. The remainder of Tom's unit would continue to do the job required of them in the days and weeks after the incident. It takes courage to climb into a boxing ring and fight, but to risk your life for your country takes courage to a completely different level.

There now seemed to be an element of certainty to my career. The European Title fight was being looked upon as a World Title Eliminator. Whoever won between Hoko and myself would be virtually guaranteed a title fight against Villasana. But it would not come without a cost. If I chose the European route and therefore didn't defend my International Title, I would lose it. It was a chance I would have to take to keep my career moving forwards.

But yet again the ground shifted beneath my feet. In late April, Hodkinson relinquished the title on the basis that Villasana was willing to give him a rematch. It pissed me off severely as I'd been desperate to get him back in the ring, but my own team had also been working hard to negotiate a deal with the Mexican. But I could understand Villasana's way of thinking. He'd already stopped Hoko once and he knew exactly what he needed to do to stop him again. As defences go, it was far less of a risk than facing an unknown quantity like me.

The European Title was now vacant, however, and it would be interesting to see who was pitted against me as a replacement. In late April, the Frenchman Fabrice Benichou was confirmed as the other contender and the date was set for Saturday, 29 May. It would be my biggest test yet.

Benichou was not your average boxer. Of French gypsy stock and with Jewish ancestry, he'd been born in Spain and now lived in Luxembourg. He'd begun his career in Italy, and fought in Venezuela, Panama and America before returning to France, where he'd built a fantastic reputation as a no-nonsense action man. He was fluent in seven different languages and turned out to be one of the nicest, most unassuming men I ever met in boxing. Like me, he was a 'fighter' rather than a boxer, relying on stamina, power and pure aggression to beat more technically gifted opponents. He'd already held a European Title and had gone on to win a World Title at super-bantamweight, successfully defending it twice.

But then it had all gone wrong. He'd lost his title in a shock defeat, in what was supposed to have been a triumphant return to the land of his fathers. The South African, Welcome 'The Hawk' Ncita, had won a unanimous points decision over him in highly controversial circumstances in Tel Aviv. That defeat had stung him and he was determined to climb back to the top of the tree, using the European Title to press his own claims for a new World Title bid. The fight promised to be a stern test of my own credentials. It would be the first time I'd climbed into the ring with a former World Champion.

Although we were keen to bring Benichou to Britain, where he would have to run the gauntlet of not just my fists but also my North-East boxing fans, the cash figures just wouldn't add up. But they did over the Channel. Two French promoters, the Acaries brothers, had secured a money-spinning deal with French television, which was pouring vast amounts of cash into the sport. Tommy Gilmour and Barry Hearn sorted the final negotiations and I was offered my biggest payday to take Benichou on in Brest, in north-west France. I nearly tore their hands off.

It would be a tall order to beat Benichou and I was stepping completely into the unknown. It was long before the days of Easyjet and being able to jump on a plane for 30 quid. Most of my fans would not be able to afford to travel, so I'd be practically alone against an extremely partisan crowd. Benichou was also eight years younger than me. But it was more than that. The odds were stacked against any British fighter winning in Europe at that time. The last 15 attempts had all resulted in defeats for British boxers, usually on points and usually with a huge element of favouritism shown to the home fighter. But I was quietly confident that I could break the trend and maybe a few other things along the way. I knew that I had the ability to knock Benichou out.

The arrangements were completely chaotic and we were getting seriously messed around. The French originally booked for us to fly to Heathrow from Glasgow until Tommy told them to fuck off. They didn't come back with new arrangements until a couple of days before we were due to leave. We had to fly to Heathrow, then jump on a bus across to Gatwick for our flight to Brest. When we got to the hotel we were supposed to be staying in, it was already full. We had to wander around Brest until we found another hotel that would take us. Talk about knowing how to piss someone off!

I was interviewed for ITV before we flew. All the talk was that I would go for a World Title if I won and the reporter asked what I thought of my chances.

'I'm going to make him pay,' I said earnestly. 'He's kept me off the drink for nearly two months. I'm going to kill him!'

It was said tongue-in-cheek, of course, but I'd watched a videotape of him in action and I knew that I had what it took to stop him, even though he had the home advantage. I was confident that I could do a proper job on him to avoid the lottery of a judges' decision.

In France, almost 20 million people were expected to tune in to watch the fight and they were in for a treat. It was one of the boxing spectacles of 1991, winning European Fight of the Year.

I nearly blew Benichou away in the first round with some strong head and body combinations. He back-tracked constantly, trying to keep out of range of my big bombs. But several times I caught him with big punches that shook him. At the end of the round, in a show of mutual respect, we touched gloves, as if to signify 'game on'.

Because of our similar fighting styles, we both knew we were in for an all-out war. But Benichou hadn't been World Champion because of his flower-arranging skills. He came back at me in the second, launching wave after wave of attacks and the pattern of the fight was set as it swung first in my favour and then in his. Twice, I nearly had him, catching him with massive right hooks that shook him to his core. Both times I was unable to press home the advantage before the round ended. But Benichou seemed to come back stronger and stronger each time. There was very little boxing, no slipping and moving. It was sheer brutality as we stood and clubbed each other in the centre of the ring, the crowd's silence underlining my dominance.

At the end of the ninth round, Tommy asked me how I was feeling.

'Fucked!' I told him truthfully. 'But he's worse than me. He's tiring fast.'

'You're ahead, John, but you'll need a knock-out to win.'

It pushed my button still further. I knew I had to go for broke, to find another big punch. I drove forward continuously looking for an opening, smashing wildly as Benichou's corner screamed at him to get his guard higher and higher, until it was practically welded to his face.

At the beginning of the 12th round, we walked into the middle of the ring and touched gloves again and embraced. We both knew that we had been part of something special and that we'd both given everything we had. Benichou knew he had home advantage but there was no way a warrior like him would settle for a points win. And it was clear that we were both going to go for broke.

The final round must have been breathtaking for the fans. Both of us gave it everything in what fans later said was an unbelievable display of endurance and power punching. We threw everything at each other, our punches as fast and furious as the very first round of what had been an epic encounter. As the final bell went, we wrapped our arms around each other in the centre of the ring like brothers. I knew that I'd put in a massive performance. I knew that in Britain I would have got the verdict. But it was in the hands of the gods and the omens were not good.

And so it proved. The decision, unsurprisingly, went Benichou's way, but I was insulted that it was a unanimous verdict. Two judges gave it to him by just one round but the Swiss judge had him winning by five rounds, which was a complete piss-take! He must have been watching *Rocky* on the monitor in front of him because he certainly wasn't watching the fight that I was in. It was a complete disgrace. I joined the long list of British fighters who had been conned by our European cousins. Bastards.

But Fabrice Benichou knew the score. Interviewed afterwards, he said, 'I had to be mentally strong to win. If I had always been so strong, I would still be World Champion. He surprised me just how strong he was and he hurt me several times. I may have won the fight, but John Davison is a true champion.'

It was the beginning of an amazing respect between us. When we met back at the hotel, he gave me a pair of miniature boxing gloves that he himself had been given when he had won his World Title. I've still got them today. As I left him for the last time, I said, 'I'll see you again,' and he smiled and nodded. He knew that I'd be knocking on his door again sometime soon and I honestly believe he was looking forward to it. He was one hard bastard.

FRENCH CONNECTION

I was philosophical about the defeat, taking heart from my performance. Benichou was, without a doubt, the finest fighter I'd ever fought but I'd proved that I could do it, that I was one of the best featherweights in the world. All I needed was a chance to prove it on the biggest stage of all.

It was now a question of 'Where do I go from here?' Although I'd lost the Benichou fight, my performance had actually enhanced my reputation. But the door was now closed on a World Title fight, at least temporarily. The plan stayed the same as always. 'Keep fighting, keep winning!' It was my own personal motto.

My team were working frantically to organise my next fight. There were tentative negotiations going on through Tommy Gilmour for a shot at the British crown. The Commonwealth Title was again discussed. It was rumoured that Gus Robinson was going to promote another WBC International Title fight in the North-East. Then, early that summer, stories started to appear that had the whole of boxing talking. It would be the biggest fight the region had even seen and certainly my biggest money-spinner. There would be no title belts at stake. It would be far more important than that! It would be local pride that was on the line.

Since I'd turned professional, everyone had mused on who would win a fight between Sunderland's bantamweight Billy Hardy and myself. We were the region's two little hardmen. We were both at the top of our game. It was a fight that would capture the imagination of the whole country, not just boxing fans. No doubt, I would have the black-and-white stripes of Newcastle United nailed to my mast, even though I fought in Sunderland and had a great rapport with the city. Meanwhile, Hardy would be draped in the red-and-white of Sunderland for the occasion.

Hardy had been fantastic in the way he'd represented the region. A professional since 1983, he'd won the British Bantamweight Title, before losing a World Title fight in Sunderland to Orlando Canizales on a split decision. He'd just lost the rematch, in the Texan heat of Laredo, when he'd been stopped in eight.

Now Gus Robinson had stated that he was going to try to get the fight on. It would sell out one of the region's big football grounds easily. It was estimated that a crowd of 40,000 could be expected. It would mean Hardy stepping up 4lb in weight to super-bantam. I would drop 4lb and we'd smash into each other right in the middle!

The press had a field day, running here, there and everywhere asking for quotes. Hardy said that it appealed to him but it would be his manager Denni Mancini's decision. He said that his path might lie elsewhere, as he was looking for a possible Commonwealth Title shot. Maybe he remembered that sparring session a few years earlier. I certainly did. When I was asked if it appealed to me, I said simply, 'I like Billy. He's a nice lad. But he won't box again after I've fought him.'

Hardy's path did lie in other places and Robinson's big plan to give the region the fight they'd always wanted came to nothing. I suppose it gives fight fans hours of fun even now, though, answering the eternal question of who would have won it. I can answer that in one word – me.

The politics surrounding various title shots continued, but when my next fight was confirmed it was a surprise even to me! I'd entered boxing to make some money, maybe to see the world. And now, I was about to live the dream.

The French promoters in the European Title fight had loved the way I'd fought. My technique of constant pressure, mixed with a violent array of punches, made for an excellent boxing spectacle. So when Fabrice Benichou's first European Title defence was confirmed, they asked me to return to France to fight on the under-card. The promoters said it was a 'thank you' to me for my performance in Brest.

The timing and location could not have been better. The fight was to take place in the South of France in mid-August and I was pitched against the American Richard Savage. Although it was my first non-title fight in almost 18 months, I still put my heart and soul into my preparations.

Savage, from Los Angeles, had represented the USA in the Olympic Games. He was a technically gifted boxer who'd won all 26 of his pro fights on the way to losing an IBF Featherweight Title fight in Korea in 1986. He was coming into the fight off the back of a winning streak, having won his last six fights. In fact, his last defeat had been to the legendary Mexican Carlos Zarate, the 'Z Man' himself, who'd stopped Savage in five rounds in Mexico City. There was no doubt Savage could box, but by now my own standing in world boxing was high. This was a fight I was expected to win.

When I'd gone to Brest for the Benichou fight, the promoters had to practically drag me there. I hated being away from Carol and the kids, especially as I'd barely seen them for two years because of my commitments to the England and Great Britain Amateur Teams. So I always tried to spend as little time as possible away from home to try to compensate. But this was different. This wasn't some horrible hotel in a grey industrial city in the North. This was the millionaire's playground at the height of summer! The sea, the sand, the sports cars... I always knew I'd make it!

The promoters wanted me in the South of France for ten days before the fight for publicity. They were putting Tommy and me up in a beautiful hotel overlooking the beach. Far be it for me to screw their plans up, especially when they needed me so badly. So, with a heavy heart, I packed my case and jumped on the plane. It was a hard job but somebody had to do it.

We flew down to Cannes and it was an amazing place. The beautiful, deep-blue sea, with its constantly changing shades of azure and aquamarine. The harbours with their gleaming white yachts bobbing gently on the water. The sun beating down, warming my bones. I don't think I saw a cloud in the whole time I was there. It was paradise and the locals were unbelievably generous. We were treated like kings.

Everywhere we went, people came to ask for autographs. We couldn't walk down the street without a café or restaurant owner calling us over and offering us free food and free drinks. It was brilliant and, even though I was on a pretty strict training regime, I still found time for a glass or two of the local rosé wine. It was just like strawberry pop and I could have drunk bucketloads of the stuff.

The fight took place in Juan-les-Pins, just along the coast from Cannes, on a beautiful Friday evening. There on the beach surrounded by the glitterati of the French Riviera, I entered the ring with memories of that bus ride to my first professional fight etched in my memory. 'Where are you going?' the bus driver had asked on my way to the Gargano fight.

I suppose I'd never really known.

Savage completely bamboozled me in the early rounds. I couldn't get hold of him as he tapped away, getting out of range as fast as possible. His movement and speed showed just why he'd been a World Title contender but he lacked any real power to hurt someone like me who had a reputation for taking a punch. It was like being back in the amateurs! His footwork was like lightning and you could tell his pedigree just by the way he moved around the ring. He was starting to grow in confidence, probably wondering why he'd heard all those stories about his so-called 'big-punching' opponent. So he started to work just that little bit closer, looking for short-range hooks and jabs, which was fine by me.

Bang! I launched a blistering tirade of punches that smashed straight into his body and head. He recoiled in shock as I let fly with another salvo, which instantly split his left eye. Then I started to close him down, hunting him around the ring as he tried to work out what the fuck had just hit him.

The pattern of the fight changed instantly. There was no way he wanted to get caught like that again. But now I was in hunting mode. I brought out more of my big weapons in the fourth, smashing cruel body shots into him that took his breath away. He was slowing down as the shock of my punches started to play havoc with his internal wiring. I'd been a big hit in France after my Benichou performance and the crowd started to get right behind me as I made yet another opponent fight my type of fight. I closed his left eye completely in the fifth with a thumping right uppercut, then I split his right eye early in the sixth. It was turning into a professional, systematic demolition job.

Savage had managed to avoid being caught on the ropes, but it was only delaying the inevitable. As his sight began to blur and his body began to throb, I was closing down more and more of his space. As we entered the final minute of the sixth, I peeled away his defences with some more massive body shots, before catching him on the ropes and opening up with left-right combinations, methodically working his body and his head. His face said it all. He'd never been hit that hard by anyone and soon he was well and truly in the shit as I unloaded shot after shot into him. The referee pulled me off him to prevent him being seriously damaged and an appreciative crowd stood to applaud me. I jumped up on to the ropes to salute them. Ten minutes later, I was in the sea with a bottle of wine.

Standing there, emptying the bottle and getting elegantly wasted, the surf lapping round my feet, I was aware of just how far I'd come. The dream continued and the desire to reach the very top was growing inside me. I'd come into boxing to win a couple of trophies for a fucking cabinet! To fight without being nicked! Success or failure had meant very little to me. But now I was desperate to win a World Title. It dominated my waking thoughts. I lived and breathed for it. And it still seemed possible, even though I was nearly 34 years old. I was fit, I was fast and, in the ring, I was furious. I'd avoided any major injuries so far and, just as importantly, any major cuts. But another slip-up after my European Title mugging and it would all come tumbling down around me. Fighters such as Benichou could afford one bad night. But I was already living on borrowed time and I had to find the missing pieces in the jigsaw that would give me a shot at the big one.

The money was actually starting to flow into my bank account for the first time in years – suddenly, I had some cash to spend. It was time for the Davison family to go shopping and the first thing we needed was a car. I checked out the latest line in Lamborghinis and Porsches, you know, cars suited to my status as one of the best featherweights in Europe, but there was really only one set of wheels I wanted and it wasn't a Sinclair C5. Soon a beautiful, red Ford Escort XR3i was parked on the drive. It was the days of hot hatches, the original boy racers, and I think the insurance was about as much as the car, but I didn't care. Everybody knew it was mine and it would have taken a pretty stupid thief to nick my pride and joy. He'd be dead before he got into third gear.

FRENCH CONNECTION

Although we could now afford to live, there was a big difference between the glamour boys of British boxing and me. And it couldn't have been emphasised more than when I signed my next 'big' sponsorship deal.

I doubt it made *Sky Sports News*. A local publican, Kevin Kelly from the Original Masons pub on the outskirts of Newcastle, offered to cover my kit and training expenses in the build-up to my next fight. The total amount he put down was a grand. It doesn't sound like a lot, but, to someone who'd spent years living on nothing, it was a godsend and a magnificent gesture.

There was an old hut behind the pub and Kevin let me train there, sweating away on a bag which was slung by an old rope over the ceiling joist. The room was tiny and I had to share it with a burger stand, the ones on wheels that you sometimes still see outside football grounds serving dog burgers. There was barely room to swing a cat, but it didn't really matter. I wasn't exactly a 'float like a butterfly' type of fighter so I didn't need much room to do my stuff.

I'd finish training and then go into the pub for some food. At the time, the chef's special was a 32oz beefburger with a mountain of chips. The deal was that, if you could eat it, you got it free. I don't know anyone who managed it and I certainly didn't try it. I'd have been fighting Bruno in the heavyweights if I had.

The sponsorship meant that I would not have to spend part of my final purse in the build-up to the fight. I like to think it proved my status as a people's champion and there was a certain irony. Even as a professional boxer, I was spending most of my time in the pub!

Word came through that Gus Robinson had struck gold yet again. In yet another coup for the North-East promoter, he negotiated a deal to bring Sakda Sorpakdee, the WBC International Super-Bantamweight Champion, to Britain to defend his crown. He would be following in the footsteps of his countrymen Srikoon Narachawat and Bangsean Yodmuaydang in attempting to beat me in front of my own supporters. The fight would give me the opportunity to make a little piece of boxing history, by becoming the first man to win an International Title at two different weights.

It was another fantastic opportunity; another International Title would keep my world ranking high, which was critical if I was to still be looked on as a genuine World Title prospect. Discussions were still ongoing for a rematch with Benichou, and the Frenchman, honourable man that he was, had indicated that he would accept another fight. Not many would do that in his position, where there was a real risk of losing. But the level of respect between the two of us was immense. He knew we had unfinished business to be resolved and there was no way that the warrior in him would turn away from the challenge.

There were also ongoing talks with the WBO Super-Bantamweight Title Champion, the Texan Jesse Benavides. If Tommy Gilmour could structure a deal, I might well be going all the way to America if I came through the Sorpakdee fight unscathed.

After all the disappointments of the past, I'd decided just to take it one fight at a time. I'd been close to a World Title fight so many times but they had always fallen through. The only thing I could do was keep on winning and keep hoping my luck would change and that something, somewhere would materialise.

But, just a month before my big night, the fight and indeed the entire future of boxing was thrown into doubt. In a brutal reminder of the dangers that all boxers faced, yet another name was added to the growing list of men killed or seriously injured chasing their dreams. But this time it was not in some anonymous smoke-filled room, where the tragedy could be sanitised through the medium of a sports reporter's written word. It was on primetime television, watched by millions and able to be replayed over and over again in graphic detail. That final punch! The sickening jolt of his head as it slammed off the lower rope. Lying unconscious, surrounded by mayhem, already suffering from a massive chain reaction of internal damage, the injured man was not some unknown soldier only recognised by dedicated boxing fans. It was Michael Watson, the housewives' favourite, the silky-smooth ring magician, who lay desperately injured in a boxing ring in the middle of a football ground on a Saturday night.

Everyone knows that boxing is dangerous, but so are many sports. Horse racing, motor racing, even the Tour de France has had its fair share of serious injuries and deaths over the years. But the argument used against boxing is that it is the only one where two athletes deliberately aim to knock each other out.

There had been high-profile casualties in the past, as well as lesser-known tragedies a little closer to home in my eyes. Mark Goult, a promising bantamweight from Norwich, had collapsed in 1990 after a Southern Area Bantamweight Title clash. He'd fought Des Gargano just eight months after me. And, just a year after I retired, Bradley Stone would collapse and die after a ten-round bout against Ritchie Wenton, a man I'd twice fought as an amateur. There's no doubt that all boxers live their lives with the shadow of injury hanging over them but they are aware of the risks and accept them. With the regulations in force these days, such as annual MRI scans, boxing is one of the safest and most regulated sports on earth.

JOHN DAVISON: LITTLE MAN, BIG HEART

For a few days after Michael Watson was injured, we were unsure if the fight would go ahead at all. There were calls for boxing to be banned. I was asked my own views. 'Of course I'll fight,' I replied. To my thinking, as long as I was super-fit, then there was less danger of being hurt.

Looking back, it was naive to think like that because, in reality, no amount of gym work can protect you. If it's going to happen, it's going to happen. But you have to believe in your own mind that there's some way of controlling the situation, or that you have a guardian angel watching over you. If you worried that you would get hurt every time you climbed in the ring, then you wouldn't put your heart and soul into it. You'd lack that killer instinct. You'd not win many fights. And surely that's the point of entering the ring in the first place?

So I had no qualms about carrying on and many people in the sport felt the same way and came out to say so. It was tragic when someone was hurt, but it was part of the risk you took, part of what made the sport of boxing so unique and, in some ways, so honest. When you climbed in the ring, it really was just you and your opponent until the end. I'd always known that and I had no thoughts of stopping now. I had Sakda Sorpakdee, the WBC International Super-Bantamweight Champion waiting for me and I had no intention whatsoever of disappointing him.

13

MATCHING PAIR

Adrian: 'Why do you fight?'
Rocky: 'Because I can't sing or dance.'
ROCKY (MGM FILMS 1976)

Aged just 19, Sakda Sorpakdee was dangerous, very fucking dangerous. He'd originally been Thai Featherweight Champion before he'd won the WBC International Bantamweight Title. At 14 years my junior, he would have a natural edge in both fitness and stamina. Trained by Thai boxing legend Naris Singhawancha, a man who knew how to groom champions, his record of 17 wins from 19 fights underlined just how hard he was. Fifteen knock-outs had propelled him up the world rankings and he was expected to move into the top ten by beating me. So-called 'experts' had said that he might lack experience because of his age. But what did age matter in boxing? After all, Mike Tyson had conquered the world at that age.

Although I was dropping down a division for the first time in my professional career, it didn't worry me. I'd wreaked havoc in the bantamweight division for two years as an amateur when I'd been captain of my country. Sure, I'd have to be more careful about what I ate but normally it was enough just to control my liquid intake to drop the necessary pounds. I was lucky in that I never had to resort to starvation to get my weight down. Other than booze, I was pretty disciplined as a boxer. Certainly, there'd be more kitchen skipping and the gas cooker might be just turned up that little bit higher but I'd still have my pre-fight piss-up to relax me before the fight.

Sorpakdee had obviously heard about my reputation, as he was leaving nothing to chance. He flew into the country two weeks before the fight, to adjust and acclimatise to the unfamiliar surroundings. Prior to that, he'd spent two months training with the Thai national boxing squad, sparring with some of their best boxers. He was determined not to go the same way as his countrymen under the weight of my punches.

Looking at him at the weigh-in, it was difficult to believe that we were from the same division. He was huge, his body rippling with perfectly chiselled muscle. Standing next to him, I looked tiny in comparison. He had the body of an Adonis, straight out of *Playgirl* magazine. I noticed some of Sorpakdee's camp smiling and gesturing towards me, looking me up and down. They obviously fancied their chances. Asked what I thought of him by a reporter, I shrugged my shoulders. 'I've chinned bigger,' I replied to general laughter.

At the press conference, I was asked how I dealt with the pressure. 'I don't feel it,' I answered honestly. 'It's my job... fighting is the way I earn my living. It's just something I do, something I love doing. Sorpakdee is just another opponent in my way.'

Glen McCrory and Billy Hardy had both recently announced their retirements, although Billy would later return to the ring in style. Much was being made of my age and one cheeky bastard asked if I would follow them into retirement if I lost.

'Why should I?' I replied. 'If I'd been boxing since I was a teenager, then maybe my time would be up at 34. But I've only been a professional for four years. I'm number-one contender in Britain, Europe and the Commonwealth. Hopefully, there's still a World Title shot on the horizon. There's plenty for me to aim for and I won't stop until there's nothing left, or until I know it's time to quit.'

'And how would you know?' someone else asked.

'My arms would fall off. Next question…'

Sorpakdee's natural power meant that he would fight on the front foot, coming forward and looking to dominate me from the off. But so would I, mainly because I didn't really know any other way. My natural instinct was to seek and destroy. So was his. Interviewed for television, I promised viewers 'this is going to be a war from the first bell'.

Yet again, Hartlepool Borough Hall was to provide the backdrop for another epic battle. The tickets were snapped up within two days for what was billed as one of the most exciting fights of the year. And so it would prove to be. I was told later that fans left the hall shaken by what they had witnessed.

I entered the hall to the sound of *Rocky*. I was smashing my gloves together as I walked, pumping up the thousands of fans, letting them see that I was up for it, I was here to entertain. John Davison was well and truly in the building! I was feeling mean, ready for battle.

I knew the size of the task ahead of me and my preparations had been perfect as always. In the final hour, I'd lain in my dressing room listening to Frank Sinatra, Ol' Blue Eyes himself, on my Walkman. I was relaxed and calm. I'd even chosen my shorts especially for the occasion. Originally, I'd been going to wear white, but after careful thought, I chose a glittering black pair, very Caesar's Palace. Carol had made them for me and they had about a million sequins on them but my rationale was simple and certainly not flash. I didn't want to ruin my new white shorts with the blood I knew would surely flow in buckets.

Sorpakdee was a good 3in taller than me and had arms like an octopus. He was fast and could throw quick combinations or big knock-out winners. I'd watched videos of him and he could take a punch well and was intelligent, switching from defence to attack in the blink of an eye. He even had age on his side. In fact, Sakda Sorpakdee had it all. All but one thing, one question that remained unanswered and which I would seek to exploit. Did he have the heart to take on a street fighter like me? Could he stay with me as I took him on a 200mph journey around the ring? He'd never met anyone like me before, of that I was sure.

Sorpakdee entered the hall to the sound of jeers from the thousands of fans, now blending into one. The crowd burst into yet another chorus of 'Blaydon Races', the hall reverberating and banging with the deafening sound, and then they moved on to singing my name over and over again – 'Dava! Dava! Dava! Dava!' It still makes the hair stand up on the back of my neck even now.

It was going to take everything I had to beat Sorpakdee. I channelled all my emotions into one raw, violent intention. Larry O'Connell brought us together in the centre of the ring and I stared at the Thai Champion, pure determination in my heart. He was in my way. He could end my World Title dream. I was going to rip his fucking head off.

In training, I'd been sharp and I'd been knocking over sparring partners like skittles. It always helps your confidence when you know that you've tested your weapons and that they're all functioning to perfection. But I knew that I would not just need my bombs and missiles. I would also need to be able to take harder punches than ever before. I was ready.

The bell pierced the night and once again I went to war. As always, I set out to fight to my strengths, readily taking punches to get inside and work on Sorpakdee's body. Neither of us was prepared to give an inch as we tried to win early control. I always treated the first round as crucial, as you can catch your opponent early and hurt them or damage their confidence. We both went for it, trying to blow each other away.

Sorpakdee circled me on the outside, driving piston-like jabs straight into my face, keeping just enough distance for him to generate maximum power. I pushed forward, right hand hanging low and poised, looking to try to open him up for my sledgehammer right. But he was clever, backing away a little and then opening up with a combination of straight left-right combinations that smashed into my head. I pushed close to him again, trying to find my own range, pure heart driving me forwards against his ripping punches. I caught him with a good right uppercut into his head, then another. It felt good to know I'd caught him with some good shots. Now I could settle into my rhythm. I pushed into him again, looking to get off some short hooks but, as we closed, he connected with a lightning jab and I was down.

The crowd's singing was cut dead, everyone stunned. I jumped to my feet. 'It was a slip! It was a slip! It was a fucking slip!' I was screaming over and over again. And it was true. As Sorpakdee had let fly, the sole of my left foot had slid across the canvas and I'd gone straight on my arse, my legs splayed wide apart. Larry O'Connell was one of the most experienced boxing referees in the world. He'd seen what had happened and thankfully he waived it away. No knock-down! No lost point! I was relieved but the crowd were now uneasy. This wasn't in the script for a Davison fight. Just how strong was this guy? Was it a sign of things to come? Was this a bridge to far?

As the round closed, they started to come back to life, trying to push me to greater efforts. We again traded punches in the middle of the ring and I answered their doubts in style, catching Sorpakdee with a sweet right hook. The thump it made when it landed was heard throughout the hall and he took it without even slowing down and came back with a flurry of his own. But I smashed another beauty into his head and that seemed to hurt him. The bell went and we both returned to our corners with purpose. Round One to Sorpakdee? Maybe. Maybe not.

Round Two started at the same frantic pace with toe-to-toe action in the centre of the ring. Who would blink first? Again, I tried to get under his jabs and work his body. As I did, he fired a slashing right which ripped open a deep cut above my left eye. Blood started to cascade over my face and I could feel the crowd's stunned reaction. 'He's cut! Dava's cut!' It rippled round the hall in one huge gasp. I could feel the wet stickiness of my own blood on my arms. Within seconds, I'd smashed two huge right hooks into him and he was visibly shaken, any mental advantage he'd got from cutting me already gone. He leaned back into the ropes, trying to avoid my onslaught as I piled in with more of the same. Head! Head! Body! Head! Head! Body! He went into a ball, desperately trying to avoid the punches raining down on him from all angles. I gave him a couple more digs before he came up and rolled away from me looking white and drained. The bell went for the end of Round Two and I was back on top. But in the corner, I was panicking.

'Is it bad, Tommy?'

'Turn your head a bit, John.'

I turned my head. 'Is it fucking bad, Tommy?'

'We'll see, we'll see,' he said, perplexed.

My cut man, Dunky Jowett, started getting to work immediately, first to stem the bleeding and then to seal it with Vaseline. It was a worrying time. There was a lot of blood and Sorpakdee could now exploit it at every opportunity, opening it up more and more with his powerful punches.

'John, it won't stop the fight,' Tommy was saying over and over again, trying desperately to reassure me. 'You won't lose this fight because of the cut. Just keep on going. Don't worry. Keep on going!'

Into the third, I picked up where I left off. I was dictating the pace of the fight. Sorpakdee seemed content to stay away from me, using his longer reach to try to out-jab me, picking up points and wearing me down. But I slipped them continuously, drilling hard crosses and some good uppercuts into his head, sucking at his energy, shaking his resolve. The crowd was going wild again, their previous reservations evaporated in a mixture of booze and adrenalin as my name echoed out over and over again. I was in control and they fucking knew it! I finished the round punishing Sorpakdee against the ropes as his own punches flew into thin air. Float like a butterfly, sting like a Davison! It was beautiful boxing.

But then the pendulum swung back again. In the next two rounds, including my favourite fifth, Sorpakdee's punching came into its own as he found another gear. He circled me constantly, moving left and right and ripping fast light combinations into me. I stood off a little, letting him come on and then counter-punching with everything I had to keep him at bay. His strength was awesome and, when he leaned into me, I wasn't always able to push him back. As Round Five closed, he smashed a thudding right jab straight into my left eye, temporarily blinding me as the cut opened up again.

I was starting to get worried. To lose a fight on a cut is the worst way to lose, especially if you're doing as well as I was. In every break in the proceedings, I dabbed my eye with my glove, trying to keep the blood from going into it. Each time, a new red sticky patch could be seen. It wasn't a good sign but, back in the corner, Tommy again reassured me as Dunky did his stuff with ready-mix concrete and superglue.

Sorpakdee had never had to box past Round Six. His opponents had all been on their arse by then. This is where my fitness would tell, I thought as I came out for the round. We started slowly after the earlier madness and mayhem, both standing off to see what each other had left, almost daring the other to push on. Sorpakdee kept his ramrod jab firing like a piston, but I slipped and moved, firing jabs of my own straight back at him. He seemed surprised but he probably hadn't thought I could jab anyway!

I tried to take my time and work a way around the Thai's defences. It came soon enough. Sorpakdee, losing patience, opened up with a barrage of his own and I smashed one clinical right screw uppercut straight into his face. His gum shield flew across the ring as he staggered backwards. I waded straight in, throwing everything I had at him, looking for a stoppage there and then. But his huge arms wrapped around me in a grip that I simply couldn't shake. He held and held, trying desperately to recover his senses and stop me getting any leverage to hurt him with further punches. He pushed me back into the ropes and I caught him again and, from then on, it was all me as I chased him round the ring, smashing punches into him at will, all technique out the window. Again, the bell broke the carnage and gave us both some respite. We were halfway through the fight but already we were tiring.

Slowly, I was starting to get on top, using sheer aggression to drive into Sorpakdee time and time again. Jim Watt compared my style to Nigel Benn's as I walked through his punches, unleashing ferocious fight-stoppers of my own. By now, I was looking sharper than Sorpakdee, whose clubbing shots were hitting my arms, my shoulders, my raised gloves, but not my face. In the ninth, I caught him with one of my trademark rights and then went in for the kill as he struggled to stay on his feet. I cornered him, hitting him so hard that his blood and sweat flew into the crowd. Even the commentator Gary Newbon started to claim excitedly that this could be the moment! But again the bell rang. Sorpakdee limped back to his corner, shaking his head in disbelief, still in the fight but stunned at the punishment I was inflicting on him.

In the tenth, he gained his revenge. He came back into the fight yet again, matching my work-rate, coming forward. In a toe-to-toe frenzy, he caught me on the ropes and opened up with an array of hooks and uppercuts. I counter-punched and slipped left down the ropes but he followed relentlessly. I stayed, happy to go for yet another slugging match, looking to block and parry then pick him off with jabs to the head. But he must have put lead weights in his gloves in the interval. He smashed a punch into the left side of my face and I swear it's the hardest I have ever been hit in my entire life. But he wasn't finished, catching me with two more jabs and then a hook into the right side of my head. He was up for it now, really fancying his chances.

Jim Watt, commentating, was telling the viewers, 'I've seen Davison come back from this sort of position time and time again, but he needs to move soon.' What he didn't know, what no one knew, was that Sorpakdee had hit me so hard with those two shots he'd shattered both sides of my jaw.

I probably should have gone down, and bought some time to recover and clear my head. But it never crossed my mind. As he launched another attack, every punch he threw grinding the bones of my shattered jaw together, I opened up myself with some massive counter-punches, drilling a combination of crosses straight into his face, watching it explode. He backed off, hurting badly as I rocked him again with yet another right hook. But he wouldn't go down. The bell went again. It was torture.

I don't remember anything about the 11th round. I fought on pure instinct, no thoughts at all. The machine had taken over. A switch had flicked inside me. Despite my massive injuries, I went forward, openly attacking Sorpakdee with all thoughts of defence now gone. Sorpakdee hit me with everything he had, but in every exchange I was getting in more punches and it was the Thai who would break and look for respite. The commentators were urging me to cover up, protect myself, but I came on time and time again, with complete disregard for anything other than landing my own punches. Sorpakdee must have felt that there was no way he could ever put me down. I'd taken his best and still stood in front of him, pouring in punches as I looked to seize his title.

We came out for the final round damaged beyond belief. Already, Jim Watt was acclaiming the fight as a British Fight of the Year contender. Tommy reckoned I was at least three rounds ahead. But I couldn't be sure. I never trusted judges and who could blame me? We hugged in the centre of the ring 'like two gladiators trading respect' as Gary Newbon poetically described it, and then we went for broke.

In the last seconds, I cornered him and I gave it everything.

But I knew that he wasn't going to go down. He was like a rubber ball; he just kept on bouncing back for more. And then the final bell went and the two of us collapsed on each other in the centre of the ring, an embrace from the eternal brotherhood of boxers. We were too tired even to make it back to our corners. Tommy ran to the centre of the ring and wrapped a towel around me. He practically carried me back to my stool.

A split decision was announced and the crowd again went mental. Fuck! I was thinking through my exhausted daze. I wasn't expecting that!

The first judge gave it to me 115-114, a margin of just one round. The second judge, from Sorpakdee's homeland, gave it to him 115–113. The crowd pelted him with beer bottles and rightly so. It was down to Larry O'Connell as referee and judge. His decision was confirmed with the words, 'The winner... and the *new* WBC International Featherweight Champion...'

I fell to my knees and kissed the canvas with relief as Sorpakdee looked on, absolutely distraught. The tension in the hall gave way to scenes of unbelievable emotion. It was relief, it was elation. No one could quite believe what they had just witnessed in the old hall. John Gibson, then sports editor at the local newspaper, would later describe the feelings of the fans in the hall: 'Fans were soaked with sweat and, having lived every single punch, felt that they themselves had been in the ring. There were points where they'd feared for John's safety, because he knew no fear for himself and would have attacked until his last breath. At ringside, the sheer power and bravery of both fighters was breathtaking, the brutality unnerving, almost primeval in its intensity. It was the most amazing fight I've ever seen.'

It turned out that there was no belt to present to me.

Sorpakdee and his team had been so confident of winning that he hadn't even bothered to bring it over from Thailand with him. Cheeky bastard!

I had to endure the agony of post-fight interviews and medicals before I was released to go to hospital. They diagnosed one fracture of the jaw and made an appointment for me to be operated on the following morning back in Newcastle.

Meanwhile, back at the house, a massive party was in full swing, with only the guest of honour and his newly won belt missing. I didn't get back home until half-three in the morning, where I drank my celebratory brown ale through a straw.

They operated that morning, wiring it up, which was an absolute fucker given that I'd been on my pre-fight diet for six weeks and was dying for some proper grub and a beer. The following afternoon, the family and my Shieldfield supporters' club arrived at the hospital with celebratory drinks hidden discreetly in pockets, rolled-up newspapers and bunches of flowers to avoid being detected by the medical staff. The impromptu party soon got into full swing as we relived the previous night, blow by blow, as we all got pissed up. Soon, the beer munchies kicked in and I demanded a plate of pie and chips. 'It's the first proper food I'll have had in weeks,' I drunkenly announced, looking for sympathy and getting fuck all.

But pie and chips were duly sneaked past the eagle eyes of the nurses. It would be the most painful pie in history. The first bite shattered the other side of my jaw, the one that the doctors had missed. I was rushed back to theatre for a further operation.

It was time to rest and bask in the glory of being the first man to win two International Titles. After two gruelling fights in just five months, as well as my little cameo role in the millionaire's paradise, it was time for a well-earned rest.

I felt that I'd put some miles on the clock and I had also ended up with steel plates in my jaw. It was now time for me to become a man of peace, to kick back and relax, to let the war wounds heal.

I would not have to make a defence of my title for six months. It gave Tommy time to again look at other options while I was recharging my batteries and blowing every penny I had on the family. As always, he was angling for the elusive 'big one', the one that would put a World Title belt round my waist. I was convinced that I would get one sooner rather than later. In anticipation, I got a new tattoo, a massive tiger down the whole of the right side of my chest. It was added to the black scorpion on my back and the names of the family on my heart. I'd had them all done during my career by Oz who owned the famous tattoo parlour in Byker and who had sponsored me for some of my early fights. It was appropriate. The eye of the tiger guiding home my right hook to win me immortality.

The word on the grapevine was that it would be Benichou that I would face in *part deux* of our European Title saga. As always, nothing was certain. It was a pain in the arse but, in some ways, I'd been glad of the rest. It would mean that, when I eventually slipped back into full training, I would be raring to go.

Early one Saturday morning, a couple of weeks after the Sorpakdee fight, I was having a lie-in with Carol when the phone started ringing. We were otherwise engaged, but it rang and rang, so, eventually, I thought it might be something important. I ran downstairs and grabbed the receiver.

'Can I speak to John Davison please?' said a voice.

'Speaking,' I said, trying to catch my breath.

'John, this is Kevin Keegan from Newcastle United Football

Club. We'd like you to come down as a guest for today's game
and do a lap of honour with your title belt. The idea would be
to have a meal in the directors' box and then...'

'Kevin Keegan?' I asked, cutting him short.

'Yes, Kevin Keegan. So we were wondering if you'd like to...'

'Kevin fucking Keegan?'

'Er... Yes. So, anyway...'

'Piss-taking bastard!' I said. 'You don't sound anything like
Kevin Keegan.' I slammed the phone down.

Seconds later, the phone rang again.

'Hello?'

'John, this really is Kevin Keegan. We were wondering if
you'd like to come to St James' Park today?' He paused. 'You
seem a little out of breath. Have I interrupted your training?'

'Yeah,' I lied. 'I run up and down the stairs 200 times each
morning. It helps build up stamina. You should get the lads to
try it...' I'd like to think I was responsible for Newcastle
United's promotion the following season.

That afternoon, I walked the pitch at St James' Park with a
lump in my throat as the whole stadium stood to applaud me,
the crowd chanting my name. It was the second time, but no
less special. I was sitting next to the chairman, Sir John Hall,
during the match. He'd only recently taken control of the club,
which was in a mess and heading for the old Third Division for
the first time in its history. One of his first acts had been to
appoint Keegan, who was looked upon as a messiah in the city.
He was a top bloke and was genuinely interested in my career.

'What's the hardest fight you've ever had?'

I thought carefully for a moment. 'Down there in the Leazes
End,' I said, pointing to the stand behind the goal and
reminiscing on my childhood fight in the toilets. I'm sure he
thought I was joking.

MATCHING PAIR

A few weeks later, I was honoured by Sport Newcastle when I was voted Newcastle Sports Personality of the Year. The award, which had previously been won by Keegan and was usually dominated by footballers, was recognition for my achievements. I was the first boxer to win it and I had the surreal experience of sitting playing bingo with Carol, Kevin Keegan and his wife at the awards ceremony. Carol shouted for the house and Keegan shook his head.

'Money comes to money, eh, John?'

'I wish I was a quid behind you, Kev,' was my reply.

The Sorpakdee win maintained my ranking as the number-one European challenger, although Tommy had his sights set further afield. A bid to bring the Texan World Champion Jesse Benavides to the region failed when a financial package couldn't be agreed with the TV companies to get enough money on the table. However, Fabrice Benichou was good to his word and 'Benichou v Davison – the Rematch' was scheduled for May 1992, one year and four days since our first battle. It would be live on Sky Sports, the first time I'd appeared on that channel.

The fight was supposed to be in the South of France, in Antibes, close to where I'd demolished Savage. We had money now so Carol booked to take the family down, along with brother Davie and Derek Frazer and his girlfriend. But yet again, the promoters fucked me right off. At the last minute, they moved the fight over to Amneville, just over the border from Benichou's home in Luxembourg. He obviously didn't fancy having to travel far to go to work. I didn't bother me, as I would have fought him in his sitting room. But family and friends were left in the South of France where they had to watch the fight in a bar instead of being ringside. They ended up persuading a bar full of French to cheer for me instead of their compatriot.

JOHN DAVISON: LITTLE MAN, BIG HEART

Since his last fight with me, Benichou had been busy, defending his European title twice and winning both by knock-out. He'd also lost a World Title fight against the Mexican Manuel Medina on a split decision.

As regards a European Title, this was do or die. I knew I would have to stop Benichou to win and I was confident that I could. I never felt I'd had the chance to unleash my biggest missiles in the previous fight, even though I had so clearly dominated it from the first bell. I trained harder than ever before. I knew I'd have to knock Benichou out to win.

The fight was a repeat performance of our earlier bout and I had Benichou in trouble in the early rounds. Gary Mason, ex-British Heavyweight Champion, who was commentating for Sky Sports, described me as 'the best-kept secret of British boxing' as I outfought the Champion every time he tried to stand and fight.

The respect between us was amazing. After the initial barrage of the first round, we touched gloves as if to welcome each other back into battle. We continued to do so at regular intervals throughout the fight.

By the eighth, I was cruising, at least four rounds ahead, although Benichou had never stopped coming at me all night. He was the kind of fighter that would never say die, the spirit of a true champion, but I had it all under control. Then disaster struck. Benichou caught me with a huge uppercut, which rocked me big style. He followed in with a combination of furious right and left hooks that put me in serious trouble, for probably the first ever time in my career. I was determined not to go down and held on grimly until the end of the round. The crowd, silent throughout, suddenly came to life as they sensed that I was in trouble.

In the ninth, Benichou, following the momentum of the

eighth, again caught me with some clean uppercuts. I came back at him with some of my own, though, and the two of us constantly had to clinch to break the brutal path of toe-to-toe slugging. As we broke, we had a stand-off in the ring and neither of us attacked as we took time to get our breath back. Then, yet again, we touched gloves, as if to signify 'game on' once more and continued the battle. It showed that the age of chivalry was still strong among true gladiators.

Former World Middleweight Champion Alan Minter, who was commentating, had me ahead by two rounds. In the studio, Gary Mason had me ahead by one, but commented that, in Europe, a British fighter had to be eight rounds ahead and then knock their opponent out to get a victory. Even after being caught by Benichou and taking everything he had, I'd still been the stronger fighter in the last two rounds. But the two judges and referee, true to form, gave a split-decision to Benichou, even though the last round had been dominated by his corner begging him to try to keep his guard up against the onslaught. I'd been robbed again and I was gutted.

'I'll fight until I'm 40 to win this title,' I told reporters afterwards.

To add insult to injury, the first person to come and see me in my dressing room after the fight was the referee. He wanted to try to justify his decision. I looked him straight in the eye, told him that he was a cheating bastard and then threw him out the room.

Benichou, yet again, was gracious in victory. He knew I'd done a job on him and was pissing blood for weeks after our fight. I told him I would challenge him again and again he smiled. We both looked forward to one more fight to see if there could be a winner in our eyes. It never happened, but I would love to go for a beer with him sometime.

Benichou would go on to fight Paul Hodkinson in his next fight for the WBC Title and Hoko would stop him in the 10th round. I always said later that Hoko owed me one for softening the Frenchman up for him. But it also made me want to face Hodkinson again even more.

14

BEST OF BRITISH

*'Men judge generally more by the eye than by the hand.
All see what you appear to be, but few really know what you are.'*
NICCOLO MACHIAVELLI 1469–1527,
THE PRINCE, CHAPTER XVIII

As one of the top boxers in Britain, I was asked to put my name behind a new initiative for a boxers' union. The Professional Boxers Association was being launched by Barry McGuigan as a way of helping retiring boxers find both employment and qualifications and to educate those earning a living in the sport as to the importance of planning for the time when the money dries up.

I was invited to London for a photo shoot with some of the national newspapers to help promote the organisation. All the top British boxers were there, including Nigel Benn, Chris Eubank, Nicky Piper, Hoko and Colin McMillan. There were some big egos stepping in front of the lenses, the sort of egos that weren't used to sharing a stage with any other boxer unless they were in a ring, but that's not surprising as it's usually a pre-requisite to being a boxer in the first place.

We were milling around trying to get lined up for pictures,

but one particular boxer kept on disappearing to check himself in the mirror and make sure his clothes were OK and that he looked the part. I won't name any names but I can confirm he's exactly the way he's portrayed to be in the media, or at least he was then.

It was nice to be invited. It wasn't that I didn't feel I deserved to be there; I know I did because I was one of the best. But all the hype that surrounds the sport used to piss me off. All the ego shit, the razzmatazz. To me, fighting was just a job, a fucking brilliant job and one in which I wanted to be the best, but it was just a job all the same. I never felt that I was special because I was a fighter, that people should look up to me, or think I was the dog's bollocks. I felt lucky to be a fighter. I was doing something I loved, something that gave me the ultimate high and it never changed me.

The British Featherweight Title had been dangled in front of me a number of times, but I'd never got so much as an eliminator. I'd always wanted to win a Lonsdale Belt, which is by far the most beautiful title belt in boxing. It's the oldest and most prestigious championship belt in the world, dating back to the early 1900s. One of the first belts had been won by 'Bombardier' Billy Wells, famous as the man who bangs the gong at the beginning of Rank films. Hand-crafted from gold and porcelain, it's a work of art. If I won the lottery now it would be the first thing I'd buy myself. I'd get one of the old ones because they were made with rose gold and were absolutely beautiful. It was 60 years since a boxer from Newcastle had won a British Title and I'd always wanted to bridge that gap.

And so it was that one man's success could be another man's opportunity. Colin McMillan, the then golden boy of British boxing, had just won the WBO Featherweight Title in London against the Italian Maurizio Stecca. McMillan was hugely popular and had even appeared on the front cover of *Loaded* magazine. He was the reigning British Featherweight Champion but relinquished this title after winning his world crown. I was declared a contender for the vacant title, along with Bermondsey's Tim Driscoll. I prayed that winning the Lonsdale Belt would do for me what it had done for McMillan and propel me to my own World Title shot.

Barry Hearns won the purse offers to promote the fight and wisely chose to stage it in the North-East, where it was guaranteed to be a sell-out. *Boxing News* had just called me 'the best-value British boxer' and, as I had a reputation for excitement, it was a fight that people would be desperate to see. A deal was done to have it televised live on Sky Sports, where it was to be the big opener to their season of live British shows. Again, it was a great chance finally to get some national exposure after years of being in the shadows.

Unlike McMillan, I still wasn't well known outside boxing. Where he had made the front cover of a national lads' magazine, I was beginning to think that the closest I would get to national exposure would be if I appeared on *Crimewatch* for those dodgy spice jars!

A number of venues were proposed before the decision was taken to stage the fight in Sunderland. Thousands of fans could be guaranteed to come from all over the region to see if I could finally lift the British crown.

Tim Driscoll was another boxer with a superb record. He'd won 16 of his 20 fights. Three defeats had been on points and one had been a stoppage. It was the only one that really mattered, however. In his last fight, he, too, had fought for the World Featherweight Title. Unlike McMillan, he had not been successful. His own challenge against Stecca had ended in failure and he had suffered a bad defeat against the former Olympic Champion. The Italian had comprehensively demolished Driscoll, who had been way behind on points when he'd had to retire on his stool at the end of the ninth round, his nose smashed to pieces. It had kept him out of the ring for almost a year.

Tim Driscoll underlined the eternal fine line between success and failure in boxing. He'd travelled to Italy with a strong pedigree, excellent record and genuinely high hopes of beating Stecca. He'd never been down in his entire career and, at 27 years old, was just entering his boxing prime, where his power and speed were at their maximum, but also blended with a high level of experience. But, because of that defeat, he stood at the crossroads that all boxers eventually reach, some far sooner than others. Win, and he was heading back up the ladder. Lose, and it could all be over. Driscoll had set his sights on the British Title as a way of preventing a slide into oblivion. The World Title defeat had cost him dear and he had to start winning again. But at least he had time on his side.

Driscoll was confident that he would beat me. He was technically superb and wasn't afraid to dig deep in a toe-to-toe slugging match. But he lacked my big-punching reputation and I was confident that that would give me the edge. The Londoner was in a bullish mood in the lead-up to the fight, making much of the fact that I was 34. He declared that I was too old still to be boxing and that he, Tim Driscoll, would put me in a retirement home where I belonged. He told anyone who would listen that I was over the hill, that my time was up and that I should make way for younger, stronger men. He even suspected that I could not go 12 rounds again because of my creaking bones. Driscoll promised that he was going to teach me a lesson and end my career. Nice.

Driscoll was judging me on the normal laws of boxing. But, if they'd applied to me, I would never have got so far in the first place. George Foreman had just lifted a World Heavyweight Title at the age of 45. By my reckoning, that gave me another ten years at least!

The sort of garbage Driscoll spoke didn't bother me. I was already starting to be described as an 'old warhorse' or a 'veteran' and I'd only been a professional for four years! All my interviews had seemed to start concentrating on 'the age factor', even though I'd just beaten a 19-year-old. So I was more than happy for Driscoll to say his piece, to underestimate me. I was more than happy to be portrayed as the underdog. I didn't need to get involved in a war of words with him or anyone else.

Some boxers like to try to wind up their opponents, even in the ring itself, telling you that they've shagged your wife or your mother, all sorts of shit. I never bothered. I never felt I had to say anything. I was the silent man, the grim reaper. Tim Driscoll would be standing in front of me soon enough and all the insults in the world wouldn't save him then.

'I'll do my talking in the ring,' was all I would say in reply. 'People might well say I'm too old, but boxing is psychological. You can fight for ever if your mind is right. I always think I can win.'

But, in a way, I knew that Driscoll was right. Lose, and all my hard work would come to nothing. The two Benichou 'defeats' were being taken for the rip-off that they were. But lose this one and my World Title credentials would be blown apart. Take a pounding from Driscoll and I'd probably never fight again at top level. So there was far more at stake for both of us than just a British Title belt. For the loser, retirement looked like the only option. I couldn't even begin to imagine life without boxing. It was a part of me now more than ever.

JOHN DAVISON: LITTLE MAN, BIG HEART

I trained for two months for the fight. My main worry was that Driscoll liked to use his head, which can lead to all sorts of problems for a fighter like me who liked to work close to my opponent all the time. The human head is a big, nasty lump of bone that can do far more damage than any fist. I should know! Driscoll was also taller than me and had a longer reach, which meant that I couldn't stand off him even if I wanted to. He would just pick me off with his left jab until he won on points.

Driscoll and his trainer Freddie King worked hard to counteract my high-pressure style. His plan would be to keep me at bay and stop me getting inside to work on his body. He was a renowned counter-puncher and would rely on this technique to break up my attacks, which he knew would come in wave after wave.

Crowtree Leisure Centre in the heart of Sunderland was packed with over 5,000 fans to see the old man of boxing do his stuff. As always, the ticket touts were making a fortune as desperate fans offered everything in their wallets to see the action. The crowd were baying for Driscoll's blood from the second he entered the ring and he showed remarkable coolness, refusing to be intimidated. He'd seen and heard it all before, of course. It was nothing new to him.

'Fucking kill him, Dava!' people were screaming all around me as I walked through the throng of people, bouncing up and down, smashing my gloves together. I climbed into the ring and instantly my whole focus was on Driscoll, standing in his own corner, rolling his shoulders. Old man? Old fucking man? We'll see who the old fucking man is! I thought as I eyeballed him. Driscoll had made a massive mistake. My whole family was in the stands, Aaron and Kelly included. Tim Driscoll thought that he could humiliate me in front of my fans, my

family and my friends. As if I wasn't going to be motivated by
the chance to win the Lonsdale Belt, he'd added fuel to the fire
by ridiculing me in the newspapers. I don't think I've ever been
more up for a fight since the Leazes Tunnel.

I started at a ferocious pace, trying to unsettle Driscoll, who
parried and back-tracked in an attempt to let me burn myself
out. The Londoner was well drilled and well prepared,
retreating to draw me forward, and then catching me with
combinations designed to pick up points and frustrate me. I
was so intent on blowing him away early that I drove forward
without any real care and Driscoll landed some good clean
shots into my head. At the end of the first, he walked back to
his corner nodding to his trainer, knowing that he'd done his
homework. He'd taken the first round easily and it was clear
that I was going to have to step up a gear.

I did just that in Round Two, catching him with a couple of
thunderous body punches that almost doubled him up. The
body shot is a great weapon to use on tall opponents as their
ribs are mainly unprotected. Driscoll showed superb defensive
skills, covering up and then slipping away from me as I went
after him, looking to smash through his defences. At least he'd
had a taste of what I could do, but I suspected that he'd shaded
the second round as well. I was still having difficulties
connecting cleanly and Driscoll's good defensive work would
have had him clocking up the points.

Then, as always in my fights, the roller-coaster effect kicked
in, with the gods determined to wring every ounce of emotion
out of both my fans and me. I was just starting to come into
the fight as the third round was coming to a close. I'd caught
Driscoll with a couple of heavy body shots that he hadn't had
time to read and which had almost crumpled him. For the
first time, I'd found my range and I was catching him with

good clean punches. I was now getting in closer, bullying him into the ropes. As I did, we clashed heads and, instantly, blood was pouring down my face. The cut was a bad one, over 2in long and right above my left eye. Blood was running down into my eye, blinding me, and it gave Driscoll the encouragement he needed. He started to target that side of my head, looking to open the cut up further. He knew it was bad and that it could win him the title if he found the target again and the fight was stopped.

At the break, Dunky Jarrett again got to work, stemming the flow of blood, which was now covering my arms and staining my shorts. For the second successive fight, I found myself asking, 'Is it bad, Tommy?'

'Dunky'll sort it, John. How are you feeling?'

'I'm boxing shite,' I said honestly.

'He's dropping his left all the time, John. He's well prepared for your right hooks and he's reading them well. See if you can get more body punches into him, and then start looking for a left hand over the top. He won't be expecting it. He thinks you can only punch with one hand!'

The fourth round was even, but in my own mind I was struggling to find a breakthrough, that one punch that would make his eyes roll and turn the fight there and then. The referee stopped the battle once to check the cut and, for a few seconds, the hall was practically silent, but he waved us back to box on to everyone's relief.

We traded punches in the middle of the ring but I, too, was starting to box. I had to protect my left eye so, instead of racing forward and risking Driscoll catching me with his head again, I slipped and moved, landing straight punches into his head. And they were starting to hit home. It was almost as if I'd been trying too hard in the early rounds. Driscoll had expected me to be gung-ho, to wade in to him. But I now sat back and he was unsure how to handle it. I drew him on, then jabbed him away, hitting him cleanly, racking up points. I started to outbox the boxer! As the bell went, I was confident for the first time that I'd won the round. It wasn't as dramatic as a big punch, but it was a turning point all the same.

Into the fifth and the crowd found its voice again, roaring me on. It sensed that there had been a shift in power and that Driscoll was now struggling to match my work-rate. Sure, he'd weathered the early storm, but the storm had continued to whirl around him and it would do so for 12 rounds if necessary. Still, he tried to use his head to catch me but, by now, my boxing had come into its own. In the past, critics had always said that I looked terrible in the ring and that I was just a crude swinging banger. My answer had always been that it won me fights. But now I used the skills I'd developed over the years to glide around the ring, picking shots with precision and controlled aggression, and then disappearing like a genie in a bottle. He was unable to catch me and his tiredness showed when I caught him full on with a straight left that made his nose explode. As the round neared the end, Driscoll's face and chest were covered in blood and he was starting to have trouble breathing. Just before the bell, I caught him with another left that saw his gum shield fly across the ring. Driscoll was starting to fall apart. In the space of just three minutes, I had seized control of the fight, in spite of the cut that, if opened up just one more time, could very well lose me the fight.

'How are you feeling, John?'

'It's just going to be a matter of time,' I said grimly. 'He's going.'

Driscoll was down for the first time in his career within

seconds of the beginning of the sixth. Trading punches in the middle of the ring, I caught him with a right hook which connected high on his head. It was so hard it rocked his whole body and he retreated hurt to the ropes, which is possibly the worst place you want to be if you're in the ring with me. It was there that I well and truly nailed him. I opened up with a combination of right and left hooks, most of which found their target. As he desperately tried to protect his head, I smashed a heavy left into the pit of his stomach. The pressure had been too much, and that final body shot ripped away his breath. He collapsed against the ropes and hit the floor as I stood rampant in the centre of the ring.

He somehow dragged himself to his feet on a count of eight. By now, the result was looking as obvious to the crowd as the laws of physics. Throw an object in the air and gravity will always make it fall to earth. Maintain this sort of pressure and it could only end one way. Only one man was going to win and it was only a matter of time. Another big body punch as the bell rang sent him back to his corner in agony.

The crowd was going crazy, their blood lust apparently not satisfied by the scarlet gash above my eye or Driscoll's shattered nose. The two of us were covered in each other's blood and the white shorts I'd saved from Sorpakdee were now ruined, stained pink.

But there was still a twist in the tale. Driscoll had taken punishment against Stecca but had still hung on. I needed to finish it sooner rather than later. I started the seventh round by again attacking Driscoll from the bell. It was a battle of sheer guts and I knew now that I was stronger, that I could bully him. I poured punches into him with both hands, catching him cleanly around the head. But Driscoll again underlined just why he'd fought for a World Title. He gritted his teeth, taking shots and counter-punching for all he was worth. One right caught me full on and, yet again, my foot slid away on the bloody floor. I was sent sprawling and, for a second, everyone thought that the Londoner had put me on my arse. I jumped up, waving my arms and laughing as if nothing had happened. As with Sorpakdee, the referee did not register it as a knock-down.

I punished Driscoll now, really fucking punished him. I launched yet another attack of good, strong combinations, which saw his gum shield fly across the ring again. This time the referee ignored it so I kept on going. I unleashed my biggest missile yet; a right hook that lifted Driscoll off his feet. He somehow stayed up, but now I rained in shots from all angles, determined to finish him once and for all. The exhausted Londoner bravely tried to rally but I bent him double with a right hook to the body, then I brought my left hand over the top, smashing a mean left hook into his head which sent him spinning to the floor.

There would be no getting up this time. As the referee counted, he rolled on to his hands and knees in a vain attempt to stand. But the signals from his brain to his arms and legs simply weren't getting through. Everything was short-circuiting. As blood poured from his nose and mouth on to the floor of the ring, he stared at his manager Barney Eastwood, shaking his head in resignation. He knew that he wasn't getting up. The referee waved his arms and it was over.

The crowd went ballistic, finally released from yet another roller-coaster ride. Carol and my mother climbed into the ring, tears rolling down their faces. Aaron and Kelly were lifted in and photos would later show me with Aaron in my arms, his white shirt smeared red with blood. The famous old belt was fastened around my waist, and I jumped up on the ropes and punched the air in jubilation. I was British Champion and things had never felt so good.

Although I was delighted finally to get my hands on the British Title, for the first time I didn't feel like I'd fought anywhere near my best, especially in the early rounds. It had been far too much for Driscoll, but not enough against my own high standards. Needless to say, the so-called experts instantly started saying that it was my age catching up with me, that the batteries were starting to run low, but that was bullshit. Everyone is entitled to an off night and I'd still beaten a World Title contender in seven rounds. And it wasn't like my fitness had been lacking. Driscoll had been able to cope with the pace I set for maybe three rounds before he'd started to wilt under the pressure. It was the first time I'd ever knocked someone out with my weaker left hand but I swear it was exhaustion as much as the punch that put Driscoll on the floor.

Boxing News's review of the fight called me a 'battered old swashbuckler', which was a new way of describing me. Its write-up of the fight basically said that the difference between Driscoll and me had been my sheer will to win. 'Driscoll couldn't have stopped him with a 12-bore shotgun...' it said quite simply.

I was determined to repay one particular friend, by the name of Geordie Punting, for the help he'd given me over the years and I knew he would love my suggestion. Just a couple of days after the fight, my newly won Lonsdale Belt was on display in the front window of his shop. Geordie lost count of the number of people who came in desperate to buy it. I announced my intention to defend it twice, keep it for real and hang it above my bed.

All the pre-fight talk of retirement turned out to be just that – talk. Being on the right end of the result, the Davison bandwagon rocked on, its journey continuing into further unknown territory. I still had the world at my feet – or, more precisely, my fists – and I now had three title belts draped across my shoulders.

But the sun was setting on Tim Driscoll's career. He fought only once more, against journeyman Derek Amory in London. He won on points over eight rounds but he knew his time had passed. His own moment of destiny had been that previous November, in Italy's Casino di Campione, when he'd been so badly injured he'd been unable to go out and face Maurizio Stecca's murderous onslaught once again. I only hoped that, if my moment ever came, I would be given the chance to grasp it with both hands.

MAKING HISTORY?

'If you can force your heart and nerve and sinew,
To serve their turn long after they are gone,
And so hold on when there is nothing in you,
Except the Will which says to them, "Hold on!"'

RUDYARD KIPLING, IF

On 30 November 1992, an unusual birthday party was held at the Four Seasons restaurant in South Shields for a celebrity guest. The party was unusual because, under the normal rules of professional sport, the star guest should never have been there.

To come into boxing so late and to achieve such things was unheard of. My whole career had been a race against time. Yet, through sheer determination, I'd climbed almost to the very pinnacle of the sport. Just one last step remained now.

The party was for my 34th birthday and, strangely enough, the theme of my cake was a boxing ring. Two decorative boxers stood in the centre, arms raised in a boxing stance. 'Which one is me?' I asked before the crowd of guests.

'That one,' replied Carol.

I flicked the other one over. 'Knock-out!' I said.

I had now lifted the WBC International Featherweight Title,

the WBC International Super-Bantamweight Title and now the British Featherweight Title. A line-up of celebrities had come along to celebrate the fact and enjoy the party. The restaurant was owned by the daughter of Jim Gayford, a bare-knuckle fighter of old and much respected in the North-East. They were all there, fellow professional boxers, street fighters of old and gangsters, mixing ·with friends, family and civic dignitaries. There was even an international pop superstar in the form of Chas Chandler from the famous 1960s group The Animals. No less than three Lord Mayors made speeches about how I had brought the region together in a way not seen before in sport. Local rivalries were cast aside when I entered the boxing ring as everyone came along to enjoy the atmosphere of a Davison performance.

At the end of the night, Tommy made a moving speech saying how he still believed that I had a World Title belt in me. Everyone believed it but, after the disappointment of the scrapped Benavides fight, the major question was really whether I'd ever get the chance to fight for the ultimate prize. Certainly, none of the UK-based fighters wanted to go near me. He went on to say how proud he was to be associated with a fighter as dedicated as me. It would have brought tears to my eyes if I hadn't been so pissed.

By now, I was the major contender across all four World Title belts. However, in a sport where money talked, the hard fact was that a deal would have to be right before any fighters would put their belts on the line against someone as dangerous as me. I could wipe someone out completely with a single, perfectly timed punch and it looked like the uncertainty I created would hold me back from a shot at the ultimate prize. My main target was still Hoko's WBC Title and Tommy was in talks with Frank Warren to see if he could get the fight on.

And then, almost against all hope, word came through that something was firming up, the cogs in the machine were starting to turn in my favour. Ruben 'The Hurricane' Palacio, WBO Featherweight Champion, had indicated that he was willing to put his world crown on the line, in Britain, against me. The deal was being put together through Barry Hearn and Tommy Gilmour. The venue would naturally be in the North-East where another sell-out crowd was guaranteed.

A fight in Britain held no fears for Ruben Palacio. He had won his World Title in London the previous October against Colin McMillan, in what was supposed to have been a relatively straightforward first defence of the Brit's newly won crown. On a night of high drama at Earls Court, London, Palacio had systematically dismantled McMillan in such ferocious fashion that he'd actually dislocated the Brit's shoulder, causing him so much damage that it would affect him for the rest of his career. A veteran of the ring, Palacio was Colombia's first World Champion in over 20 years and he was worshipped there as a god.

The Colombian had a fantastic record. He'd been a pro since 1981 and had won the Colombian Title at three different weights. He'd lost an IBF Super-Bantamweight Title bout on a judges' decision in 1985, but had kept on clocking up the wins. Then came the biggest performance of his life against McMillan. He was at the very top of the fight game and would travel to Britain as firm favourite.

The news was broken to me in a phone call from Tommy. 'We've got him, John! We've got him!' he shouted excitedly.

'Which one?'

'The Colombian. We've got him!'

'Bring it on!'

The fight was scheduled for 6 February 1993. At last, D-Day!

I'd been desperate to hear those words since I'd first demolished Narachawat to win my first International Title.

The North-East was buzzing with the news that I finally had a World Title shot. One paper ran with the headline 'FAIRGROUND FIGHTER CAN CONQUER THE WORLD'.

To capitalise on boxing's high profile in the region at the time, the country's newest World Champion decided to pay the region a visit as part of his 'Meet the People Tour'. Lennox Lewis had recently chosen to fight professionally in British colours, the country in which he had been born, rather than for Canada, where he had been raised. He'd represented Canada as an amateur, winning a number of amateur titles that culminated in a gold medal at the Seoul Olympics.

I was asked to go to Gateshead's Metro Centre shopping mall for a photo shoot. It was going to be the 'Little and Large' of British boxing! Lewis had with him his WBC World Title Belt, famously picked out of the bin where Riddock Bowe had thrown it after refusing to fight him. He was Britain's first Heavyweight World Champion of the 20th century and there were great hopes that he could go on to be an undisputed champion. I was hoping to add one to my own little collection just a few weeks later.

We had met years earlier at the World Boxing Championships in Nevada when Lewis had struck gold for Canada and I had lost my own semi-final on a split decision. We shook hands and I kicked off the banter. 'You'll remember me then,' I said to Lewis.

'Er... yeah... I mean... course I do...' said the perplexed heavyweight.

'Yeah, you borrowed $50 off me in 1986. I'm here to collect.'

He burst out laughing. 'You've got a few belts there,' he said, gesturing to the three title belts I had draped all over me as the photographers snapped away.

'I know – and I fought for every single one of them.'

His reply was unprintable as he gave me a sly dig on the arm.

Not long after, I had a call from Frank Warren. 'Are you vacating the British Title?' he asked.

'No. Why should I?'

'You've got your World Title shot.'

'Yeah, but why should I vacate it? I only won it a few weeks ago.'

'It's a gentleman's agreement. It's always been done. It's a national title and you're fighting for a world crown.'

I was in love with the Lonsdale Belt and didn't want to give it up without a fight.

'I might lose the World Title fight,' I argued. 'I could defend the British Title in Newcastle and sell out. I'd make 30 grand.'

'If you give it up, I'm sure that you'll get another shot at it if you lose to Palacio.'

It was a hard decision because I really wanted to win one outright. Far lesser boxers have had one to keep on their mantelpiece and, after pursuing it for so long, it seemed ridiculous just to hand it back. But I had no real choice; Warren was right. It was a gentleman's agreement and I relinquished the title a few days later. My sights were now global, and there's always someone in boxing who is looking for that next stepping stone, just as I had always been.

I began my preparations for Palacio almost immediately. This would be my moment of destiny and I wanted to be in the best shape of my life. My training had always been fanatical but now I prepared myself to push further than ever before, such was my determination to win the fight. I knew exactly what to expect from Palacio, I knew exactly what he could do to me if my body and mind were not at their peak of performance, hardened to absorb any form of physical pain, able to take the onslaught of 'The Hurricane'.

As the weeks went by, my body hardened and my mind tuned in. In the gym, I was starting to punish my sparring partners. On the road, I was eating the miles. I was calm but I was determined and my preparations enhanced not just my body and mind but also my confidence. When Palacio came, I knew I would be ready for him.

On Christmas morning, the Conroy household had just finished unwrapping its presents when there was a knock at the door. 'What the fuck are you doing here?' Tommy asked me incredulously as I stepped inside with my kit bag.

'I've got to train, Tommy. I'm burning up this morning. I've got to train.'

'It's Christmas Day!'

'Merry Christmas,' I said, offering him a Christmas card. 'Come on, just a couple of hours,' I begged.

He shook his head. 'Come on then. Just a couple of hours, though.'

'Any chance of calling up a spar?'

Now I was starting to reach my fighting peak, both physically and mentally. I pushed myself to the limit, feeling the power within me beginning to grow into an irresistible, overwhelming force. Palacio would have to match me for work-rate to beat me. He would have to match me for power. That natural boxer's confidence started to come through as I went through my training schedule. I knew I could beat him.

In the weeks leading up to the fight, my training level was increased still further beyond anything I'd done before as the excitement started to build. I was destroying sparring partners daily and Tommy was desperately trying to find more for me to test myself to the limit. As always, it was coming together. I knew I could hunt Palacio down and turn the fight into a living hell for him. And I knew he couldn't put me down because no one ever had. I would simply walk through his punches and I would knock him out. I knew I could destroy him.

Ten days before the fight was due to take place, word came from Colombia that Palacio was not flying to Britain. He'd injured his foot in training. It would require surgery so the fight was postponed until 13 March.

I was gutted. My pre-fight training schedule was almost complete and I was on fire, the fittest I'd ever been. Everything had gone right and I was raring to go. I drank a bottle of wine that night and slept almost the whole of the following day. I then set about trying to maintain my almost superhuman level of fitness. This was no easy task. The human body is designed to go to a certain limit and no further. But I had no choice. I knew it was the only chance I would ever have.

The weeks passed by more slowly as I maintained my momentum and my focus. I was fast, fit and furious that I'd already wasted three months' preparation. I harnessed this anger. Palacio would go in my favourite fifth round to teach him a lesson. One reporter who interviewed me in the lead-up to the fight asked how my training was going.

'I'm flying. I'm the strongest I've ever been.'

'Are you confident?'

'Confident?' I asked, smiling. 'I'm going to kill him! He's kept me off the drink for three months.'

Although I had a huge amount of respect for Palacio, it wasn't unknown in boxing for a fight to be delayed due to a fake injury claim. This could have a catastrophic effect on an opponent's training schedule and also his mental preparations. I worked hard to ensure that this would not happen to me.

The pre-fight build-up began again and there was a feeling of déjà vu about my preparations. On the road, then in the gym... on the road, then in the gym. A never-ending cycle of physical and mental enhancement so that every sense would be fine-tuned for that single hour that I'd craved so long. There was a buzz of anticipation everywhere I went. John Davison – WBO Featherweight Challenger. No one would have believed I'd get that far. It had a nice ring to it. But not as nice as John Davison – World Champion. Just days before I was to step into the ring, there was a further devastating call.

Palacio was injured again, this time he had some sort of problem with his stomach and needed a further operation. The fight was rescheduled again, this time for Saturday, 17 April.

I drank another bottle of wine and had another day in bed. Then I started yet again, desperately trying to maintain my fighting fitness. By the time I climbed in the ring, I would have been in hardcore training for over six months, compared to my usual two. It didn't take a genius to work out that this was going to cause me massive problems. My body had already peaked twice and, just as importantly, so had my mind. It's hard to maintain focus for a fight you think may never happen. It's hard to keep pushing yourself in the gym. But still I kept it together, working hard every day and praying that it wouldn't all go wrong.

And still it came together, still my body obeyed the demands I placed upon it. The buzz and the hype surrounding a World Title fight is huge and it helped spur me on.

Palacio finally landed on British soil on Saturday, 10 April, seven days before the fight. He was to acclimatise to the North-East, which is just that little bit colder than Colombia, as well as all the promotional work that comes from being World Champion. The relief I felt when it was confirmed that he had finally landed in London was unbelievable. He was here. The fight was going to happen at last. My chance was not going to be stolen from me.

Palacio travelled to the North-East on the following Monday. The first time I met him was at the pre-fight press conference. We stood looking at each other – the man I had been so desperate to face, the moment of destiny I had been so desperate to grasp. Palacio had the look, the strut of a World Champion. But, when I looked in the mirror, so did I and I knew I could take him out.

Palacio trained at Tommy's gym on the Tuesday night as the excitement for the up-and-coming fight grew to fever pitch. He looked sharp, according to the media who saw him train. I would have expected nothing less. But I felt on top of the world, despite the delays. My mind, the strongest muscle I possessed, was overriding any feeling that my body was tired. Even after six long months of training, that feeling, that snap was still there. It was in my feet, it was in my fists. I could feel the power. It flowed through me like a mystical presence. I knew I would win.

And then, that fateful Thursday afternoon, the call came from Tommy. There was a problem. A big problem. The biggest fucking problem there could possibly be. In 1993, the British Boxing Board of Control was the only regulatory board in the world, other than Nevada State, to have recognised the risk of an emerging new illness that could be transmitted through bodily fluids such as semen, saliva and blood. HIV and AIDS were seen as a new plague, a potential epidemic of biblical proportions and a doomsday scenario for mankind. One of the USA's biggest sports stars, Magic Johnson, had retired from the LA Lakers 18 months earlier after being diagnosed as HIV positive. The tennis legend, Arthur Ashe, ex-Wimbledon and US Open Champion, had died only two months earlier of full-blown AIDS. His story was particularly tragic. He had been infected during heart surgery and had gone on to infect both his wife and child. People had seen in graphic detail the effects of this terrible new illness on billboards across the world, courtesy of the Benetton Fashion Company's infamous poster campaign, which showed an emaciated AIDS victim just minutes from death. HIV and AIDS were killing indiscriminately, causing mass hysteria across the globe. The death of global superstars such as Rock Hudson and Freddie Mercury had shown that no one was safe. And now HIV had infected boxing, the only sport where opponents literally traded in blood. And it had infected a high-profile victim, a World Boxing Champion – Ruben 'The Hurricane' Palacio.

I was stunned. 'It can't be...' I told Tommy. 'Palacio only fought in London a few months ago – he would have had to pass an HIV test then. What the fuck's going on?'

But it was true. Palacio had failed his first test two days earlier, on the Tuesday. He had not been informed but his manager had been told that there was an irregular result on a blood test. The World Boxing Organisation had also been informed. Their initial reaction was that it could be a positive test for a banned substance and the re-test procedure kicked in. The second result that Thursday had sealed Palacio's fate. The President of the World Boxing Organisation, informed of the crisis while in France, had been literally shaking with shock.

Within minutes, the news was being transmitted down the wire to media agencies all over the world. It would go on to make front-page news in the *Washington Post* and the *New York Times*. Within an hour, the World Boxing Organisation had issued a statement. It had acted in the only way it could; Palacio could not fight carrying the HIV virus, so he could not defend his title. If he could not defend his title, then it had to be stripped from him. The impending fight was cancelled and the title declared vacant.

Ed Levine, the World Boxing Organisation official overseeing the fight, commented, 'We cannot risk the life of another boxer by letting him [Palacio] fight... It's the kind of disease that can be spread via blood contact and boxing is a sport where that is likely to happen.'

In the mass hysteria that followed the announcement, I went back home to my wife and children, the very reasons I had pulled on boxing gloves in the first place. In a room, by myself, I broke down and cried. I cried for the chance I had lost, knowing I would never get another. I cried for the injustice of what had happened. And I cried for Ruben Palacio, a man I had barely met, but someone I felt I knew so intimately. A man who was part of the boxing brotherhood, a man I respected so much for his bravery in the ring and because he had been willing to give me my chance, when all others had refused. I knew that Palacio was dedicated to his family. I knew that, like me, he was a father of two young children. I unbolted the defences I had built through the months of training to be a warrior and became, once more, a man.

Late the following day, the Friday afternoon, I got yet another call which again blew me away. The fight was back on. Barry Hearn had searched the whole of Europe for a replacement and one had been found. Welshman Steve Robinson, possibly the only fight-fit featherweight in the country, had accepted the fight and the WBO had nominated him as their other contender for the now vacant title.

Robinson had only an average record of 13 wins from 20 fights and had been in training for a British Title Eliminator, the title I'd relinquished without so much as lacing a glove. He was far better than his record suggested, however. Like me, he'd previously lost dubious decisions to hometown fighters. But in no one's eyes was he a World Title contender. Tim

Driscoll had stopped him in five rounds on the way to his own World Title challenge.

For Robinson, it was the opportunity of a lifetime. In his wildest dreams, he could never have imagined he would reach such dizzy heights. I'd never even heard of him. He'd never been on my radar as I'd pursued Hoko, Villasana, Benavides and co around the world of boxing. Until just two months earlier, he'd been working for 50 quid a week as a storeman in a Cardiff department store. He'd left this job in one last attempt to break into the big time. Now he'd suddenly found himself one of the biggest ladders in the history of the sport while I seemed to be standing on the snake.

I was shot to pieces. I'd barely slept on the Thursday night and my mind was in complete turmoil. At 4.00am that Friday morning, I'd been walking the streets alone, sick at heart and trying desperately to make sense of what had happened. I'd arrived back home as the sun was rising, mocking my feelings of despair. To have come so far and then have it all snatched away. I'd given everything in the gym for over six months. I'd given everything in the sport for five years. Now my body, maintained for so long in peak condition, had collapsed on me as soon as the news of Palacio's illness had broken. I had already prepared myself to announce my retirement. And then came the news that there was still a chance.

I shrugged my shoulders. I had come too far now to consider anything other than fighting. 'Game on,' was all I could say. I picked up the pieces and put them back together. The world would see John Davison climb into that boxing ring.

At 7.00pm that night, I knocked on Tommy's door. He'd also been through the mill and hadn't slept for two days. He looked as bad as I felt.

'John, what are you doing here?'

'I've got to train, Tommy. You've got to get me a spar from somewhere.'

'You can't spar! It's 24 hours to your fight.'

'I've got to!' I insisted through gritted teeth. 'Get me a fucking spar. Anyone!'

A few calls were made and, by 8.00pm, Chip O'Neil, a local boxer I'd sparred with many times before, was being laced up in the other corner.

As the sun faded that spring evening, casting its long shadows over the River Wear, as the city centre hummed with the anticipation of yet another hectic Friday night's partying, passers-by may have noticed a light shining in Tommy Conroy's Professional Boxing Gym, nestled on the banks of the river. I was inside, John Davison – WBO World Featherweight Contender, about to try to pull it together and save my World Title dream.

After a few rounds, Tommy called a halt. 'John, I think you should stop now.'

Chip was taking my shots with ease and dishing out more than a few of his own. I was uncoordinated and cumbersome, my body tight and tense after the frustrations of the previous two days.

'Not yet,' I said fiercely.

'You don't want to fuck yourself up.'

'One more round, Tommy,' I said desperately. I had to see if I had something left; I had to see if I could shake away the lethargy that had enveloped me.

The bell rang and I went at Chip for all I was worth. He tried to back me off, counter-punching hard enough to make Tommy wince but, at last, something clicked and I caught him with a beautiful combination, driving him back against the ropes and catching him with some big shots. Tommy rang the bell and I took the gloves off and stared across the river. I could and would fight with everything I had, but I knew the sharpness wasn't there. It had all gone terribly, terribly wrong. I prayed that the bottle of wine on the kitchen table would help me get some sleep.

I came into the ring to a tumultuous reception from my fans, over 6,000 of them, packed into the hall with millions more watching on television. They had come to see my finest ever performance, to see me anointed as the best in the world. I was their star, someone they all associated with because they all knew that I was one of them. Just an ordinary guy from the street made good. Normally, I bounced into the ring, hyped up and full of power and vibe. But my mind was in pieces, my preparations blown apart. The last 48 hours had stolen from my mind what the previous six months' solid training had stolen from my body. I was exhausted both mentally and physically but I would let no one see that. So I came in as a man of steel with raw determination in my heart. I stared ahead, seeing no one and nothing but the task before me. 'I can still do this,' I told myself, 'I can still win my title.'

But, from the first bell, I knew that things were badly wrong. The energy, the snap that a boxer feels when he's on top of his game just wasn't there. I'd never felt like that before. Even warming up in my dressing room, Tommy had been desperately trying to rev me up, telling me that I could still do it, that I still had enough. But I was weak, as if my internal engine was running with one cylinder misfiring. Robinson was fresher, stronger, and he had nothing to lose as he looked to take this unforeseen opportunity with both hands. Where I had been trying for three years to get this chance, being constantly disappointed along the way, for him it had literally fallen into his lap. He was going to make the most of his opportunity and could fight with no fear.

I tried to fight my normal fight, working close to the Welshman and using my strength to dominate him, but it was Robinson who was making the pace. Nothing I tried would work, my punches missing by millimetres, where they would usually have hit home and worn him down. He took the first round and, by midway through the second, to the untrained eye, it looked as if it were Robinson who was the real challenger and I was the late substitute as he constantly scored points.

Through the third round I toiled, desperately trying to find some sort of momentum. But Robinson's punching was cleaner and crisper and he was scoring points time and time again. Twice in the third, he rocked me with strong right hooks that had me clinging and holding on to him. By the end of the fourth, he had taken a big lead and I knew I was in serious trouble. I was struggling to maintain anything like my normal pressure. I was struggling to fight on my terms. It was slipping away and I knew it.

Sitting on my stool, with Tommy trying desperately to rally me, I looked into the abyss. If I faltered now, if I let my exhaustion overwhelm me, Robinson would take me apart. All I had achieved in my career flashed through my mind. I couldn't let it end like this. Not after everything I'd been through.

As the bell went for the fifth round, I clipped my gloves together once as if to signify that a line had been crossed, a decision had been made. I'd dug deep before and pulled off what people thought was the impossible for me. Now I had to go back to the well one last time. I had to do something because I could not let it end like this. Not after all I had achieved. If Robinson wanted the World Title, he would have to have to fight through hell to win it.

Through mind-numbing exhaustion, I set about turning it around. I detached any feelings of pain, of tiredness and I fought. I fought for my family, my friends, my fans who drove me on time and time again. The noise was deafening as I forced Robinson back, creating a war zone inside the ring. My fans pushed me forwards and I was scoring points, winning rounds, finding a way through Robinson's previously solid defences. It wasn't pretty but, then again, I never had been. It wasn't my best, but it was starting to be enough. Every time I connected, the roar of the crowd got louder and louder as they willed me to finish it as I had so many times before. Unbelievably, the fight was back in the balance as we moved into the ninth round and still I came and came.

The pace was frantic as I pressured Robinson, but without being able to find that single killer blow. I hunted and harried the Welshman who, strong though he was, was unable to stay in the same place for more than a few seconds without risking being annihilated. Moving into the last round, most observers would have scored the fight even. But it was only the judges that would count and both Robinson and I knew that. As we came out for the final three minutes, Jim Watt, who had commentated at my most famous victories, told the viewers that it was all on the last round. Both Robinson and I knew it was all to fight for in those last three precious minutes. I had pushed myself far beyond the level of human endurance and the tanks were on empty, but just one more round and I would reach the Promised Land.

And then it happened. Yet again, I went toe-to-toe with Robinson, looking to finish the fight there and then but, as I opened up, the Welshman caught me with a left uppercut that shook me to my core. It was without a doubt the hardest punch I ever took. He knew I was hurt and he came in for the kill, following up with an avalanche of punches, scoring eight direct hooks into my head. But I would not go down. I somehow held and then came back at him, out on my feet and fighting purely on an inner determination not to lose, counter-punching through rapidly failing senses, hurting Robinson and forcing him back into a full retreat.

The last 60 seconds were torture for the two of us. It was too close to call. No one could guess what was on the judges' scorecards. I knew that I needed a knock-out to be sure, but my energy was spent. I'd been hurt, but I had come back. I was still the one driving forward and sometimes such things could make all the difference in such a close contest, especially as I was the favourite and was fighting in my own heartland. Again and again, I closed Robinson down, desperately trying to find a way through his defence. Gone was the thought of winning. It was about who was the hardest and I would never, ever give up. I looked for one more big right, one more punch in a million. But it never came. The bell rang for the last time and it was over. We were both carried back to our stools to await the agony of points.

'Have I got it, Tommy?' I was slurring through sheer exhaustion.

'It's close, John.'

'Have I got it, Tommy?'

'It's too close to call. I don't know. I just don't know.'

I sat slumped back, my head resting on a rope, my arms hanging listlessly by my side. I could barely move them. I was tired beyond words and hurting beyond meaning.

The referee called us to the centre of the ring and grasped me by my left arm. A split decision was announced. The very closest you can get in separating two men who have maimed each other for 12 rounds of brutal boxing.

The first judge, the American Al Wilensky, scored it 115–114 in favour of Steve Robinson. The crowd howled its disapproval. My face showed no sign of emotion. I had nothing left to give.

The second judge, Samuel Conde from Cuba, scored 115–114 in my favour. The hall was in uproar as the tension dripped from the ceiling. My heart was like stone.

The third and final judge, Knud Jensen from Finland, scored it 116–114. The new WBO Featherweight Champion of the World was... Steve Robinson.

WHEN THE PARTY'S OVER

'All the world's a stage
And all the men and women merely players.
They have their exits and their entrances
And one man in his time plays many parts.'
WILLIAM SHAKESPEARE, AS YOU LIKE IT

After the World Title fight, I disappeared into the arms of my family. I stayed away from the gym. I stayed away from the media. I locked myself away from the outside world so that I could repair my exhausted body and my shattered mind. Steve Robinson's performance that night had been worthy of a true champion because he'd taken all the leather I could throw at him, but I was devastated at what fate had done to stack the odds so firmly against me in the build-up to the fight.

In my own mind, I'd retired. I tried to forget that I could ever have been Champion of the World; indeed, that I'd even been a boxer. It was time to look to a future away from the sport I'd grown to love. A sport which had given me so much but had ultimately been so cruel.

JOHN DAVISON: LITTLE MAN, BIG HEART

I'd gone from World Champion to over the hill in the blink of an eye, on the decision of one judge. It's right what they say about boxing – no matter how good the good times are, how high the highs, ultimately, it gets you in the end.

But I was still a big name, still a crowd-pleaser, and a ticket-seller. I could carry on if I wanted to, but why? I was closing in on my 35th birthday; what could I now hope to achieve in boxing? What was there left for me to do? I was shot and, deep down, I knew it. The Palacio experience had put miles on my clock. I felt like I'd run to the moon and back.

So, yet again, it was decision time. Would I go on, try to make some more money, becoming a punchbag for young pretenders who needed a big scalp on their records? Fighters with their futures in front of them, not behind them, as mine was. Strangely enough, that option just didn't appeal to me.

I was still number-one contender for the British Title, the one I'd given up when the World Title fight had been agreed. I'd fallen in love with the Lonsdale Belt and I'd wanted to defend it. But then along had come Palacio to blow my world apart.

I had to speak to my family and Tommy, to listen to what they felt was right.

We talked for weeks and it always came back to the same decision. I'd run out of time. The journey was over. I should announce my retirement and get on with my life.

Then, in the October, Frank Warren phoned me. 'I want you to fight for the British Featherweight Title in December against Duke McKenzie. You'll be topping the bill in Manchester.'

'Frank, I'm finished,' I said truthfully. 'I couldn't knock out a fly.'

'I'll give you 30 grand.'

'Get the fight on,' I said instantly. This one would be for the money, I thought. This one was for my wife and kids.

WHEN THE PARTY'S OVER

I phoned Tommy to tell him and he went ballistic. 'What the fuck are you playing at, Dava?' he exploded.

'You can't deny me the chance to make 30 grand, Tommy, not you or anyone else.'

'You said yourself, you're finished. It's over.' He was genuinely incredulous.

'It's not over until I say it is,' I said acidly.

'John, you can't do this. You've got nothing left to prove.'

'I'm getting in that ring, Tommy, whether you're there or not!'

'But you've got your whole life ahead of you, John.' There was a pause. 'I don't want to see you get hurt,' he said quietly. 'No one does.'

'Duke can't hurt me Tommy. No one can. Remember?'

'John, I really don't think...'

'I'd rather you were there,' I said quietly.

There was a long silence. 'See you in the morning, bright and early,' he said, trying to sound cheerful and failing miserably.

I was back at the gym the following day and we started the old routine. It was a struggle, getting back into full training after months of inactivity, but I started feeling stronger quickly. I worked on stamina initially, back on the road, on the bags and pads, looking to try to build up to go 12 rounds again. I tried to be my old cocky self but, deep down, I knew that I was fooling no one. No matter how hard I tried to convince myself, Duke McKenzie would be no pushover. He was a brilliant boxer, the first British boxer to lift three World Titles at three different weights in the 20th century. He was smooth and stylish and he had fast combinations. But he could also punch and was intelligent in the ring. He'd been a pro since 1982, beginning his career in the flyweight class, where he'd won the British, European and World Titles over a six-year period before stepping up to bantamweight. A World

Bantamweight Title had soon followed and he'd stepped up again to beat an opponent I'd tried so hard to get in the ring, Jesse Benavides, for the super-bantamweight crown.

McKenzie had now stepped up again, to featherweight, looking for a fourth World Title. Greedy bastard.

The training wasn't going according to plan. Tommy took me to one side. 'How do you feel?'

'I feel great,' I lied.

I could tell Tommy felt very awkward. 'John, it isn't happening for you.'

'It's going OK,' I said indignantly.

'John, yesterday in sparring,' he said, struggling to find the words he needed, trying to be kind. 'You were... er... getting knocked about a bit.'

'Was I?' I hadn't even noticed.

'Yes.' He nodded sadly. 'There's no shame in pulling out, you know. No shame at all. It could be another injury. Maybe your hand again.'

'I can't do that, Tommy,' I said sadly. 'I have to go through with this. I came into boxing with nothing. I don't want to leave the same way.'

There was nothing he could say.

The fight was a week before Christmas at a packed MEN Arena. Newcastle United had been playing in Manchester that day and the place was decked with black-and-white flags as thousands of fans had made their way straight from the football ground for one big party. But Ham, one of my oldest friends, and someone who had been to practically every one of my fights, amateur and professional, told me the day before that he wasn't going, he couldn't get away from work in time. It was only years later he admitted that he didn't want to see me get hurt.

It seemed my fans knew what I was thinking. Most said afterwards that they'd come down to see me one last time, to say goodbye, hopefully with the Geordie Hammer landing a big right just one more time.

If it was going to be my last fight, there was an outstanding debt that I wanted to pay to someone who had believed in me in the beginning. Across the back of my gown, I had emblazoned 'John Davison – Sponsored by Viv Graham' to thank the man who had done so much to help me financially at the beginning of my professional career and even prior to that, when I was an amateur international. However, the television company banned me from wearing it, deeming it to be unauthorised advertising. I had to enter the ring with white tape stuck all over the back of my gown so that the cameras wouldn't broadcast it to the nation.

Viv Graham would be murdered just two weeks later in what was described by the media as a 'gangland shooting'. I never did get a chance publicly to thank him when he was alive, but years later I revealed what he'd done to help me in a book about his life, which was written by North-East author Stephen Richards. I also gave the gloves I'd worn to win my first International Title to his kids as a posthumous thank you. Viv was a great bloke, as generous as could be and I'm sure he's resting in peace.

When I emerged to the sound of my *Rocky* anthem, the roof was lifted off the hall. 'Dava! Dava! Dava!' The warrior within me knew that McKenzie couldn't hurt me. The man inside knew this was my last dance. But I was as determined as ever to give my all and put on a good show and, as soon as I heard the crowd singing my name, the previous months of pain evaporated. Once again, I was John Davison the fighter, the underdog who could destroy reputations. Once again, I felt unstoppable. Once again I believed.

JOHN DAVISON: LITTLE MAN, BIG HEART

'Dava! Dava! Dava!'

My whole life had been one crazy roller-coaster ride since I'd first stepped inside the West End Boxing Gym ten years earlier. Even at the age of 35, I had more power than most in my division. 'All it takes is one punch,' I kept on telling myself. 'Stay close, keep the pressure on, catch him once and he'll go. It's not like I'll ever go down.'

The bell went to a crescendo of noise and I was in McKenzie's face like a bat out of hell. I was straight into my normal pace, pressuring him, hunting him as he constantly back-tracked. I never gave him time or space to settle into his own rhythm. The crowd roared me on, the volume reaching breaking point each time I connected. Two punches snapped into his face and were heard throughout the arena despite the noise of the crowd. McKenzie shrugged them off and kept dancing, darting both left and right and launching jabs of his own. He was silky smooth as he moved around the ring, maybe the best boxer I ever fought. The first round was even, me getting in the bigger punches, him the more numerous. It was a good start and McKenzie seemed unsettled by how hard I'd hit him. No doubt, he'd been told that my power was on the wane.

The second round started as fast and furious as the first. McKenzie tried to take me on toe-to-toe. I got the better of the exchanges, getting inside his defences and launching some of my trademark body blows. The sheer power of my punching forced him to back away and dance rather than stay and be hurt. It was looking like the start of another epic, as if I could defy the odds just one more time. He came in again, his punches so fast that I barely saw them, let alone had time to avoid them. Two connected crisply with my head, dimming my vision. I went after him, but he'd already gone. Seconds later, he was back, launching another barrage of straight rights and lefts that I took full on, trying once more to get inside his defence. Again, he was gone, but I shook my head. He wasn't fucking hurting me.

He came again and we traded blows. I clubbed him once with a straight left and, for a split-second, I'd seen the chance to launch my right hook. But it was gone even as I saw the opportunity. In the past, I wouldn't have even thought, it would have already been off and connecting with his face. As the second round closed, my rate of punches was already slowing and Duke McKenzie was moving and punching like the triple World Champion that he undoubtedly was.

'You're tiring, John.'

'Am I fuck, Tommy,' I lied, as I tried to regulate my breathing, taking big controlled gasps of air. 'I'm keeping my energy for Round Twelve.'

'You're taking shots, John. Stay away from his left hook. Stop coming straight at him. You're walking on to his punches.'

To be fair, I wasn't actually meaning to. I wasn't exactly enjoying being hit.

'I've got to get in close.'

'I know, I know. But, if you start taking too many shots, I'm pulling you out.'

'Don't you fucking dare! If you stop this fight, I'll never speak to you again!'

'But, John…'

'I fucking mean it, Tommy! We'll be finished!'

He shook his head and put my gum shield back in.

I slammed my gloves together. 'Come on!' I shouted, revving myself up. As the bell for the third rang, I was up and at McKenzie like a raging bull.

I'd always been fit, always been strong. My style had always been based on relentless pursuit of an opponent. But, in the third round, anything I'd had left from the Palacio mess ebbed away on to the floor of that boxing ring. I tried to go forward but McKenzie stopped me dead with hard jabs. I tried to get inside his guard to open up but he was too fast for me. He'd be away out of danger, then straight back at me with an attack of his own. I was taking shots I would never have taken. I was missing opportunities. McKenzie took the third round easily. The curtain was finally falling.

'That's it, John, I'm pulling you out,' said Tommy as I slumped on my stool.

'You can fuck off!' I replied. 'There's no way you're stopping this!'

'You can't take much more.'

'It's my decision, Tommy,' I said through clenched teeth. I had to get back out there. I had to turn it round.

'He's hurting you.'

'He's not!' I looked at Tommy desperately. 'I just need one punch, Tommy! Just one punch. He'll go. I know he will.'

Tommy grabbed my head and pulled me close. 'Just one punch, John, do you hear?' Our eyes locked and I understood exactly what he was saying. I'd given my all, but now it could never be enough. We both knew it. 'You've got to take him this round. You've got to knock him out.'

I nodded and stood from my stool to go to war one final time. I was no longer John Davison the professional boxer. He was gone for ever now. In truth, he'd been gone for months. I was just a man, left with nothing but the determination never to give up. I was John Davison, husband, father, son, brother and friend. I clipped my gloves together one more time and looked at Tommy.

'Go on, son. Go and finish it,' he said. He rammed the gum shield into my mouth and I stepped off the end of the world.

* * * *

The following day, I announced that I was retiring a proud man. In the space of ten years, I'd gone from a complete novice, to England Captain, to one of the best professional featherweights in the world. I'd been the first man to win two International Titles, the first Newcastle man to win a British Title in 60 years. My performances had won Scottish, British and European Fights of the Year. What's more, I'd done it in almost complete defiance of the laws of boxing. Looking back at some of the people I fought gives me a glow of real satisfaction.

The Frenchman Fabrice Benichou would fight twice more for the ultimate prize after his fights with me. He was still boxing as late as 2005.

Sakda Sorpakdee would still be in contention for World Title honours as late as 2004, losing a WBF Super-Middleweight Title fight to the Australian Shannan Taylor.

Steve Robinson, the 'Cinderella Man' as he called himself after his dream victory against me, went from zero to hero overnight. He would defend his World Title seven times, beating the cream of British boxing, all the men who had not been prepared to get in the ring with me in my prime. This included Sean Murphy, Paul Hodkinson and Colin McMillan. He would also knock out Duke McKenzie in the eighth round of their bout in Wales. Robinson went from unknown to the dominant force in British featherweight boxing overnight. As I've always maintained, he was a worthy World Champion. He would eventually lose his title to the enigmatic brilliance of the little Prince Naseem from Sheffield, the boy who once upon a time had said he wanted to be just like me.

People often say I must be gutted when I see what Robinson went on to achieve, that it should have been me who was defending my World Title so emphatically. Robinson went on to pack the halls of Cardiff; could John Davison not have filled

St James' or Roker Park to the rafters? The answer is that, yes, I think I could have done, if I'd have won. As I said earlier, 'if' is the most used word in boxing.

Before the original delays in the Palacio fight, we'd agreed a deal for me finally to get Colin McMillan in the ring for my first title defence. He'd already been nominated as the mandatory challenger and I'm sure that that one would have been huge. My other move would have been to try to unify titles by taking on Hoko for his WBC version. Again, it would have been one of the biggest fights in the whole of the world that year.

Things had changed, however, by the time I climbed into the ring to face Robinson. By that point, Tommy and I both knew what the crisis had done to me mentally and physically. Tommy's own idea would have been to choose an easier defence, which every champion does sometimes, and then try to talk me into retiring as an unbeaten champion. I doubt that his plan would have had much success, but it's all academic. Robinson beat me and that was that. It's never kept me awake at night, wondering what might have been, howling at the moon about how unlucky I was. I've never looked on it as a missed opportunity. Sure, it would have been nice to have the extra money in the bank at the end of my career but, in my eyes, it was a triumph that I got in the ring that night in the first place, given the mess I was in, and I still got closer to beating the Welshman than any of the other people he went on to fight.

So how good was I in the greater scheme of things? If you want to know how good I was, ask Paul Hodkinson, or Fabrice Benichou, or Steve Robinson what I was capable of. They can all tell you first-hand, as can many others I demolished along the way. The only performance I ever regretted was against Duke McKenzie. I was shot to pieces and I didn't do myself justice. It wasn't the real John Davison. When the referee stopped the fight towards the end of the fourth round, I was taking shots, but I'd come through far worse before. Benichou in his big eighth; Sorpakdee on the night he shattered both sides of my jaw; even Robinson in the final round. But, in those fights, I had something to give back. Against McKenzie, I had nothing and the referee could see it. It's the one performance that pisses me off. I've never watched the footage and I never will.

Losing the World Title fight, although a pisser at the time, was not the tragedy of epic proportions that you might imagine for me. But it was for my opponent in the fight that never was. Certainly, what happened in those fateful months all those years ago ended my career prematurely. But it was Ruben Palacio who was to pay the ultimate price. After he was stripped of his title, he flew back to Colombia and into a media storm. For months, he denied that the test results had been accurate which, in the highly macho culture of Colombia and the connotations that the illness had with the gay community in the early 1990s, was, perhaps, understandable.

Fourteen months after the cancelled fight, he was arrested at Miami International Airport with 6kg of heroin stitched into his clothes. Indicted by a Federal Jury on charges of heroin importation, which carries a maximum sentence of life imprisonment, Palacio faced his biggest ever fight.

At his trial, his defence pleaded for clemency saying that, as he could no longer fight, he had been forced to work for the cartels to provide for his wife and young children and to pay for his HIV medication. This, in itself, would have been horrendously expensive for a man stripped of his only way of making a living, the only thing he knew. Although sympathetic to his plight, the United States was in the middle of a global drugs war. It could not afford to take a lenient approach with such a high-profile offender. Palacio was given ten years in prison, which was in itself a life sentence, given his illness. He died of AIDS in 2003 aged just 40.

At the time he was diagnosed with HIV, his wife was four months' pregnant with their third child. Neither had contracted the virus. Palacio also passed the same test in October of the previous year in London prior to his World Title fight with Colin McMillan. It's possible that the World Champion was infected during the surgery that postponed his original scheduled fights with me in early 1993. Like so many others in the early 1990s, he may well have been the unknowing victim of infected blood, the virus being passed to him during a routine blood transfusion. His child, a son, was born in September 1993 and the former World Champion named him John Palacio, in my honour.

So where am I today? I can still be found punching people for a living, although these days it's far less violent than in my boxing career or in what I would call my 'previous life' on the streets of Newcastle. When I first left the ring, I got my manager's licence and I managed fighters for a couple of years, passing on the wisdom I gained from being involved in the fight game. I knew every scam in the book so there was no chance of my being ripped off. But it wasn't the same as being in the ring. I missed the buzz of fighting but, unlike others from the 'trade', I never thought of a comeback. You have to know when it's over, when you can't maintain the performances that make you special, when you've used up the gift that you were given.

I made another little bit of history when I trained the first female boxer to fight in the North of England and, just a couple of years ago, I was working with a young lad who looked like he could be the next me. John Sayers, a Geordie lad born and bred, was certainly the best young amateur boxer I'd seen in many years. He had a similar style to me, was hard as nails and as brave as they come. But he suffered from 'away' points decisions in the same way that I did. It's sometimes better to be a lucky boxer than a good one.

When I retired, I also used some of the money to open up my own shop – John Davison Knock-Out Discount Prices. It sold groceries, hardware, that sort of stuff. The place was always mobbed with friends and family and, at first, I thought it was my popularity. But I soon realised the real reason. Every time I looked in the till, it was full of IOUs. Everyone I knew was getting their stuff on tick! I got rid of the place after a few months. I think it was the only time I lost money buying and selling!

Unfortunately, Carol and I split up a few years ago. We had great times together and have two wonderful kids. Kelly is beautiful and independent and everything a dad could want from a daughter. Aaron is one of my best mates. He's always loved boxing and could easily turn professional if he wanted to. But his talents for entertaining people are completely different to his dad's. He's a singer-songwriter, with a really soulful voice. He's working hard to get his big break and he could go all the way.

I now live with my partner Caroline, whom I met at the gym when she used to come to my classes. I think she liked the tight cycling shorts I used to wear. We hit it off straight away and we're happy and looking forward to the future. I've become a father figure to her two sons Dominic and Patrick, who are great kids when they're not kicking seven colours out of each other!

I've still got a passion for antiques and I'm always looking for that Da Vinci painting in second-hand shops and car boots. I still make appearances at boxing shows and I'm still signing autographs and getting fan mail from around the world. I'm always proud that the fans remember my performances. They're still shown on Sky Sports Classic and Bravo *Fight* programmes and people are always surprised when they see that I don't look a day older now than I did when I was fighting! I still do the odd celebrity appearance and I'm available for weddings, funerals and bar mitzvahs, but I'd draw the line at *Celebrity Big Brother*. I'd maybe consider *Love Island*.

These days, I like to sit with a glass of wine and watch the fish in the pond in my back garden. I've done my fighting now, although there's still plenty of fire in me. I did an exhibition fight in 2006 at a white-collar boxing event, the first ever in the North-East. I hadn't been in a ring competitively since Duke McKenzie and I entered wearing the shorts I wore in my epic 12-rounder against Sakda Sorpakdee. All those old feelings came flooding back as I walked into the hall, the hairs standing up on the back of my neck as my title belts were carried in front of me and the crowd sang my name. The hunger for glory, the desire to get in the ring and fight, it's addictive, possibly the most powerful drug in the world. I realised then that 13 years had not dimmed the craving. Deep down, it's always there and it always will be.

I'd like to think that I had many fine moments in my boxing career and that I gave fight fans something they will always remember. But I count my finest moment as a man, and my biggest victory, as the night I pushed Steve Robinson to the very limit for the Featherweight Championship of the World.

WHEN THE PARTY'S OVER

When my moment of destiny came, I had the courage to reach out and grasp it with both hands. I looked deep inside myself and I was not found wanting.